THE BATTLE OF
THE FOUR COURTS

MICHAEL FEWER enjoyed thirty years as an academic and a practicing architect, and was a Fellow of the Royal Institute of Architects of Ireland, when he took up writing full-time in 2000. He has written twenty-two books since 1988, on walking, travel, history and architecture, and his recent nature book for children was a bestseller. He was a consultant contributor to the *Encyclopaedia of Ireland* and has featured in RTÉ television programmes and on RTÉ Radio's 'Sunday Miscellany'.

ALSO BY MICHAEL FEWER

Travelogues
By Cliff and Shore
By Swerve of Shore
Walking Across Ireland
Rambling Down the Suir
Michael Fewer's Ireland

Biography
Thomas Joseph Byrne: Nation Builder
(with John Byrne)

Anthology
A Walk in Ireland

Architectural History
The New Neighbourhood of Dublin
(with Dr Maurice Craig and Joseph Hone)
Doorways of Ireland

History
The Wicklow Military Road: History and Topography
Hellfire Hill: A Human and Natural History

THE BATTLE OF
THE FOUR COURTS

The First Three Days
of the Irish Civil War

MICHAEL FEWER

An Apollo Book

This is an Apollo book, first published in the UK in 2018
by Head of Zeus Ltd

9 7 5 3 1 2 4 6 8

A catalogue record for this book is available from
the British Library.

ISBN (HB): 9781788546645
ISBN (E): 9781788546638

Typeset by Adrian McLaughlin
Maps by Jeff Edwards

Printed and bound in Great Britain by
CPI Group (UK) Ltd, Croydon CR0 4YY

Head of Zeus Ltd
First Floor East
5–8 Hardwick Street
London EC1R 4RG

WWW.HEADOFZEUS.COM

CONTENTS

To Teresa

INTRODUCTION

Dublin's Four Courts have been the centre of legal life in Ireland for over two hundred years. While researching a biography of T. J. Byrne, the chief architect of the Office of Public Works from 1923 to 1938, I came across a report on the condition of the buildings in the Four Courts complex after the battle that had occurred there in June 1922. The National Army had laid siege to the courts, which were then occupied by an armed force that had rejected the Treaty which had been signed between the government of the United Kingdom and representatives of the Irish Republic, and the battle that ensued had resulted in considerable damage to the courts and the surrounding buildings. It also led to the destruction of most of the priceless archives held in the Record Treasury of the Public Record Office. I was surprised to find in Byrne's report that the basement of the Record Treasury had not been greatly affected by the fires that destroyed the archives stored above, and particularly to learn from Byrne's photographs and documentation that no explosion had taken place there.

Most histories I had read blamed the destruction of the Treasury's irreplaceable archives of political, legal and social documentation on the explosion, deliberate or otherwise, of a store of munitions, or a 'great mine', placed in the basement of the building by the anti-Treaty garrison of the Four Courts. I knew that the Record Treasury, and most of its contents, had been destroyed on Friday, 30 June 1922. I was intrigued, however, by how Byrne's report rebutted this conventional wisdom, and I wondered if I could work out, from contemporary technical information, photographs and reports, the facts of the matter, even at this late stage, nearly a hundred years later.

Although the attack on the Four Courts by the National Army in June 1922 was perhaps one of the most important events in modern Irish history, no comprehensive account of the siege has been published. Much of what transpired, in the midst of the confusion, fear and the adrenaline rush that attends violent armed conflict, will probably never be truly known, and even the later accounts by those who were there, for a variety of reasons, are not necessarily fully accurate. While narratives of the siege by historians seem to be generally correct, their reporting of the 'great explosion' is not always accurate. Although information on the matter was readily available at the time and in the months and years afterwards, it was often either not consulted, or was simply ignored. More recent accounts of the siege continue to perpetuate the inaccuracies of earlier writers. In some cases, historians seem to have failed to understand the sequence of events that took place during the three days that the siege of the Four Courts lasted, and, for others, knowledge of the layout of the Four Courts complex and the streets around it, a critical factor in understanding the reality of how the siege played out, is clearly absent. In some recent publications, maps depicting the layout of the complex are incorrect, showing only three, not the four, buildings that occupied the site in 1922.

The only substantial published written account of the occupation and siege, by a member of the garrison of the Four Courts, is to be found in *The Singing Flame*, a book that is based on a collection of manuscript and typed notes written by Ernie O'Malley, which were edited to produce the book twenty-one years after his death in 1957. O'Malley was a member of the executive council of the Irish Republican Army (IRA) which established the Four Courts as its headquarters in April 1922, and he was the officer in charge of the military garrison in the last hours of the siege. His dramatic account is understandably partisan and full of bravado, and some of his recollections, in particular those regarding the different buildings on the site, are demonstrably inaccurate. Equally, there is only one substantial account from the National Army side, *Sleep Soldier Sleep*, the edited memoir of Commandant Padraig O'Connor, published in 2011. This more simple account of the battle, and indeed its author, should be better known. I found it most useful in relation to understanding the details of the assault on the complex by the National Army, and owe my thanks for using material from it to its editor, Padraig O'Connor's nephew, Diarmuid O'Connor.

The Four Courts has been, since its completion in the early nineteenth century, a significant physical presence along the Liffey quays in Dublin, and because fighting was mainly confined to the area immediately surrounding it during the first hours of the Civil War, the battle drew large crowds of spectators, and the action was comprehensively recorded in photographs and film. Many of the photographs that still exist, however, some of them containing critical evidence, have been incorrectly catalogued, and my search for relevant subjects therefore involved trawling widely through an enormous number of images of the period in various archives. For instance, in the National Library Photographic Archive, I found an informative photograph of the roofless Record Treasury taken shortly after the siege in June 1922 captioned 'Dublin Ruins 1916'. The same photograph appears in the 1998 publication *The Irish Civil War* by Tim Pat Coogan and George Morrison, entitled 'The ruins of the *Freeman's Journal* presses'. When assembled, however, a collection of these photographs assisted me in understanding what had happened before, during and after the siege.

My background as an architect helped me to identify, from architectural details, obscure locations depicted in photographs, and it was also useful in enabling me to create three-dimensional digital models of the buildings, which allowed me to work out the trajectory of artillery shells fired, and to interpret technical reports and building plans. I was fortunate to have available to me T. J. Byrne's photographs of the Four Courts after the siege and during reconstruction work, and I also learned much from contemporary newspaper reports and correspondence. Since I knew little about artillery or explosives, two important elements of the siege that have been argued about for nearly a hundred years, I sought the advice of an army artillery officer on the matter of the 18-pounder guns, and an explosives engineer on the question of the 'great explosion'.

As in all wars, the first shot fired in the Irish Civil War in June 1922 was but the beginning of a series of chaotic developments, with little subsequently turning out as expected by any of the protagonists. It was a war between solidly entrenched idealists and political pragmatists, and before the conflict petered out, ten months later, many of the leaders, including Michael Collins, Arthur Griffith, Rory O'Connor and Liam Lynch, would be dead. This work deals primarily with the first sixty hours of organized hostilities between the two sides, from the firing of the first shot in the Battle of the Four Courts, early on the morning of Wednesday, 28 June 1922, to the surrender of the garrison on the afternoon of Friday, 30 June. In order to put the siege into context, however, my account begins with an examination of the complex political and military developments in Ireland in the months that led up to it.

I hope I have told the story of the battle with accuracy, identifying some stories about this historical event that have no basis in fact, and in each case setting the record as straight as it can be set at this remove. I am sure that I am mistaken on some matters, but am hopeful that those who know the truth will correct any errors I have made. It is a story that has long deserved to be told, and I hope I have done it justice.

CHAPTER 1

PRELUDE

'The Four Glorious Years', as Éamon de Valera called them, from 1918 to 1921, were not so glorious for many in Ireland. Dissatisfied with the limited autonomy offered by Home Rule, Sinn Féin had declared an Irish Republic in December 1918 following its election victory. An armed campaign against British rule, which became known as the War of Independence, followed, and life in some parts of the country became increasingly chaotic and hazardous as fighting intensified. By 1920, patrols of armed British troops were a familiar sight on the streets of Ireland's cities and towns, and on occasion pitched gun-battles took place, during which what Americans now call 'collateral damage' was widespread. Dubliners, in particular, had lived since 1916 with a constant reminder of the destructiveness of revolution: great swathes of the centre of Ireland's capital city had lain in ruins since the Easter Rising of 1916, when British artillery and fires had wreaked widespread destruction on O'Connell Street and the surrounding area. Only towards the end of 1918, after the First World War had ended, did work begin on what must have been Ireland's biggest building boom since the late eighteenth century: the reconstruction of O'Connell Street, Middle Abbey Street, Princes Street, Eden Quay and North Earl Street.

Dublin was not the only urban centre in Ireland to be so affected. In September 1920, a mixed party of rampaging Auxiliary Police and Black and Tans burned down Balbriggan's famous hosiery factory and twenty-five houses in the town. In December of the same year, a mob of Black and Tans rampaged through the city of Cork, and over 40 business premises, 300 residential premises and Cork City Hall were deliberately burnt down, laying waste 5 acres (2.02 hectares) of the city.[1] The reconstruction costs would come to over £2 million, equivalent to nearly £30 million today.[2]

The burning of the Custom House in Dublin by the IRA on 25 May 1921 was the last act of major destruction of the Irish War of Independence in the south of Ireland. Less than two months later, on 11 July 1921, the British prime minister, David Lloyd George, announced that he had invited Éamon de Valera, the president of the Dáil, to meet him for talks in London, and that de Valera had agreed. At noon on that day a truce came into effect in the south of Ireland between the British forces and the IRA. There was no truce in the north, where sectarian violence was rampant: the day before the southern truce came into effect, 161 Catholic homes in Belfast were burnt down, and 15 people, 10 Catholics and 5 Protestants, were killed. An American White Cross delegation in Belfast noted that 1,000 Catholics were sheltering in old stores, stables and schools.[3]

Following the formal signing of the truce, a Truce Liaison Office was established in the Gresham Hotel, Dublin. Initially it included, acting for the British army, Gen. Sir Nevil Macready, the officer commanding British forces in Ireland, Col. J. Brind, and Alfred Cope, assistant under-secretary for Ireland, and acting for the army of the Republic, Commandant Robert C. Barton TD and Commandant E. J. Duggan TD.*

On the British side, the following points were agreed:

1. No incoming troops, Royal Irish Constabulary, auxiliary police and munitions. No movements for military purposes of troops and munitions, except maintenance drafts.
2. No provocative display of forces, armed or unarmed.
3. It is understood that all provisions of this Truce apply to the martial law area equally with the rest of Ireland.
4. No pursuit of Irish officers or men or war materiel or military stores.
5. No secret agents, noting description or movements, and no interference with the movements of Irish persons, military or civil, and no attempts to discover the haunts or habits of Irish officers and men.

---

* The Oireachtas or parliament of Ireland consisted of two houses, Dáil Éireann, the Irish parliament, and Seanad Éireann, the Irish Senate; TD is short for Teachta Dála, or member of parliament.

6. No pursuit or observation of lines of communication or connections.

On the Irish side, the following points were agreed:

1. Attacks on Crown forces and civilians to cease.
2. No provocative displays of forces, armed or unarmed.
3. No interference with government or private property.
4. To discountenance and prevent any action likely to cause disturbance of the peace which might necessitate military interference.

General Sir Nevil Macready, the officer commanding British forces in Ireland, arriving at the Mansion House in Dublin to arrange the terms of the Anglo-Irish Truce on 8 July 1921.

The signing of the truce led, in its early stages, to relative peace in the south of Ireland between the IRA and the British army, as lengthy and complex discussions commenced in London between representatives of the Irish Dáil and the British government, seeking agreement in broad principle on what British newspapers called 'the Irish Question'. Five months of intensive negotiations culminated in the Anglo-Irish Treaty, which was signed in London in December 1921 by representatives of the British government and an Irish delegation. The Treaty brought the War of Independence to an end, providing for the establishment of an Irish Free State as a self-governing dominion within the Commonwealth of Nations.

The news of the signing of the Treaty in London was greeted with surprise by some of the leaders at home. Rory O'Connor,* who was to become a leading figure in the anti-Treaty faction, asked his opinion immediately after the Treaty was signed, is reported to have replied, 'Oh we must work it for all it's worth,' then, after a slight pause, added, 'but if I could get enough to support me, I would oppose it wholeheartedly.'4 It was also reported that Éamon de Valera, meeting with his Dáil colleagues, Austin Stack and Cathal Brugha, before the return of

---

* Roderick (Rory) O'Connor (1883–1922) was born in Dublin and educated by the Jesuits at Clongowes. He studied engineering and arts at the National University, and afterwards worked as an engineer on the Canadian Pacific Railway. He returned to Dublin in 1915, and served in the GPO in 1916. During the War of Independence he was Director of Engineering of the IRA, and for a time officer in command of the 2,500 Volunteers based in England. He was executed by the Provisional Government in December 1922.

5

the delegation to Ireland, appeared to support the Treaty, but Stack later persuaded him to change his mind.

Rory O'Connor addressing a crowd early in 1922.

The Anglo-Irish Treaty was debated in Dáil Éireann, held at the National University of Ireland at Earlsfort Terrace, Dublin, during December 1921 and early January 1922. The arguments for and against it dramatically exposed a deep division between those who saw the Treaty as a not entirely satisfactory, but still a realistic way forward, and those who were vehemently against everything for which it stood. The recorded proceedings of the debate allow fascinating insights into the minds of political activists of the time and the wide range of policies, beliefs and aspirations of the disparate individuals who represented the people of Ireland in the Dáil. Many of those taking part were conscious of the fact that, although the first Dáil had been democratically elected by the Irish people in 1918, its leadership in the struggle, as representing the will of the people, had been accepted by the IRA only in 1920, and then with some reluctance.

In the early twentieth century there were few examples, to reference and learn from, of nations negotiating their way out from under the rule of the British Empire; 'a political experiment' was the future Minister for Justice Kevin O'Higgins's apt summing up of the tortuous Anglo-Irish Treaty negotiation process. While the proceedings of the Treaty debate in the Dáil reveal the depth of the passion and resolve of Dáil deputies, whose navigation through a morass of legal principles and democratic ideals is suffused with with idealism and revolutionary rhetoric, agreeing the Treaty's terms posed many complex questions that were not easy to unravel. Indeed, as a reading of the record shows, their discussions frequently descended into slapstick and slanging matches.

Éamon de Valera believed that the Treaty compromised republican ideals and everything for which the War of Independence had been fought. The process that had begun during his first meeting with Lloyd George the previous year had not gone the way he had expected, and he had come to the realization that much of the work that had filled all his waking time since then had been in vain. During the debate, as he saw his idea of a republic unravelling, he complained, uncharacteristically, 'I am sick and tired of politics, so sick that no matter what happens I would go back to private life.' Todd Andrews, a young Volunteer who had joined up in 1916 at the age of fifteen, and who attended the Treaty debates, describes in his memoir

Dublin Made Me how during these years he was very much an idealist: he believed that great men were leading them into a new Ireland. Listening to the debate, however, he realized that these 'great men' were mostly very average, some were below average, and others were malevolent and vicious. Only de Valera, whom Andrews saw as a man of compassion and dignity, impressed him.[5]

After eleven long days of discussion and argument, on 7 January 1922 a vote was taken on the Treaty. De Valera led the deputies who voted against it, but it was carried by sixty-four votes to fifty-seven. Two days later he resigned as president of the Dáil, and refused to take part in the election of Arthur Griffith in his place, stating that Griffith, as chairman of the delegation that had signed the Treaty, was bound by it to set up a state that would subvert the republican ideal. Wishing to absent himself from the election of the new president, he staged a symbolic walk-out with his followers, amid unseemly insults being shouted by both sides. Although the official 'walk-out' photograph (right) shows the group displaying stern expressions, British Pathé film clearly indicates that, before the photograph was taken, there was a jovial atmosphere and some laughter, and even de Valera and white-bearded Count Plunkett were smiling broadly.

Arthur Griffith was then unanimously elected as the new Dáil president, following which he announced the names of those members he intended to appoint to his cabinet. The anti-Treaty faction returned to the Dáil for the next session of the debate, and proceedings came to an end on a reasonably cordial

The official, posed photo of the de Valera 'walk-out' from the Dáil.
There are solemn faces all round: Éamon de Valera is on the right,
and Cathal Brugha is in front holding his hat.

note. There was a forewarning of times to come, however, when
Éamon de Valera enquired of the newly nominated Minister
for Defence, Richard Mulcahy, how the army was to be run
as a single force. Mulcahy replied that the army would remain
the army of the Republic. There was general applause for this
reply, but this vision of an Irish army did not come to fruition.

With the Treaty formally ratified by the Dáil, the long and
complicated process of the handover of power began, together
with a myriad of peripheral related activities, such as the over-
printing of George V's image on British postage stamps used
in the south with the legend '*Rialtas Sealadach na hÉireann
1922*', and the painting green of the red postboxes throughout the country. The green paint failed, of course, to disguise

the elaborate scrolled initials of the British sovereigns, 'V R', 'E VII R' or 'G V R', embossed on the cast-iron boxes, and indeed, many of these fine examples of metal engineering are still in use in Ireland to this day.

An Edward VII postbox.

Overprinted postage stamps.

At the time the Treaty was signed, the IRA, organized into sixteen divisions, had an estimated nominal membership of 114,652 officers and men, many of whom had joined subsequent to the truce. A very small percentage of these Volunteers were experienced, active members.[6] In common with the end of most wars, those who had been intensively involved in the fighting found it difficult to come to terms with the peace of the truce. Many units took the opportunity to run training camps during this period, keeping the Volunteers occupied. The commander of the British army in Ireland, Gen. Sir Nevil Macready, complained that these might turn what had hitherto been 'a disorganized rabble' into a 'well-disciplined, well-organized and well-armed force'.[7]

However, for many of those who had been for four years in the thick of the fighting against the British army – in addition to the Black and Tans, the Auxiliaries and the Royal Irish Constabulary – there was an unaccustomed leisure time in which to indulge in broad-reaching political discussions with their comrades. Arguments and analyses of the situation served to fan the flames of the frustration of some at having to accept a twenty-six-county Free State, a much watered-down version of the fully fledged and independent republic, encompassing the entire island of Ireland, for which they had fought so hard and seen many of their comrades die. The truce took many active IRA Volunteers by surprise, particularly those in the south and the west, remote from the happenings in Dublin. As Tom Barry, Commander of the 3rd West Cork Flying Column of the IRA, put it, they were 'dazed at first and uncertain of the future, as no one considered during those early July days that the truce would continue for more than a month.'[8] As time went on, however, months of inactivity, particularly for young Munster Volunteers, who had been busily involved in warfare for most of their adult lives, led to prolonged and increasingly bitter discussions about the new cordial relations between the

Provisional Government and Britain. Although their erstwhile enemy, the British army, was gradually being withdrawn from barracks around the country, those soldiers who still remained were very visible, particularly in Dublin, where they walked about in safety, protected by the truce.

As the representatives of Sinn Féin in the Dáil had become divided over the Treaty, members of the IRA who were not politically involved also began to take sides. The IRA headquarters staff in Dublin and some units based in the Irish midlands supported the Treaty, but many of the Munster and Connacht units rejected it. All members of the IRA who wished to continue in the military were encouraged to join a new National Army, which was being armed and equipped by the British as part of the Treaty, but most of the anti-Treaty Volunteers stood apart, held onto their arms and remained with their units, unsure about what was to happen.

Although the British army gradually withdrew and was shipped back to Britain, the new National Army had not yet the numbers in some parts of the country to replace it, so the Provisional Government reluctantly agreed that, in these cases, the barracks should be taken over by the local IRA, irrespective of its attitude to the Treaty.

The mood in the wider community differed too. Although it is difficult to accept at this remove, in 1921 many people, particularly urban dwellers, still saw Ireland as part of the United Kingdom, and filled in their nationality on forms as 'British'.

Over 200,000 Irishmen (it is difficult to obtain figures for Irish women) fought in the First World War, of which well over 30,000 died: while some may have joined the British army to defend other small nations, many joined for economic reasons and one cannot discount loyalty to Britain. Armistice Day continued to be a major commemoration in Dublin well into the 1930s: British Pathé newsreels show crowds of tens of thousands gathered each year at the Wellington monument in the Phoenix Park on the occasion, waving Union Jacks and military banners. Even in 1922 many Irish newspapers still retained vestiges of their erstwhile provincial British status, and the *Irish Times* gave regular prominence to London fashions and the activities of the royal family. Articles with headings such as 'Court and Personal' did not refer to legal matters, but informed readers of what the different members of the aristocracy were up to. In May 1922, for instance, the paper related news items about the Marquis and Marchioness of Milford Haven, where they were going to spend their holidays, what ball they would attend on their return to London, and that the Duchess of Oporto, recently arrived from Madrid, was staying at the Ritz Hotel.

In Dublin's Mansion House on 14 January 1922, a Provisional Government, with Michael Collins as chairman, was elected by the Dáil, the southern Irish parliament, in accordance with Article 17 of the Anglo-Irish Treaty, by those members who had voted for the Treaty, together with the four Unionist members for Trinity College. This temporary administration was to govern Ireland's twenty-six counties until the Free State was fully established, and it moved without delay to take over the various departments of state necessary to do this. Two days later Michael Collins led a government delegation to Dublin Castle, for centuries the most powerful symbol of British rule in Ireland, for the formal handover of the twenty-six counties of Ireland from Britain to the new administration. A large crowd had gathered outside the great granite castle gateway since early morning to witness this historic occasion, the end of British rule in Ireland, and they cheered Collins and his colleagues as they arrived in taxis. One castle official is said to have greeted Collins with the words, 'We're glad to see you, Mr Collins,' to which he replied, with a grin, 'Like hell you are!'

The members of the Provisional Government were met by the lord lieutenant of Ireland, Lord FitzAlan, to whom Collins presented a copy of the Treaty. The lord lieutenant formally acknowledged the existence and authority of the Provisional Government, then introduced the heads of the various civil service departments of the British administration gathered at the castle to their new ministers. The civil service chiefs were struck by the youth of most of the new government ministers: Sir Henry Robinson, who had run the Local Government Board, commented on how they seemed scarcely out of their teens, and how they all looked pale and anxious. The Minister for Education, Eamonn Duggan, at forty-seven, was by far the oldest, and W. T. Cosgrave, Minister for Local Government, was forty-two, but the rest were in their early thirties. Michael

Collins, Robinson wrote, shook hands warmly with the civil servants, 'with the greatest bonhomie'.[9] At the end of the ceremony, Lord FitzAlan and his party left the castle in three cars and a pony-and-trap to the cheers of the crowd.

On their return to the Mansion House, Michael Collins announced to the Dáil that members of the Provisional Government had received 'the surrender of Dublin Castle at 1.45 p.m. today. It is now in the hands of the Irish Nation.'

Kevin O'Higgins, Minister for Justice, leads the way out of Dublin Castle after the official handover by the British administration on 16 January 1922. He is followed by Michael Collins (marked with an x) and Eamonn Duggan.

Since the signing of the truce, work had been going on quietly, with the assistance of the British, to establish a new Irish National Army. The uniforms were to be supplied by the

WAS IT FOR THIS THEY DIED?

An anti-Treaty cartoon by Grace Gifford Plunkett depicting Collins,
watched disapprovingly by seven of the 1916 leaders, kowtowing
to the British at Dublin Castle on 16 January 1922.

British army, but they would be dyed green. In some respects
the Irish kit was superior, however. For instance, British soldiers
wore puttees, a strip of cloth that had to be wrapped around
the lower leg from boot to knee to protect against water or
debris entering the soldier's boots. Puttees were first adopted
by the British army in India in the second half of the nineteenth
century, and they continued in use until 1938. The Irish army
had, instead, smart-looking leather gaiters. The new army was
being supplied with the standard British infantry gun, the Lee
Enfield bolt-action, ten-round, magazine-fed rifle. This had
been the British army's main rifle since its introduction in 1895,

and the fact that it did not become redundant until 1957, after 17 million had been produced, is testimony to the excellence of its design.

The new army also had a different rank structure to the British army: the rank of commandant, which had been used in the Volunteers since 1916, and which equated with the rank of major in the British army, was continued. What stands out is what appears to be a predominance in the new army of very youthful senior officers: a large number of the generals were in their early twenties. Emmet Dalton, who played a central role in the Civil War, was twenty-four when he was appointed a major-general early in 1922.*

It had been considered early in 1922 that a regular army of between 4,000 and 12,000 men would be appropriate, and by April 3,500 men had enlisted. The majority of those accepted had seen service in the War of Independence, but some were

---

* Emmet Dalton (1898–1978) was born in the United States, but grew up in Dublin. In 1913, at the age of fifteen, he joined the Irish Volunteers, and two years later, as a 2nd Lt., the 7th Battalion of the Dublin Fusiliers. He served throughout the First World War. In 1916 he joined the 16th Irish Division under Maj.-Gen. W. R. Hickie, where he became friendly with Lt. Tom Kettle MP, who commanded a company during the Battle of the Somme. On 9 September, towards the end of the battle, Dalton and Kettle were advancing with their companies near Ginchy, when Dalton saw Kettle killed by enemy fire. Dalton advanced regardless, leading other companies who had also lost their officers. Later, almost singlehandedly, he made an attack that resulted in the capture of a German officer and twenty men. For his conduct during the battle he was awarded the Military Cross by King George V at Buckingham Palace. By the end of the war he had been promoted to major. On his return to Ireland in 1919 he rejoined the Volunteers, which soon afterwards became the Irish Republican Army, and took an active part in many important operations.

ex-British army or had served with other armed forces. This did not always work out well. In 1924, Gen. Richard Mulcahy commented that 'Old soldiers, experienced in every kind of military wrong-doing, were placed under the command of officers necessarily inexperienced and the resulting state of discipline is not to be wondered at.' Commandant-Gen. Dermot MacManus, director of training for the Dublin Guards, commented later: 'Many of the officers in the Free State Army were of a very rough type, poorly educated, tough and not really amenable to discipline.' Some of the new recruits were 'transfers' from units of the anti-Treaty IRA in the city. In the IRA they had been receiving a basic allowance, but many of them were unemployed married men and could not sustain their situation. There were also recruits from the refugees who had come south with their families to escape the sectarian violence against the Catholic community in Belfast. J. A. Pinkman, who had been a member of the Irish Volunteers in Liverpool, joined the National Army at Beggars Bush in Dublin in March 1922. He wrote afterwards that many of the new recruits had to wait some time for their uniforms, but that did not prevent them from being instructed in drilling with their weapons by other new members who had been in the British army. They were all very enthusiastic, and even practised their drill in their spare time during the evenings.[10]

The full training period envisaged was eighteen months, but in many cases this was shortened by unfolding events, and plenty of soldiers went into action with little training in the use of their new rifles. Recruits were paid 3s 6d per day, with a generous family allowance of 4s per day for a married recruit and 6s 6d for each child (up to two children). The economic security that wages like this (£1 in 1922 is the equivalent of £534 in 2017) could provide must have attracted many, including the IRA Volunteers who had an antipathy towards the Treaty.

In June 1922, the Department of Finance projected that the expenditure on the army for 1922/23 would amount to £7.2 million, 27 per cent of the total national expenditure on public services. As the Civil War unfolded, there is no doubt that the costs increased dramatically.

The first time the Free State's new army was seen in public was on 30 January 1922, when the Dublin Guard, as it became known, then a detachment of forty-three men, led by Capt. Paddy O'Daly and Lts. Padraig O'Connor and Joe Leonard, formed up at the Gough monument in the Phoenix Park and marched into the city, with the Fintan Lalor pipe band providing martial airs. Four months later these three men were to play crucial roles in the ending of the occupation of the Four Courts. The troops had not had their new Lee Enfield rifles for long, and were unused to the weight of the weapons on their shoulders. To add to their troubles, they had to march with bayonets fixed, because the order for their leather equipment had not included a bayonet 'frog' or sheath. The detachment marched down the Liffey quays, across Grattan Bridge and up Parliament Street to City Hall, the temporary home of the Provisional Government.

The National Army military guard at City Hall turned out

The Dublin Guard marching along the cobbled quays of Dublin, past
St Paul's Church, near the Four Courts, on 30 January 1922. Led by
Capt. Paddy O'Daly, Lts. Padraig O'Connor and Joe Leonard, they were
on their way to take over Beggars Bush barracks from the British army.

and saluted the parade, while Arthur Griffith, Michael Collins
and other ministers watched proudly from the top of the steps
as the soldiers passed by, answering the command 'Eyes right!'
They passed down College Green and along D'Olier Street,
where the crowds of onlookers were so dense that there was
hardly space for the column to pass through. The parade continued on to Beggars Bush barracks, which was to become the
National Army's headquarters, and which was the first of the
Dublin barracks to be handed over by the British.

The official announcement that this parade would take
place, and the parade itself, seems to go against at least the

spirit of the undertakings the Irish gave in the Truce Liaison Committee, that there would be 'no provocative displays of forces, armed or unarmed'. The *Irish Times* reported that 'early in the afternoon Dame Street and College Green were crowded with spectators' and the detachment's 'passage along the quays evoked numerous cheers, which increased in volume as they turned across the river towards the City Hall... where a dense crowd awaited their arrival.' The men were all members of the Active Service Unit of the Dublin Brigade of the IRA, which had an illustrious record of military action during the War of Independence. As opposed to most Volunteers at the time, the men of this unit were full-time paid soldiers, and they took their orders from Michael Collins, rather than from IRA headquarters.

O'Daly and his men marched into Beggars Bush and formed up on the barracks square. Richard Mulcahy, Minister for Defence, presented Capt. O'Daly with a large tricolour, saying, 'the entry of this small band into possession of these buildings is an event of which they cannot at present estimate the importance.'

Beggars Bush had been occupied by a force of Auxiliaries who were less than happy to hand over the barracks, and were unwilling to do so in a joint ceremony with the National Army. Having paraded in the barracks square before Capt. O'Daly and his men arrived, they lowered the Union Jack, cut down the flagpole and left in lorries. Similar flag-pole-felling was carried out by departing British units in Kilkenny and Portobello Barracks, Rathmines, and there were other cases of rather childish efforts at demonstrating unhappiness with the outcome of the Treaty, such as the occupants of the barracks in Bray, Co. Wicklow, blocking the chimney of the kitchen oven with masonry. In most cases, however, the takeover of barracks was an orderly affair.

British army strength in Ireland had stood at 40,000 in October 1921: while most of these troops had been evacuated by May 1922, at least 5,000 were still camped in the Phoenix Park awaiting evacuation. The British government was not in a hurry to complete the evacuation until it could be seen that the Irish had fulfilled all the agreements in the Treaty, and Gen. Macready, commander of the British forces in Ireland, monitored developments from his headquarters at the Royal Hospital, Kilmainham, reporting weekly to the cabinet in London. A number of bases scattered about the country, such

The changing of the guard: National Army troops,
on the right, march into Richmond army barracks,
while British troops, on the left, march out.

as Marlborough barracks in Dublin, and the RAF station at Collinstown, north of Dublin, were still garrisoned by the British, and British servicemen in uniform continued to be a common sight in city streets as they went about collecting supplies or enjoying their leave.

Soldiers in the green uniforms of the new National Army were also increasingly visible around the barracks they had taken over and guarding government buildings and, later, banks.

The general public was also becoming aware of a third active army, which during the War of Independence had been rarely seen. The IRA, heavily armed but in civilian clothes, was now parading and patrolling streets throughout the country. While the new National Army was referred to as 'regular IRA troops' or 'Official Forces', the break-away republicans insisted

There is no ignoring the menacing appearance of these anti-Treaty troops on patrol in Grafton Street, Dublin, in about March 1922.

that *they* were the IRA, but they were increasingly referred to as the 'Executive Forces', the 'anti-Treaty IRA', the 'Irregulars' or the 'Die-Hards'.

Gen. Macready had written to Frances Stevenson, Lloyd George's secretary, in February 1922, suggesting 'The only way… the Irish question will ever be settled is to let the two parties fight it out together.' The challenges confronting the newly established but inexperienced Provisional Government were formidable. It had the task of assembling a governing civil service from the tattered remains of a British administration that its supporters had spent the previous four years trying to demolish, while being heckled by former comrades who were vehemently against everything they were doing. Minister for Justice Kevin O'Higgins, at thirty years of age the youngest of the ministers, when commenting later on the atmosphere in Ireland at the time, told the Irish Society of the University of Oxford that 'the country had come through a revolution and… a weird composite of idealism, neurosis, megalomania and criminality is apt to be thrown to the surface in even the best-regulated revolution.' He described the Provisional Government as 'simply eight young men in the City Hall standing amidst the ruins of one administration, with the foundations of another not yet laid, and with wild men screaming through the key-hole.'[11] The undercover 'alternative' government departments which had been established by the Dáil during the latter part of the War of Independence had not been particularly effective, but they did succeed in undermining much of a British-backed civil service. Replacement of the old bureaucracy was going to take time, and meanwhile local government throughout the country was dysfunctional; there was also no effective police force and the judicial system was fragmented.

British laws had prevailed for centuries, and now new Irish laws had to be enacted to replace them.* The Royal Irish Constabulary (RIC), an armed police force set up in the early nineteenth century under the control of Dublin Castle, which had become a target of the IRA, was now almost non-existent. Many of its officers took the generous severance packages provided for by the Treaty and emigrated to Canada, Australia and New Zealand. For those who remained, life was often precarious. Old grudges were being avenged, and over twenty ex-RIC men were murdered in the twelve months after the Treaty was signed. The new Garda Síochána police force was still in its infancy and not yet an active entity. In his Truce Liaison Office in the Gresham Hotel, Maj.-Gen. Emmet Dalton, the Provisional Government's military representative, complained about the 'brigandism' that was sweeping the country, and reported that he was receiving daily reports of armed hold-ups and motor thefts.[12] Part of the reason for this was that anti-Treaty IRA divisions were finding it increasingly difficult to feed, clothe and house their Volunteers around the country, because the Provisional Government,

---

* It was not until 2005 that the Dáil repealed many of the old English laws, such as the Suppression of Wears Act 1297, which forbade Englishmen from wearing Irish clothing, or having their heads half-shaved in the Irish custom, leaving the hair on the back of the head to grow long, and the Adulteration of Coffee Act 1718 which provided a penalty of £20 'against divers evil-disposed persons' who found ways to add substances to coffee to increase their profits.

concentrating its resources on establishing the new National Army, refused to pay their costs. So, as they had done before the truce, local commands had continued to appropriate food and goods from shops, and hold up post offices and trains to provide financial resources. Some of the raids on trains and railway stations were in connection with the Belfast Boycott:* the Midland and Great Western Railway suffered about 150 armed raids between 28 March and 22 April 1922, the raiders claiming they were searching 'by order of the IRA' for 'Belfast goods'. During the same period there were numerous raids on post offices, when money and registered letters were stolen, and letters were censored by the IRA.[13]

The anti-Treaty IRA was not alone in causing disruption among the civilian population. Gen. Richard Mulcahy, Minister for Defence, received many complaints from outraged citizens about harassment by National Army troops. A letter from the offices of the Labour Party and the Trades Union Congress, received on 27 April 1922, criticized the way in which 'military lorries and cars have been rushed, at "auxiliary speed" through the streets of the city; of "hands-uping" [sic] and searches of

---

* The Belfast Trade Boycott, originally instituted by the Dáil during the War of Independence (1919–21), was established in reaction to the requirement of Protestant employers in Ulster for prospective employees to sign a declaration of loyalty to the British government. It was also felt that trading with Belfast meant endorsing the ongoing Orange atrocities there. The Dáil urged people in the south to do no business whatever with Belfast banks or companies, saying that it was the sacred duty of every Irish man and woman to make the boycott effective in every way possible. The boycott was cancelled by Michael Collins on behalf of the Provisional Government in January 1922, but was continued by the anti-Treaty IRA.

civilians by military men; of indiscriminate shooting, i.e., firing at any moving object after an attack or alleged attack, to the danger of civilians in the streets' and an 'awful readiness to use the gun'.[14]

At the insistence of Rory O'Connor, Liam Mellows and several other leading figures in the anti-Treaty IRA, Gen. Mulcahy called an army convention on 18 January to establish an agreement between the pro- and anti-Treaty factions of the IRA. At the convention, Michael Collins appealed to the anti-Treaty officers to be patient and not withdraw allegiance to the Dáil, as they had been threatening to do. It was essential, he contended, that there should be no hold-up in the continuing British military withdrawal from Ireland. IRA resistance to accepting the authority of the democratically elected Dáil might cause the British government to slow down the evacuation of the army, or even to halt it completely.

While the convention did not achieve much agreement between the two sides, Collins did succeed in holding back, at least for a while, the hawks among the anti-Treaty group; he managed to persuade them that he was concerned to keep the British happy until he could get them to complete their withdrawal from Ireland. It was a delicate balancing act: at the same time as placating those who were against the Treaty, Collins was actively assuring the British army commander, Gen. Macready, that he was keeping the anti-Treaty faction in line until the planned general election was held, an election that would effectively put the Treaty to the people for ratification.

Certain IRA officers were, however, becoming impatient.

Just over a month after the army convention, on 22 March, Rory O'Connor, who was beginning to be accepted as the de facto leader of the hardline IRA, held a press conference, during which he made a number of crucial statements. Claiming to represent the 80 per cent of the IRA who were against the Treaty, he repudiated the authority of the democratically elected Dáil, and of the National Army headquarters. In 1920, the IRA had given allegiance to the lawfully constituted Dáil, elected by the people. The IRA had previously been controlled by an executive, and in 1920 this executive dissolved itself in order that there should be no ambiguity as to the Dáil's authority. The Dáil, in turn, confirmed that the IRA was the National Army of defence, and that Ireland and Britain were at war.

O'Connor was now rejecting the decision of two years before. He stated that the IRA was 'in a dilemma, having the choice of supporting its oath to the Republic or still giving allegiance to the Dáil, which it considered had abandoned the Republic. The contention of the army [by which he meant the anti-Treaty IRA] is that the Dáil did a thing that it had no right to do.'[15] He further declared that the IRA was no more prepared to stand for de Valera than for the Treaty. Asked if this meant the setting up of military dictatorship, he made the ominous reply 'you can take it that way if you like'. Although there seems little doubt that O'Connor and some of the more militant leaders of the anti-Treaty IRA were turning their backs on democracy, others felt that he talked too much and was not an ideal spokesman for the IRA, and that this particular statement was a political embarrassment.

The following day, in open defiance of the Provisional Government, the anti-Treaty IRA published an announcement in the press, signed by over fifty senior officers, calling for another army convention on 26 March. Over 220 predominantly anti-Treaty delegates attended this meeting at the Mansion House in Dublin. Knowing that the government did not want the meeting to take place and might make access to the Mansion House difficult, members of the 1st Southern Division of the IRA arrived there in an armoured car. There was, however, no interference. The assembly unanimously reaffirmed allegiance to the Republic, and decided that the anti-Treaty IRA would be placed once more under the command of an army executive, whose sixteen elected members would appoint a five-member army council. It was unanimously decided that the Provisional Government and its National Army would be ignored.

Two days later the newly elected army executive, which included Rory O'Connor, Liam Mellows, Liam Lynch and Ernie O'Malley, issued a statement asserting that the Minister for Defence no longer exercised any control over the IRA and that recruitment into what they called the 'Beggars Bush troops' and the new police force, the Garda Síochána, should be halted. On 26 March, exercising his new-found military authority, Rory O'Connor led an armed 'punishment' attack on the premises of the *Freeman's Journal* newspaper in retaliation for what the IRA regarded as that paper's misleading reports on the IRA convention, and its general support for the Treaty. Founded in 1763, the *Freeman's Journal* was the oldest nationalist newspaper in Ireland and always exercised moderation in its reporting, a moderation that was increasingly out of step with the upsurge of radical nationalism. The attack on 27 March left the newspaper's printing presses destroyed and some 400 men unemployed. Months before, a similar raid by the IRA would have attracted the attention of the British army or the Auxiliaries, who would have turned up in force and a fire-fight would have ensued, as had happened during the IRA attack on the Custom House in May 1921. Now, the British were no longer involved, and the Provisional Government, still hoping for an agreement with the anti-Treaty faction and not ready to confront them militarily, turned a blind eye.

On the same day as the attack on the office of the *Freeman's Journal*, the British Admiralty supply ship *Upnor* was intercepted off the Cork coast by members of the 1st Southern Division of the anti-Treaty IRA. Its cargo, a large amount of military materiel, including rifles, ammunition and explosives, which was being brought back to England from the evacuated army barracks, was captured.

The general election was scheduled for 16 June 1922, and political meetings were being held around the country by both sides. Pro-Treaty meetings were constantly disrupted by anti-Treaty activists. On 5 April, Michael Collins wrote to Joseph McGarrity, an Irish-American political activist:

The opposition are making it almost impossible for us to hold useful meetings. The crowds assemble alright, but twenty, or thirty, or forty, interrupters succeed in most places in preventing the speakers from being heard. That apparently is official policy, accompanied by blocked roads and torn up railways to prevent the excursion trains from bringing the people to our meetings. Evidently, they are going a step further now. Some of our Volunteer cars were fired on in Dublin yesterday. I greatly fear that the civil war which they have been threatening is now close at hand. So far as we can see, the result of that will really mean the destruction of all our hopes, and the return of the English. The prospect is certainly not very enticing.[16]

A few days before, in Castlebar, Co. Mayo, a meeting that Collins was addressing had been broken up by an exchange of gunfire between opposing parts of his audience, and he had had to be dragged into the safety of the nearby Imperial Hotel.

On 9 April, the anti-Treaty IRA convention reconvened. One proposal put to it was that the IRA should declare a military dictatorship, sideline the Provisional Government, and prevent a plebiscite from taking place on the matter of the Treaty. While Cathal Brugha, a former chief of staff of the IRA, opposed this motion, it was voted down by only a narrow majority. The army executive appointed an army council consisting of Liam Lynch as chief of staff, Joseph McKelvey, deputy chief of staff, Florrie O'Donoghue, adjutant-general, Ernie O'Malley, director of organization, Joseph Griffin, director of intelligence, Liam Mellows, quartermaster-general, Rory O'Connor, director of engineering, Seamus O'Donovan, director of chemicals, and Seán Russell, director of munitions.[17]

The newly elected army council was concerned about the fact that funds accumulated through Republican loans and bonds issued in Ireland and the United States were no longer coming to the IRA, but were now being used by the Provisional Government to pay the National Army and subvert the very republic they were collected to maintain. This meant that local contingents of the IRA around the country had to commandeer goods, foodstuffs and cash in order to maintain their men. The army council therefore made a decision to 'officially' carry out raids on banks in Dublin and around the country to provide the necessary funds for the maintenance of the IRA, during which 'official' receipts for the money handed over would be provided in the names of the officers commanding the raids.[18] Not all such raids were carried out in a 'gentlemanly' manner; in Tullamore, a bank manager was shot dead by raiders for refusing to open a safe: the safe was taken to a waiting lorry and driven away.

Michael Collins had admitted in a speech in Wexford on 9 April 1922 that the country was in a more uncontrolled and chaotic state than it had been during the time of the Black and Tans. As many as 331 raids on post offices and 319 raids on trains were recorded during the months of March and April. The new Garda Síochána had not yet appeared, and with no police force in the country, for many months robberies and lawlessness went unchallenged. The president of the Dublin Chamber of Commerce, William Hewat, put the general situation in a nutshell when he stated that the country 'was pervaded with fear... fear to purchase anything, fear to have anything for sale, fear of violence, fear that your life's work may be destroyed before your eyes, fear of being driven from your home.'[19]

CHAPTER 2

OCCUPATION

Dublin's main Four Courts building, which accommodated the Exchequer Court, the Court of Chancery, the Court of King's Bench and the Court of Common Pleas, was built on a site by the River Liffey and was completed in 1802. By 1922, it had been the centre of legal life in Ireland for 120 years. The original designs for the building were those of Thomas Cooley (1742–84), a brilliant young English architect. He came to Ireland having won, at the age of twenty-six, a competition for the design of Dublin's Royal Exchange, the building that is now Dublin City Hall, where the Provisional Government had its offices for much of 1922. In Ireland Cooley had a very busy career, but at the age of forty-two he died of 'a bilious fever' in his house at Anglesea Street. On his death, James Gandon, another English architect who had settled in Ireland, took over the courts project, and the great domed Four Courts that we know today, the foundation stone of which was laid in 1786, is mainly Gandon's design. In the same complex as the Four Courts building stood the Public Record Office, the Land Registry Office and the Solicitors' Building, all built later in the nineteenth century.

The Four Courts today.

The Easter sittings in the Four Courts opened every year with 'a splendid assembly in the Round Hall after the levee given by the Lord Chancellor'. He would arrive at the front entrance of the courts in his 'court dress, velvet suit, and long knee breeches with lace ruffles at neck and sleeves'. Preceded by two tipstaves and a mace-bearer, and followed by his train-bearer and purse-bearer, he would make a grand entrance and take his place on a scarlet carpet under the clock. The other judges then entered

The Lord Chancellor and members of the Irish judiciary
early in the twentieth century.

and passed before the Lord Chancellor in order of precedence,
following which he led a procession to the Benchers' Chamber
at the rear of the building where the customary meeting for the
opening of the term was held.[1]

Between midnight and 1 a.m. on 15 April 1922, only days
before this ceremony was to take place, a motorized force under
Maj.-Gen. Rory O'Connor arrived outside the Chancery Street
gate of the Four Courts. The policeman on guard was requested
to open the gates. He nervously refused, but was overpowered
from behind by men who had climbed over the railings into
the complex elsewhere. They locked him up in a nearby office.
The gate was then opened and the convoy of lorries drove into
the courtyard at the back of the main courts building. Soon

afterwards, a police sergeant and two constables arrived, and they too were restrained and locked up. All four men were later released. A short time later, a detachment of Tipperary anti-Treaty men formed up outside Barry's Hotel in Little Denmark Street, and marched to the Four Courts to join their comrades.

Up until then, the headquarters of the anti-Treaty IRA had occupied the Gaelic League Hall in Parnell Square, but it was proving too small, and it had no suitable office equipment, or sleeping accommodation for the Volunteers who guarded it. On 13 April, the army council decided that it should have a proper military headquarters in Dublin. It is not clear who first came up with the idea, but after what seems like very little discussion, the Four Courts with its capacious site and buildings was chosen, and orders were issued to occupy the complex. So, on 15 April, in one of the best-known buildings in Ireland's capital city, the general headquarters of Óglaig na hÉireann, otherwise known as the Irish Republican Army, was established. It was close to the sixth anniversary of the beginning of the 1916 Rising, and some of the 150 men that entered the Four Courts that Saturday had also been part of the garrison there in 1916.

The foreman/housekeeper of the Public Record Office, John J. Tucker, had living quarters with his son in three rooms in the basement of the Record House part of the building. He was in residence when the occupation took place, and initially he was allowed to stay. He had been evicted by the Irish Volunteers when the Four Courts was occupied during the Rebellion of 1916, and had claimed £54 4s 9d compensation for the 'looting' of the contents of his flat. On 30 April 1922,

The Four Courts Hotel in 1922.

he was evicted from his accommodation again, this time by the IRA army executive.

A group of armed men entered the nearby Four Courts Hotel, and 'refreshments' were seized and brought back to the courts. Other men visited Kennedy's Bakery in Britain Street and Donnelly's bacon-curing factory in the Coombe and returned with a lorry-load of bread and bacon. When one examines the events of the months following the Treaty debate, and the gradual intensification of unlawful activities of the anti-Treaty IRA, it is difficult not to believe that Rory O'Connor and his comrades were attempting at every stage to goad the Provisional Government, and indeed the British army, into a military confrontation, believing that such an event would bring down the infant state. If indeed this was their agenda, up until this point the anti-Treaty adherents had been unsuccessful, partly because of Collins's efforts to reunite the IRA and partly because, militarily, the Provisional Government was not ready for such a contest. Rory O'Connor and Liam Mellows could not have seen the occupation of the Four Courts, to provide what Mellows called 'a decent headquarters', as a serious military occupation. Although it was more defensible than the Gaelic League Hall in Parnell Square, very little planning was carried out, or measures put in place, then or later, for a realistic military defence of the Four Courts complex. It is possible that the taking of the country's main law courts was a spontaneous and symbolic act, with no long-term plans and little thought about the consequences. There are indications that O'Connor and Mellows fully expected to be confronted at this particu-larly outrageous provocation, and were initially disappointed when, in spite of Griffith's anger at the event, there was no reaction from the Provisional Government.

Liam Lynch, the IRA chief of staff,* was clearly preoccupied

---

* Liam Lynch (1893–1923). Born in Co. Limerick, at seventeen he com-menced an apprenticeship in the hardware trade in Mitchelstown, Co. Cork. He joined the Volunteers after witnessing a shooting by the RIC, and by 1919 he was commander of the Cork No. 2 Brigade of the IRA. He gained such a reputation as a guerrilla leader that he was made commander of the 1st Southern Division in April 1921. Increased deployment of British troops later in the year put his division under significant pressure, and he was relieved when the truce was called, although he did not believe it would last long. He opposed the Anglo-Irish Treaty, but was not happy with the split in the Republican movement and, up until the beginning of the Civil War, he worked for a compromise with erstwhile comrades who were now pro-Treaty.

with the army negotiations at the time of the occupation, and had been optimistic about their outcome, but his optimism was fading. When the Four Courts was occupied, he also expected to face an attack, and even considered that artillery might be used. On 18 April he wrote to his brother, Tom:

> We have at last thrown down the gauntlet again to England through the Provisional Government... I write this from G.H.Q. Four Courts not knowing the hour we will be attacked by machine-gun or artillery, we have a well-armed garrison of about 150 men with G.H.Q. Staff & we need only call on the Dublin Brigade or any part of the country when support will come in any numbers. I am absolutely certain that the Free State was sent to its doom by our action last week... Sad it is to risk having to clash with our old comrades but we cannot count the cost...[2]

This letter indicates that Lynch was aware that the occupation might be the last straw for the Provisional Government, but, strangely, in spite of the expectation of an attack, he gave no orders to prepare for it. The occupation did, however, drive a final and solid wedge between the two sides involved in the army negotiations, and confirmed for some members of the British government their worst fears – that the Anglo-Irish Treaty was in serious trouble.

The general membership of the IRA countrywide was clearly emboldened by the Four Courts occupation; following it, there was a dramatic increase in 'IRA outrages'. Richard Mulcahy, the Provisional Government's meticulous Minister for Defence, made notes of all the IRA activities that were reported to him. On 20 April he wrote: 'six armed men in a motor car called at Messrs Eastman's butchers shop, Thomas Street, demanded and received 85 lbs [38.5 kg] of meat. They gave a receipt signed IRA and said they required the meat for the use of the garrison in the FC.' On the same day, 'a quantity of mutton, butchers['] tools etc, value about £14 taken by five armed men from the Royal Army Service Corps section of the Corporation Abattoir, NC Road. A receipt was given signed by Seán O'Mullen, GHQ, Four Courts barracks.'

Two days later, 'Mr Kidd of 22 York Street, while conveying cigarettes value £30 in his motor car, to the RIC depot, was held up outside his premises in York Street by two armed men who compelled him to drive them to the Four Courts where they took the cigarettes from him and brought them into the Four Courts.' The same day, 'Six armed men who said they were from the Four Courts seized a quantity of fish, value £6 and 4s from Mr Shine in the Corporation Markets. The leader gave a receipt signed IRA.' An unusual hold-up took place the following day, in the name of the Belfast Boycott: 'The Irish Needlework Co. in Molesworth St was raided and £360 worth of ladies and children's wearing apparel, silk etc. was taken.'[3]

In 1922, the Four Courts and its ancillary buildings occupied a site of more than 2 hectares (4.9 acres), surrounded by sturdy wrought-iron railings 2.5 metres high. There were four gateways into the complex, the principal of which was a covered porte cochère, a two-storey gatehouse, opening onto Chancery Street.

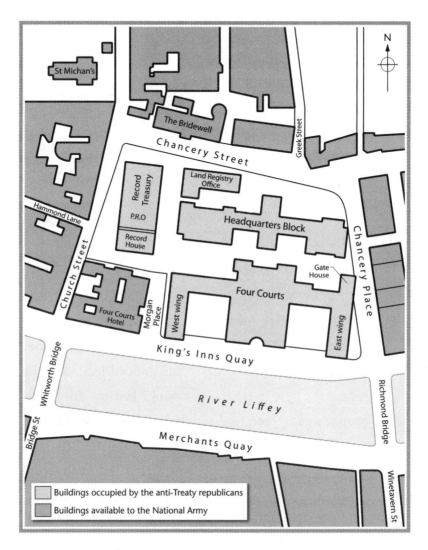

Layout of the Four Courts complex as it was in April 1922.
Note the isolated location of the Public Record Office (PRO), and how it is almost surrounded by the Four Courts Hotel, the buildings on Church Street and the Bridewell. Also note the proximity of St Michan's Church, the tower of which overlooked the roof of the PRO.

The copper-domed Four Courts building was, and still is, a substantial rectangular block, housing four main court-rooms, one in each corner, set off diagonally from a large and grand rotunda known as the Central Hall. Above this a cylindrical drum, over 21 metres (69 ft) in diameter, rises high above the surrounding roofs, topped by a peristyle of twenty-four Corinthian columns surmounted by the large and familiar green dome. Two L-shaped wings of three floors plus basement, accommodating mainly offices, extend east and west from this central block, the whole making up a riverside façade over 130 metres (427 ft) long.

To the north-west of this building was the Public Record Office, a purpose-designed national archive repository. From the earliest period of the Norman Conquest, the representatives of the English monarchs in Ireland created a bureaucracy that produced increasing amounts of written documentation such as letters, grants of lands, writs, orders, mandates, petitions, financial accounts, memoranda, court proceedings, statutes, parliament rolls and charters; effectively, the records of the administration of Ireland and the Irish. By the late thirteenth century, as these documents began to accumulate, they were gathered into the repositories of the different administrations they related to.

Occasionally documents were stolen, lost to vermin or damp, or destroyed by fire, as in St Mary's Abbey in 1304, the Birmingham Tower in Dublin Castle in 1758 and in the old Custom House in 1711. What remained, however, constituted a prodigious amount of material rich in information for historians examining aspects of Irish history, such as the Anglo-Norman settlement in Ireland, relations between Irish kings and English monarchs, land holdings, land values and the development of Irish towns. In 1867 most of these records were gathered together, for safety, into the new Public Record Office on Church Street, and by the early twentieth century the public records of Ireland had been brought into an ordered and manageable state for the first time.[4]

The Public Record Office consisted of two parts, the largest of which was the Record Treasury, where the archives were stored, a building of cast-iron construction with a six-storey

The Public Record Office as it was before the Battle of the Four Courts in June 1922. The four-bay, three-storey part on the left is the Record House, accommodating offices and a public viewing room; on the right, with the tall windows, is the Record Treasury, where the archives were stored. The two parts were separated by a fireproof link. The lamp-post and railings on the extreme right mark the south-western corner of the block that was used by the anti-Treaty IRA as their Headquarters Block.

central roof-lit atrium, surrounded by galleries of steel storage shelving. The walls were granite-faced, with tall, three-storey-high round-headed windows. The other part of the Public Record Office, at the southern end of the block, was the Record House, which housed administrative offices, a strong room, a public Reading Room, and basement accommodation for a foreman/housekeeper. The stairway in the Record House, which today houses the Courts of Appeal, is an elaborate tour de force of sand-coloured Portland stone and elaborately detailed hand-rails with wrought-iron balusters.

The Record Treasury was separated from the Record Office by a 3-metre (9 ft 10 in.)-wide fireproof link to prevent any fire that might break out in the 'living and working' area of the building spreading to the storage area. At the time of the occupation, the Public Record Office had a staff of thirty-five,

The north-east corner of the Headquarters Block, seen from across Chancery Street, during reconstruction works in 1926. The dome of the Four Courts can be seen behind, and part of the Four Courts east wing can be seen on the extreme left.

under Herbert Wood, who was then the deputy keeper of records. It had been officially handed over to the Provisional Government by the British administration on 1 April 1922, fourteen days before the beginning of the occupation of the Four Courts.

To the east of the Public Record Office and north of the Four Courts was a building of three floors over basement that was constructed in parts between the 1830s and the 1860s, and was known as the Solicitors' Block. It housed a range of accommodation including several courts and offices, chambers for solicitors and barristers, a dining-room, the Incorporated Law Society's premises, and the headquarters of the Benchers of the Honorable Society of King's Inns. This building was selected, according to Ernie O'Malley,* by Liam Lynch to house the offices of the IRA's headquarters, and I will refer to this building throughout the text as the Headquarters Block.

North of the Headquarters Block, facing onto Chancery Street and opposite the Bridewell police barracks was the Land Registry Office, an L-shaped, three-storey-over-basement building completed in 1912. Ernie O'Malley makes no reference in his narrative to it, and it has been left out of maps in three

---

* Ernest O'Malley (1897–1957) was born in Co. Mayo and was studying medicine at the National University when the 1916 Rising occurred. He joined the Dublin Brigade of the IRA in 1917 and saw active service in Dublin, Co. Tyrone, Co. Monaghan and Co. Cork, where he got to know Liam Lynch and with him captured the first British army barracks to fall to the IRA. He was imprisoned in Kilmainham Gaol but escaped, and went to Munster, where he was put in command of the 2nd Munster Division of the IRA, and saw further action in Tipperary, Kilkenny and Limerick.

recently published books that deal briefly with the siege of the Four Courts. There is no mention of it or its garrison in either Ernie O'Malley's or Padraig O'Connor's writings, but the *Freeman's Journal* of Saturday, 1 July says that it was occupied by anti-Treaty men, and Mr Glover, the registrar of the Land Registry Office, reported that the damage done to the building appeared to be caused by the 'explosion of the mine, and by the

The entrance and west façade of the Land Registry
Office, before the Battle of the Four Courts. It was very close
to the north wall of the Headquarters Block, which can be
seen immediately to its right. On the extreme right, inside
the railings, is the north-east corner of the Record Treasury.

armed forces that were in occupation.'⁵ One photograph I have come across shows that the roof was fortified with sandbags.

The impressive façade of the Four Courts addressed the River Liffey and cobbled, tram-lined King's Inns Quay. To the north of the complex, opposite the Land Registry Office, lay the Bridewell Police Barracks and a courthouse. Contemporary maps give a good impression of the surroundings of the Four Courts at the time. To the east, facing Chancery Place, there was a warren of densely inhabited tenement blocks, while on the west side facing Church Street were more tenements, the Maguire & Patterson match factory, the only manufacturer of such products in Ireland, part of the Hammond Lane Foundry and Sheridan's Eagle Foundry, where bronze bells were cast. Between Church Street and Morgan Place a block containing a number of houses, shops and the Four Courts Hotel projected, like a Trojan horse, into the south-west corner of the Four Courts complex. Windows in these buildings were no more than 11 metres (12 yds) from the south façade of the Public Record Office, and 16 metres (17.5 yds) across Morgan Place from the west wing of the Four Courts. If there had been a serious intention of defending the Four Courts against a military attack, these buildings should have also been occupied by the anti-Treaty IRA that April.

Substantial amounts of barbed wire and sandbags were brought in by lorries over the first days of occupation to fortify the buildings. The men who had been in the courts during the rebellion six years before were particularly useful, for they were already familiar with the general layout of the buildings, and the main Four Courts block. It must have given them a strange feeling of déjà vu to be barricading the same windows with tables, leather-bound law books, bundles of files and legal documents as they had done in April 1916. The two gateways facing the river as well as the opening onto Morgan Place were blocked with sandbags and barbed wire, and later landmines were laid to prevent them from being used. Entrance to and exit from the complex was limited to the main gateway opening onto Chancery Place, controlled by an armed guard detail stationed in the gatehouse. Later on, a Rolls-Royce armoured car, popularly named 'The Mutineer', equipped with a Vickers

'The Mutineer' Rolls-Royce armoured car with
its Vickers machine-gun in the Four Courts.

machine-gun in a revolving armoured turret, was stationed in the entrance courtyard, covering the gate.

The Headquarters Block was, perhaps, the building in the complex least exposed to possible gunfire from outside, protected as it was by the Four Courts to the south, the Public Record Office to the west and the Land Registry Office along part of its north side. According to some accounts, a 'chemical shop' was established in this building, involving the use of 'inflammable substances'.[6] As we shall see, it was also chosen for the storage of explosive materials to be used in the manufacture of mines and hand grenades in the adjacent Public Record Office. Members of the IRA executive chose offices for themselves in the Headquarters Block, Ernie O'Malley selecting a suite on the second floor, with roll-topped desks, typewriters and comfortable furnishings. The office accommodation in the building was luxurious in comparison to what the executive had been used to in Parnell Square, and there was a stationery office in the basement that supplied all that was needed in terms of notepaper, files and other office materials. O'Malley's description of the exciting atmosphere that prevailed as they all settled into their new quarters has a *'Boys' Own'* feel to it; he saw it as an adventure, and recalled how Liam Mellows could be heard singing songs such as 'The Croppy Boy' and 'Come all ye Brave United Men'. The Four Courts was a convenient Dublin base for Mellows and he continued to attend meetings of the Dáil up until the time of its dissolution at the end of May 1922.[7]

Una Daly, Liam Mellows's secretary, claimed that she was the

Two members of the garrison of the Four Courts display their
prowess with arms. On the left is William Doyle, who was one
of those who initially took the pro-Treaty side, only to
change sides and join the men in the Four Courts.

first woman to enter the Four Courts with the occupying garrison, and that they had 'a very posh office'. She also remembered
that 'Mrs Terry McSwiney' was there. She was the widow of
Terence McSwiney, author, political activist and Lord Mayor
of Cork, who had died on hunger strike in Brixton Prison on
25 October 1920. Daly said that there was quite a big staff,
that she did not 'live in' but went home at night, and was not
there when the siege started.[8] Todd Andrews had originally
aligned himself with the pro-Treaty side, and had worked for

Emmet Dalton making arrangements for the handover by the British of army and police barracks, but he threw in his lot with the anti-Treaty side after the convention of 26 March, and went to work in the Four Courts as a clerk in Ernie O'Malley's office. He admired O'Malley, although he found that the man was not generally liked. He was regarded as a martinet and, even worse, an intellectual: when the men were sitting around the fire gossiping, O'Malley held himself aloof, and sat in the corner reading some obscure work of classical literature. Andrews was surprised to find that O'Malley had a frivolous side, however: he recalled him going into town with Seán MacBride every morning to stroll in Grafton Street where they would meet girls from the university for coffee in Mitchel's or Roberts'. He also remembered accompanying O'Malley and MacBride when they commandeered a car from some 'harmless citizen' just to go for a drive in the country.[9]

It soon became clear that there would never be enough sandbags, law books and ledgers to protect all the windows: as O'Malley recalled in his book, *The Singing Flame*, 'the building swallowed them up'. Rory O'Connor and others had justified the occupation on the grounds that their Parnell Square premises were not big enough, and that the Four Courts would be sufficient to accommodate all the operations of a proper headquarters. What they did not mention was the need for premises that would be suitable for setting up a factory for the manufacture of military explosives, such as landmines and hand grenades, and that could provide suitable storage space for the explosives, detonators and arms they were accumulating from around the country. The Four Courts campus also provided secure parking for the lorries and other vehicles a modern army needed, all this evidence of the serious intent of the IRA at least to be prepared to return to military action.

On 1 May Liam Lynch wrote: 'We are absolutely convinced of wiping out this supposed Free State, but we don't mind giving it a slow death, especially when it means the avoidance of loss of life & general civil war… There is no strain here, a

The interior of the Record Treasury of the Public
Record Office early in the twentieth century.

fight would in fact relieve any such, especially if the English interfere.'[10]

O'Malley wrote that lathes and motors had been installed in the Public Record Office, where mine cases and hand grenades were being manufactured and filled with explosives. He saw 'a jumble of lathes, moulds and mine cases; hand grenade bodies lay in heaps; electric detonators, electric wires and explosives were piled between the racks which held the records... In the lower rooms there were explosives, including a large amount of TNT.'[11] The Public Record Office was, because of its isolation from the other buildings, the most appropriate location in the complex for the manufacture of mines and hand grenades. However, its large areas of glazing and its closeness to the back of the Four Courts Hotel and the buildings on the west side of Church Street also made it the most vulnerable building. The choice of the Public Record Office for the manufacture of munitions might suggest that the anti-Treaty IRA executive foresaw, and indeed expected, that its Four Courts headquarters would come under military attack, and that the existence of the precious archives in the Record Office and the danger of damage to them would create at least a reluctance on behalf of the National Army to launch such an attack. One wonders why it was that this most exposed post, with no safe way to get supplies of ammunition and food to its occupants if it came under fire, was garrisoned by 'young lads', a section of Na Fianna, under the command of Tom Morrissey. While some of the young men, such as eighteen-year-old Thomas Wall, had been 'active' with the IRA for a few years, the lads of Na Fianna were usually younger than that, and their normal duties would have been as messengers and in other non-combatant roles.*

Subsequent events and other anomalies in O'Malley's recollections provoke one to ask if he had a clear memory as to exactly which building was used to store explosives. It would be standard practice that the manufacture of munitions would never take place in close proximity to an area where explosives were stored: if such were the case, even a minor accident could become a major catastrophe. Early in the occupation, Seamus O'Donovan, the IRA director of chemicals, had his hand accidentally blown off while experimenting with grenades in the 'munitions factory'.[12]

The Record Treasury consisted of a central open space five storeys high, with galleries along the sides running the length of the building. With regard to O'Malley's statement in *The Singing Flame* that 'In the lower rooms there were explosives, including a large amount of TNT':[13] 'lower rooms' rather than 'in the basement', seems to suggest there were upper rooms in the place he remembers, rather than this one great space. Evidence, as we shall see, points to the TNT 'store' being in one of the rooms at the western end of the Headquarters Block, easily accessible and close enough to the Record Treasury, which became known as

---

* Na Fianna was an Irish Republican youth movement founded in 1909 by Countess Markievicz (1868–1927). In 1913 Liam Mellows took on the task of making it a countrywide movement. Although they received instruction in the use of firearms and were often involved in actions against the British, the normal work of Na Fianna in the IRA was to act as orderlies, passing messages between staff officers and serving food in the mess.

the 'munitions factory' or the 'munitions block', but far enough away for safety. Such would not be the case if explosives were stored in the basement of the Record Treasury.

The main canteen to feed the garrison was established in the Central Hall of the Four Courts, a vast, echoing, marble-floored space under the dome. It was overlooked by four magnificent bas-relief panels representing great events in British history: William the Conquerer establishing Norman laws, King John signing the Magna Carta, King Henry II landing in Ireland, and King James I abolishing the Brehon Laws. The food, however, served in this impressive canteen was anything but magnificent, and soon earned a poor reputation. Todd Andrews relates in *Dublin Made Me* how the meat and vegetables that were commandeered from local shops were the best to be had, but had been ruined by the time they reached the table. O'Malley commented that the cooks 'might have learned their trades in a sailors' dive on the quays.' Headquarters clerical staff, mostly women, preferred to leave the Four Courts to go out to lunch. From time to time unusual delicacies were passed around among the garrison, 'appropriated' by the teams under Leo Henderson, the commandant in charge of the Belfast Boycott, which was carrying out armed raids on premises selling goods produced in Northern Ireland and 'confiscating' them.

Strangely, the occupation of the Four Courts drew scant immediate attention in the Irish press. An article in the *Irish Independent* reported on 16 April that 'the occupation of the Four Courts prompted a degree of curiosity, but people were not in an excitable mood.' On 15 April the paper published an interview with Rory O'Connor, whom the media seems to have accepted as the leader of the occupation. He declared emphatically that the IRA occupation of the building should not be taken in any way as a *coup d'état*, nor did it indicate the beginning of a revolution. There is going to be no revolution, he said.

On 18 April *The Times* of London was scathing about the occupation and was clearly unaware of the anti-Treaty faction's highly efficient methods and success in financing its operations, noting that the maintenance of a considerable garrison 'must be a costly business, and it is quite possible that Mr O'Connor's adventure may be no more exciting than that of the Duke of York who marched his troops up the hill and then down again.' The newspaper went on to comment that it expected that the Constitution of the Irish Free State, 'which has now been completed', would be published within days, allowing the electorate adequate time to study it before the general election to elect a new Dáil under the terms of the Treaty, which was to take place later that month. Work on the Constitution was not, in fact, completed in April, and the election was postponed until June.

For the ordinary Irish public trying to fathom what was going on politically, it must have been a very confusing period. For a while, when there was a split in the executive council of the IRA between the Four Courts garrison and those who sided with Liam Lynch, there were three separate anti-Treaty factions, including de Valera's newly formed political party, Cumann na Poblachta. Winston Churchill, the British Secretary of State for the Colonies, referred in the House of Commons to

The east (Chancery Street) gate during the occupation of the Four Courts:
the south-eastern corner of the Headquarters Block can be seen on the
right. Note the sandbags in the first-floor windows of the gatehouse,
and the very modern-looking 'Drive Slowly' sign on the gatepost.

the genuine Republicans as 'a comparatively small number of
armed men, violent in method, fanatical in temper, but in many
cases disinterested or impersonal in motive'. Behind them,
however, there was

> a larger number of common, sordid ruffians and brigands,
> robbing, murdering, pillaging, for their personal gain or for
> private revenge, or creating disorder and confusion out of
> pure love for disorder and confusion. These bandits – for
> they are nothing else – pursue their devastating course under
> the so-called glamour of the Republic and are inextricably
> intermingled with bona fide Republican visionaries.[14]

During the War of Independence, individual divisions of the IRA in the provinces, while accepting the leadership of the Dublin headquarters, carried on their local operations independently without necessarily seeking the sanction of headquarters. This policy continued during the truce and, increasingly, provincial bodies of the IRA, disillusioned with the Treaty and feeling more than ever disconnected from the happenings in Dublin, were carrying out actions that were on occasion close to common banditry. A report in the *Irish Times* for 13 May gives a typical example of this. The article relates that early in 1922 anti-Treaty forces had evicted the Coast Guards from their station at Banbeg, Co. Donegal and occupied the place. On 12 May they held an auction, in which they sold off all the furniture, fittings, bedsteads and other contents of the building, after which they set fire to it, commandeered a car and were last seen heading for Letterkenny. Local people hurried to the scene before the building was fully burnt out, and removed everything of value that remained, taking away even the doors.

Even while this and other similar acts of lawlessness were happening around the country, in Dublin, negotiations continued between the anti-Treaty IRA and the National Army. During these discussions Liam Lynch ordered that some of the buildings in Dublin, such as the Kildare Street Club, which had been occupied earlier, were to be evacuated and handed back, to demonstrate good faith. The Kildare Street Club, a gentleman's club founded in 1782, was a bastion of the Anglo-Irish Protestant ascendancy. After being used temporarily to accommodate Catholic refugees from the pogroms in Belfast, it was handed back on 3 June. The *Irish Times* reported that a formal handover took place, with Brigadier Oscar Traynor representing the occupiers and Sir Frederick Shaw representing the club. Shaw is reported to have commented that 'except for injuries to a window and a billiard table, not much structural damage has been caused anywhere', and he 'thought that the occupying party had done their best to preserve everything – rolling up the carpets and covering up the pictures.' Before the handover, however, some members of the garrison departed wearing clothing belonging to club members and even waiters' uniforms, leaving the premises short of many cigars and 10 gallons (45.5 litres) of whiskey.[15] Ernie O'Malley recalled a visit to the Kildare Street Club when it was occupied and seeing anti-Treaty men sitting in leather upholstered chairs puffing leisurely on long cigars, some of which found their way into the quartermaster's stores in the Four Courts: he remembered being given a pocketful. The club subsequently made a claim for compensation in the amount of £5,400, and received £4,180, which was regarded as a satisfactory result.

Meanwhile, the Provisional Government, wary of further occupations that might be attempted by the anti-Treaty forces in Dublin, put armed guards on many premises around the city, including the GPO, the Shelbourne Hotel, Hopkins and Hopkins, the jewellers, and Jacob's Biscuit Factory, 'as a precautionary measure'.

Although Liam Lynch was chief of staff of the army council, he had his office where he stayed in the Clarence Hotel; the Four Courts was only a few minutes away on foot. Neither he nor Joseph McKelvey, deputy chief of staff, who was very much part of the occupation and remained in the Four Courts until the end, took much interest in the military aspects of the occupation. Rory O'Connor and other members of the IRA army council such as Liam Mellows, who had their offices in the Four Courts, also avoided direct involvement in the maintenance and defence of the headquarters. To look after these matters, they appointed Paddy O'Brien of Dublin No. 1 Brigade as the officer commanding the garrison. One of the members of the garrison, Donegal socialist Peadar O'Donnell, said later that the presence of members of the IRA army executive undermined O'Brien's authority.[16]

O'Brien seemed unclear about the extent of his powers as garrison commander, and when he made strong recommendations to Lynch regarding what needed to be done about the proper fortification of the complex and establishment of defensive positions around it, his suggestions were ignored. Lynch did, however, find the time to write a letter to O'Brien on 19 May complaining about the state of sanitation and cleanliness of the headquarters, telling him that they were not receiving the attention they deserved: 'Scarcely any disinfectants are being used even in the lavatories and the corridors are very often not swept. The entrance to this [GHQ] block is usually in a most untidy condition. Disinfectants should be used unsparingly all over the barracks.'[17]

He went on to say that the kitchen of the officers' mess was in an 'bominable' [sic] condition, and that if it were not thoroughly disinfected, there was the 'grave' danger of it being the cause of sickness, since food cooked or stored there would not be wholesome.

O'Brien passed the letter to the 'Medical Officer' for his 'immediate attention and explanation' [sic]. There is no evidence that he received one. He must have been furious, however, that while urgent and crucial military decisions were not being made, the chief of staff was concerning himself with such minor matters as disinfectants. He had no choice but to be satisfied with the most basic and simple objectives within his control, such as identifying the locations that attackers might occupy around the Four Courts complex, setting up defence posts to counter an attack, and having each man ensure that his rifle sights were properly distance-adjusted. O'Brien did have an agenda of his own, however. He suspected that Lynch was going to order that more of the properties that had been occupied in Dublin should be evacuated and handed back, as the Kildare Street Club had been, and that his garrison might be ordered to vacate the Four Courts. He told Ernie O'Malley that he would burn or blow up the place rather than hand it over. O'Malley agreed with him, and for this purpose he and O'Brien had 'barrels of petrol and paraffin... stored in the cellars and in dark corners, unknown to the rest of the Headquarters Staff.'[18] The Limerick-born Republican Seán Moylan later confirmed this plan, saying that 'barrels of paraffin were brought into the courts on the Sunday before the attack, and men were sent to distribute them among the buildings.'[19]

★

Although Arthur Griffith and other members of the Provisional Government were in favour, from the beginning, of forcibly evicting the occupiers of the Four Courts, Michael Collins, like Liam Lynch among others on the anti-Treaty side, believed that negotiations between the two groups would eventually bring about a resolution of their differences, which would lead to the courts and other occupied buildings being peacefully vacated. Collins was certain that taking a hard line at this stage would only worsen the split and, anyway, there was no appetite as yet among the officers of the new National Army to take up arms against their former comrades. There was also concern that the National Army was not yet sufficiently up to strength, its men inadequately trained, and it was still lacking in proper discipline and organization. One man who had joined the National Army simply changed his mind after a week and went back to his farm: his absence went unnoticed until some time later. Some enlisted men only reported on paydays,[20] and others were still swopping 'sides'. After waiting around for some four weeks at Beggars Bush barracks to be commissioned into the new army, an aspiring recruit called Hughie Early gave up, walked to the Four Courts, and threw in his lot with the anti-Treaty faction.[21]

The months of April and May 1922 were characterized by an increasingly frenetic series of long-drawn-out meetings and negotiations, the circulation of position papers, statements and counter-statements, as desperate efforts were made to find a consensus on the matter of the Treaty and its fallout. In parallel with time spent debating theories about the meaning of such terms as the 'Free State' and the 'Republic' with the anti-Treaty faction, those who were members of the Provisional Government were working day and night on the Herculean task of putting the country back in order and running it as an independent state. In a room at the Shelbourne Hotel in Dublin, the Constitution for the new state was in the process of being written: Michael Collins was the chairman of the Constitution Commission, but attended only the first meeting. Long hours and overwork were taking their toll on all the members of the Provisional Government: Collins was exhausted and suffering from stomach pains, head-colds and lack of sleep, and Arthur Griffith was swiftly losing the imperturbability for which he was so well known.

The occupants of the Four Courts, in spite of the commandeering activities and bank robberies that they were overseeing around the country, and their continued planning to destabilize the north, were unrestricted in their activities. While it is to be assumed that the place was being watched and the government was receiving reports on what was going on, there was no military cordon around the complex and the leaders and other personnel were allowed to come and go unhindered. Most members of the garrison left the complex during their time off. The barrack adjutant, twenty-three-year-old Seán Lemass, issued stiff cards as passes, which he signed and stamped on the back with the wax seal of the Lord Chief Justice of Southern Ireland. Barry's Hotel in Little Denmark Street was a popular drinking spot for both National Army men and anti-Treaty IRA men, and at the Plaza Hotel in Gardiner Row, men from

Meeting at the Mansion House in Dublin, 8 May 1922, and still
talking: Seán MacEoin (pro-Treaty), Seán Moylan (anti-Treaty),
Eoin O'Duffy (pro-Treaty), Liam Lynch (anti-Treaty),
Gearóid O'Sullivan (pro-Treaty) and Liam Mellows (anti-Treaty).

the two factions drank together and argued about the Treaty
late into the night.

The Four Courts covers a city block, and is not so extensive
that, had the National Army had sufficient men, it could not
have been easily encircled by a strong, dug-in military cordon.
Such a tactic could have effectively confined the occupiers
indefinitely without access to food, ammunition, supplies and
communications. There was concern, however, that such action
would disrupt the negotiations and bring a swing in public
opinion in favour of the besieged. There was also the possibility
that there could be serious clashes or worse, if other anti-Treaty

Barracks pass from the Four Courts, signed by Seán Lemass,
barrack adjutant, and stamped with the seal of the
Lord Chief Justice of Southern Ireland.

factions in the capital, particularly Oscar Traynor's Dublin
Brigade, came to the aid of the garrison.

What is not certain, but must be considered, is how Michael
Collins's membership of the Irish Republican Brotherhood
may have been an important factor in his disinclination to
order an attack against fellow members of the brotherhood.
Another reason for not moving on the Four Courts was the
deteriorating situation in Northern Ireland, which was troub-
ling Collins deeply. Northern Catholics, in particular, felt they
had been abandoned by the Treaty, and were suffering from

the lack of police protection from Loyalist mobs: indeed, the overwhelmingly Protestant Special Constabulary was behind much of the shootings, intimidation, burnings and the driving of Catholics from their homes. Sectarian violence worsened during the month of May, and many suffered injury and death. From January to the end of May, 237 people – 87 Protestants and 150 Catholics – died in the violence. During the month of May alone, 75 people, including 42 Catholics, were killed in Belfast.[22] What is particularly telling about the casualties, many the result of sniper fire, is the number of women and children killed and wounded: nine women and three children were shot dead in the last ten days of May 1922. By the middle of June about 23,000 Catholics had had to leave their homes, and 8,750 were driven out of their employment. Public support, which had been essential to the IRA all over the country for the waging of the War of Independence, had dropped away severely for the northern divisions of the IRA, whose members were demoralized. The northern counties had been for decades a problem, a stumbling block, to the achievement of Irish independence, and had become a pawn to be strategically played by either side. Since as early as 1912, the idea of as many as twenty-eight counties seeking independence from Britain, leaving the remaining four behind, had been seriously considered by some. In spite of the horrors occurring during the pogroms in Belfast, little had been said in the Treaty debate about Northern Ireland which, long before its borders were established formally, had been a functioning state for a year by then. This may have been partly due to Collins's assurances that the Boundary

Commission would leave the Unionist north an unworkable entity, allowing the Free State to have Derry city, Fermanagh, Tyrone, south Down and south Armagh. This, of course, did not happen.

Throughout the period of the negotiations and the truce, Michael Collins, in parallel with working towards fulfilling the Treaty agreements, was secretly engaged in finding ways to protect the northern Catholics and continue the war in the north through the anti-Treaty IRA. Indeed, the Four Courts played a central part in an undercover operation that was in place during this period, with the help of Minister for Defence, Richard Mulcahy, to supply arms to the northern divisions of the IRA. The youthful Seán MacBride had been arranging shipments of arms from Germany before the Treaty had been signed, and he continued to do so after the signing, with the encouragement of Collins and apparently other prominent members of the pro-Treaty side, after the signing. In MacBride's memoir, *That Day's Struggle*, he later wrote: 'Collins promised to give us all the assistance he possibly could so that the struggle would continue in the north. Arms were handed over in substantial quantities, in lorry-loads, to the IRA in Dublin, to us, to Rory O'Connor.'[23] In an article in *The Republic* newspaper which Rory O'Connor wrote from his cell in Mountjoy Prison before his execution, he made it clear that both Mulcahy and Eoin O'Duffy, the National Army chief of staff, were also involved in what was going on. He mentioned a meeting which these two, and also Mellows and Lynch, had attended, during which they discussed co-ordinated military action against 'N.E. Ulster', and agreed to appoint one officer who would command both Republican and Free State troops in the region. The meeting also dealt with the National Army passing on to the anti-Treaty IRA in the south new Lee Enfield rifles received from Britain. Great efforts were made to ensure that the Royal Ulster Constabulary would not capture rifles from the IRA which had only just been handed over by the British to the National Army, so rather than supply the north directly, elaborate arrangements were put in place by which some of the new rifles supplied by the British for the National Army were given to southern divisions of the IRA, while their own, older rifles went north. Even up until mid-June rifles and ammunition were being 'sent to and fro between the Four Courts and Beggars Bush barracks and many officers were sent with equipment to the divisions in the north.'[24] Todd Andrews remembered being puzzled by lorry-loads of rifles being delivered to the Four Courts from Beggars Bush, and other arms being sent back to that barracks.

In July 1922, as the Civil War intensified, the Kildare Brigade of the anti-Treaty IRA was to find itself inadequately armed because its rifles had been shipped north through this complicated system and had not been replaced, and were unlikely to be replaced at that stage, by rifles from the National Army shipments.[25]

Matters in the south were, however, Michael Collins's priority. There had been talk in the newspapers of a possible civil war as early as March. In that month Kevin O'Higgins, Minister for Justice, wrote, 'Mr de Valera is at present leader of a motley coalition which contains within itself elements so conflicting that it can only be held together on a destructive programme.'[26] As March ran into April and then May, minor armed clashes between National Army and anti-Treaty forces around the country were increasing. The frequency of skirmishes between the two sides was such that two full months before the siege of the Four Courts began, Richard Mulcahy commented, in relation to a request by Western Command of the new National Army for more armoured cars, rifles and mortars, 'we must face it that we require them at once, even if we had not in this "Civil War".'[27]

In spite of his reduced influence with the anti-Treaty faction, Éamon de Valera fanned the flames of violence in many of his remarks: he called the Provisional Government 'the new Castle', referring to Dublin Castle, which for centuries before the Treaty had attracted the hatred of the Irish. He told the people that if, in future, they dared to aspire to the fullness of their rights, they would have to turn their swords against their fellow countrymen. In speeches in Carrick-on-Suir and Thurles on 17 March, de Valera told his listeners, which included armed members of the anti-Treaty IRA that, if the Treaty was ratified, they would have to wade through Irish blood, and the blood of Irish government soldiers, and perhaps the blood of some members of the new government in order to get Irish freedom. In Killarney the following day he repeated his warnings, and condemned majority rule, making, for him, the strange remark, 'the people never have the right to do wrong'.[28] All this in spite of his earlier comment in the Dáil that he would never commit himself to any course to which it would not be possible to secure the assent of the majority of the people. 'I will never put myself in the ridiculous position of an engine running away without the train.'

By the beginning of May there had been eight fatalities and forty-nine wounded in armed skirmishes between the National Army and the anti-Treaty faction around the country, and it was becoming increasingly apparent that unless there was a meeting of minds very soon, more serious hostilities would inevitably occur. There was also the possibility that the British, who still had a considerable number of combat troops in Ireland, would be drawn into renewed warfare. Early in May, in a further worsening of activities, the anti-Treaty IRA carried out raids on twenty-six banks throughout the country, during the course of which over £156,000 was 'handed over'.[29] There seemed to be little public concern about this – banks were not particularly popular with the general public – but the success of the raids and the continuing lack of reaction from the government emboldened the IRA executive. There is little doubt that a portion, at least, of this money never saw the IRA vaults, and it is said that numerous businesses were set up around the country after the Civil War with money from train and bank robberies. Indeed, there is evidence that an IRA member was expelled from the Volunteers by a court comprising Commandant Maurice (Moss) Twomey and Seán MacBride, for misappropriation of monies gained in raids – the expelled individual later set up a successful motor business and became a prominent member of Clare Co. Council.[30]

The army council in the Four Courts spent much time discussing a destabilization campaign in the newly created state of Northern Ireland, and devising plans for attacks on the British army and the police there. For these 'invasions', a sufficient number of cars and lorries were being 'commandeered' around Dublin and brought to the Four Courts to transport a large military force to the north. There was no subterfuge about this: in an interview for the *Cork Examiner* on 29 May, Rory O'Connor stated that his people controlled three-quarters of the arms in the country, and that an attack on Northern Ireland was ready. He knew that these developments were being watched with growing concern by the British government, and it seems clear that he and his fellow council members hoped that such provocative acts would force British military intervention, which would result in the National Army and the IRA reuniting in resumed hostilities against Britain.

It seems certain that the Four Courts-based army executive member who was most enthusiastic about re-establishing the influence of the IRA in Northern Ireland was twenty-four-year-old Joseph McKelvey, from Stewartstown, Co. Tyrone. He had commanded the Belfast Brigade of the IRA during the War of Independence, and his hardline attitude towards the Treaty must have been born out of the long-running pogrom suffered by Catholics in the north which he had witnessed at first hand, and the betrayal he felt the Treaty represented. In August 1920

Joseph McKelvey.

his brigade had been involved in the locating, in Lisburn, Co. Antrim, of District Inspector Oswald Swanzy. The previous March, Tomás MacCurtain, Mayor of Cork and commander of Cork's No.1 Brigade of the IRA, had been shot dead in front of his wife and young son by a group of men with blackened faces. The men with the blackened faces were members of the RIC, and the shooting was in revenge for the killing by the IRA of one of their fellow officers. The coroner's inquest on MacCurtain's death had passed a verdict of wilful murder against the British prime minister, David Lloyd George, Lord French, the lord lieutenant of Ireland, and some named high-ranking members of the RIC.[31] One of those named by the coroner's jury was Oswald Swanzy, and for his protection, he had been transferred from Cork to the overwhelmingly Loyalist town of Lisburn. With the assistance of McKelvey's brigade, however, IRA intelligence tracked him down there, and he was killed as he left a Sunday religious service by three members of the Cork Brigade, one of them using Tomás MacCurtain's personal handgun. The killing had created a vicious sectarian backlash in Lisburn and the surrounding countryside. In three days of rioting, nearly 1,000 Catholics had had to flee the town when their homes and shops were burnt down, causing half-a-million pounds' worth of damage. About 100 business premises had been destroyed, including Protestant shops that burned when the fires got out of control. The local IRA was hunted mercilessly, and Joseph McKelvey had to flee to Dublin and lie low for some time. During his sojourn there, he had got to know many of those working in IRA headquarters. Back in the north, his brigade suffered many setbacks, and after the truce was signed, he went to Dublin to argue against the acceptance of the Treaty. His arguments appealed to many and he had been elected to the IRA army executive.

The general election to the Irish Dáil was finally set for 16 June and, mutually concerned to avoid it cementing a split in Sinn Féin, de Valera and Collins met on 20 May to try to find sufficient common ground to allow the election to go ahead fairly and smoothly. They agreed that both factions would present a united front in the election, and that they would recommend that pro-Treaty voters give their first preference to the pro-Treaty

candidate, and their second preference to the anti-Treaty candidate, while anti-Treaty voters would do the reverse. The pact
could lead to both pro-Treaty and anti-Treaty members sitting in
the Provisional Government. Hugh Kennedy, the government's
law officer, told Collins that the strategy could be contrary to
the Treaty, because each member of the Provisional Government
had to accept the Treaty in writing, and this was unlikely to
happen if there were anti-Treaty members.

The pact was also not entirely legal, working as it did against
smaller parties such as the Labour Party, the Farmers' Party
and the Southern Unionists, but it shows the desperation with
which both de Valera and Collins viewed the deteriorating situation. Arthur Griffith was strongly opposed to the pact, but
Collins managed to get the cabinet to endorse it. It was roundly
condemned by a furious British government, who saw the possibility of any unity of pro- and anti-Treaty factions as a dangerous
development. The evacuation of British troops from Ireland was
halted, and Collins and Griffith were summoned to London to
explain themselves.

By the end of May 1922 it was becoming apparent to the
general public that the Four Courts occupation might not be just
a temporary affair, and that if the occupiers did not evacuate the
buildings soon, it might become a battleground between anti-
Treaty forces and either the British army or the National Army.

One can imagine that the judges, solicitors and barristers
whose offices, files and personal belongings had been inacces-
sible for some weeks were becoming frustrated, and there was
growing concern that should fighting take place in the Four

Courts, the large quantities of legal documentation and records stored in the complex might be lost. There was particular concern among scholars and historians about the priceless archives stored in the Record Treasury of the Public Record Office. They were right to be worried: the Record Office had had a small garrison during the occupation of the Four Courts complex in 1916, and the place could easily have come to grief then. The Royal Dublin Fusiliers had set up a machine-gun at the western end of Hammond Lane, and hosed down the western façade of the Record House. The contents were not harmed, but Thomas Allen, one of the Irish Volunteers occupying the building, was killed. Among the vast collections of documents stored in the Record Treasury were census records, military records, details of law cases, court records and records of land transfers. There were also a number of medieval chancery rolls, collections of medieval records of all sorts, including wills, writs, fines and letters, transcribed onto parchments, which were stored by being stitched together head to foot and then rolled up. The oldest document was said to be a papal grant of AD 916, creating the Chapter of Christ Church in Dublin, and there were also letters and legal documents from the time of Henry II. A typical example of the more modern material was the magnificent 149-volume set of the manuscript Journals of the Irish Lords and Commons, bound in crimson morocco leather, with each volume lavishly tooled in gilt. Irish book bindings of the eighteenth and nineteenth centuries were much superior to those of many other countries; this particular set was described by the early-twentieth-century chairman of

Sothebys, G. D. Hobson, as 'probably the most majestic series of bound volumes in the world.'[32]

In an interview with the *Irish Times*, the day after the occupation of the Four Courts in April, Rory O'Connor was quoted as saying that they would safeguard all the records that were in the Public Record Office, which, he understood, could never be replaced.

Constantine P. Curran, senior counsel and registrar of the Supreme Court, wrote letters to the Provisional Government, Éamon de Valera and the occupants of the Four Courts regarding the importance of the contents of the Public Record Office.* Correspondence was also received by those in the Four Courts from M. J. McEnery, president of the Royal Society of the Antiquaries of Ireland (RSAI). He explained at length that it was on account of potential danger to these public records in the past, scattered as they were in various locations around the country, that the Public Records (Ireland) Act had been passed in 1867 to ensure that a safe, national central storage location was established for the records, where they would be readily accessible to the public. He pointed out how 'disastrous it would be for the nation if any of the archives therein should suffer any harm', underlined the enormous importance of the Public Record Office to the nation and hoped that 'no steps will be taken which will jeopardise this magnificent collection of the archives of Ireland'.[33]

---

* Curran is perhaps better known today as an art historian and for his lifelong friendship and association with James Joyce.

One copy of McEnery's letter went straight to the IRA in the Four Courts and a reply dated 30 May was received from Óglaigh na hÉireann general headquarters. Signed by Maurice Twomey, for the IRA chief of staff Liam Lynch, it stated, 'I quite realize the importance of guarding this Office against any damage being done to any documents etc. stored there, and every precaution has been taken to insure [*sic*] that they are not interfered with.'[34] On notepaper headed 'The President's Department, Dáil Éireann', Arthur Griffith's secretary replied on 6 June, 'I have been instructed by President Griffith to say that the matter is receiving attention.' On 10 June, de Valera's secretary, Kathleen O'Connell, wrote, 'Mr De Valera has received your letter and wishes to assure you that he fully realizes the importance of the Public Record Office. He will use every influence to see that no harm comes to it.' De Valera brought the society's concerns directly to the Four Courts, subsequent to which the RSAI received a second reply from that address dated 12 June in which Donal O'Leary, who signs on behalf of the 'adjutant general', assured McEnery that the archives would not suffer in any way. Early in the same month, Constantine P. Curran turned up at the Chancery Street gate of the Four Courts and was taken to see Rory O'Connor. Curran again warned O'Connor about the irreplaceable documents stored in the Public Record Office, and told him that it would be inexcusable if anything should be allowed to happen to them, particularly in view of the extensive empty cellars under the main Four Courts to which the documents might be removed for safety. He left without receiving a satisfactory reply. Three weeks later, Curran would have the sad task of inspecting the destruction caused by the siege of the Four Courts.

The anti-Treaty IRA executive had been stockpiling components, materials and explosives for the manufacture of munitions in the Four Courts since the beginning of their occupation in April. According to Ernie O'Malley, even before this exchange of letters, they had already decided to use the ground floor of the Record Treasury as a munitions factory. Mines and grenades would be manufactured here under the direction of Frank Cotter. The building became known among the members of the garrison, and indeed, as we shall see, among the headquarters staff of the National Army, as the 'Munitions Block'. In O'Malley's descriptions in his book, *The Singing Flame*, he not only refers to the Record Treasury as 'the Munitions Block', but later he seems to be using the same name for the Headquarters Block.[35]

There is little in the way of records to tell us what explosives were brought into the Four Courts between April and the end of June, other than Volunteer Seán Brunswick noting in his Witness Statement that he brought a batch of 3,000 detonators from Limerick on Rory O'Connor's orders,[36] and references in various accounts to two lorries parked in the courtyard between the Four Courts and the Headquarters Block loaded with 'thousands of sticks'[37] of gelignite. In the garrison were a number of men highly experienced in the manufacture and use of electrically detonated mines: Rory O'Connor, director of engineering of the army executive, was himself an expert in the matter, having worked on the Canadian Pacific Railway as an engineer. Some of the mines manufactured in the Record Treasury 'Munitions Block' were laid in critical locations around the Four Courts complex, to be electrically detonated should the National Army attempt to break in. Mines were also laid in the streets immediately surrounding the Four Courts: one went off 'by accident', leaving a large crater.[38]

Besides the manufacture of munitions, arms and ammunition were being stockpiled in the Four Courts, and continuing efforts were being made to obtain more. Eighteen-year-old Seán MacBride was, despite his youth, assistant director of operations, and he travelled abroad on arms-buying missions for Liam Mellows, which included a ten-day mission in Germany in June 1922, from which he returned on 18 June.[39]

One of the concerns of Paddy O'Brien, officer commanding the Four Courts garrison, was the vulnerability from gunfire from outside the complex, if it came under attack, of anyone passing through the open spaces between the buildings. In order to ensure safe passage from building to building, work was begun on tunnels between them, probably at basement level, through which personnel could pass without being exposed to gunfire. The large brick-constructed sewers that passed under the complex were surveyed with a view to using them as escape routes. The barracks adjutant, Seán Lemass, fell into one and O'Malley noted that 'he smelled to heaven'.[40] This particular option, however, was abandoned when they found that the sewers flooded at every high tide.

★

In Northern Ireland, meanwhile, the atrocities continued. Headlines in the *Irish Times* on 2 June trumpeted 'Woman Set on Fire: Diabolical Outrage in Belfast'. The previous night, over thirty houses had been burnt out in the Millfield–Peter's Hill area, a Roman Catholic locality, in reaction to the shooting dead of Special Constable A. Roulston and the wounding of Special Constable S. C. Campbell. Trains from Belfast continued to bring refugees to Dublin, women and children mostly, carrying their personal effects in pathetic paper parcels.

On 3 June the last major British army parade in Ireland took place, when 9,000 soldiers paraded through the Phoenix Park to celebrate the birthday of King George V. With them, marching and saluting the Union Jack, were red-uniformed, bemedalled pensioners from the Royal Hospital, Kilmainham and the boys of the Royal Hibernian Military School. There was a good attendance of onlookers, including many ex-soldiers. It was noted that hats were lifted when the various colours of the regiments passed by, and that many officers of the National Army and the anti-Treaty IRA were recognized among the onlookers, in plain clothes.[41]

CHAPTER 3

ESCALATION

Towards the end of May 1922 it had seemed to some that agreement between the anti-Treaty and pro-Treaty sides might be near. The National Army chief of staff, Eoin O'Duffy, seemed to think so anyway. On 22 May he made a request to his superior, Richard Mulcahy, for permission to resign his position. He said that he had agreed to serve as chief of staff only while he was working towards army unity with the anti-Treaty IRA, and he was now optimistic that this was on the verge of being achieved, so it was time for him to move on. There seemed to be very few obstacles left, and he felt that it was only a matter of agreeing on jobs, making decisions on who would be the principal staff officers of the unified army and the make-up of the army council, and even which offices would be allocated to whom in Portobello barracks, the National Army headquarters. Who would command the National Army was discussed: as late as 8 June, Liam Lynch gave a guarantee to Mulcahy that if he were appointed chief of staff, he would work to maintain the stability of the army, and would not try to overthrow the government returned after the coming general election, even if de Valera and his followers, the political wing of the anti-Treaty faction, were not members of that government.[1]

While all these negotiations were going on, however, there were members of the cabinet of the Provisional Government on the one side, and of the IRA executive, mainly those in the Four Courts, on the other, who were, at best, reticent about what was being agreed. One gets the impression of a complex series of discussions taking place between different individuals, and there being no one person on either side who had an overall knowledge of what was being determined upon, or who had the overriding authority to make solid agreements. In addition, it seems clear that some leaders, particularly those in the Four Courts, had little interest in unity, but were glad to have the additional time the long-drawn-out talks gave them to complete their preparations to resume the war with Britain. Indeed, two days after Lynch's guarantee to Mulcahy, the Four Courts faction decided that the talking had gone on too long, and they were not prepared to negotiate further on the issue of unity after 12 June.

On 14 June the IRA executive met in the Four Courts to hear Liam Lynch report the results of his latest discussions with Mulcahy. While Lynch was not enthusiastic about what was on the table, he was prepared to go along with what had been agreed, in the name of unity. This, however, was rejected by the majority of the executive, who had already decided that it was time to end negotiations, and 'take whatever action may be necessary to maintain the Republic against British aggression.'[2]

The following day, twenty-four hours before the general election, the Constitution of the Irish Free State, which had been in the making for the past six months, was published. The aspiring republican language of its early drafts had been severely watered down by the British, and while this final document declared that 'all powers of government and all authority, legislative, executive and judicial… are derived from the people of Ireland', it also set down that the legislature would consist of 'the King and two Houses, Dáil Éireann and Seanad Éireann', and that an oath of allegiance to the king had to be taken by each elected member of the Dáil and Seanad. Michael Collins, who was attending an election meeting in Cork, received the final wording of the critical clauses of the Constitution by telegraph. He realized that, in spite of all the efforts of the previous months, there was little chance now, once the hardliners on the anti-Treaty side had read it, that a complete split could be avoided. During a public speech in Cork, he departed from his election agreement with de Valera, and urged his listeners to 'vote for the candidates you think best of'. This form of words was seized upon by anti-Treatyites to mean that Collins was repudiating the pact. This may have been so, but his speech was not reported dramatically in any of the newspapers on the following day, and it is doubtful that it had any significant effect on the election results. His comments, however, together with the publication of what they saw as a travesty of a Constitution, were probably the last straw for the anti-Treaty faction.

On the same day, the British cabinet received the monthly report on revolutionary activities in the UK prepared by Scotland Yard Special Branch. Suspected subversive movements in Britain, including those of the Communist Party, some trade unions, the No More War Movement and even some unemployed groups were infiltrated and spied upon by Special Branch. Irish clubs and associations were also carefully watched, and in this particular report 'well-informed Irishmen' predicted that 'we have not seen the end of our troubles here or in Ireland.' The storm, they thought, was not far off and a pro-Treaty victory in the general election would merely have the effect of hastening the outbreak. It was thought that de Valera might try to avoid civil war, but the general opinion was that Rory O'Connor and his Irregulars would get out of hand.

Polling in the general election took place on 16 June and, although the results would not be issued for a further eight days, all indications were that the pro-Treaty side had won a majority of seats in the new Dáil. There was a growing sense among the anti-Treaty faction that they were becoming marginalized.

On 18 June, another army convention, called by Liam Lynch, took place in the Mansion House. When the results of Lynch's negotiations were put to the convention, they were met by angry protests. Tom Barry, commander of the 3rd West Cork Flying Column, moved that, rather than discussing the negotiations any further, they should agree on renewing the war by attacking the remaining British forces in Ireland. This caused an uproar, with even some other hardliners rejecting outright Barry's radical proposal. The proposal was put to the vote, however, and it was passed. There was horror in the room among the moderates, but war with the British was averted when the result of the vote was objected to on technical grounds, and after a fresh vote, Barry's proposal was narrowly defeated. The harm was done, however, and yet another new split was opened. Liam Lynch was still urging moderation, but the level of disagreement with his policy of continuing to negotiate was so widespread that he felt, in the circumstances, he could no longer continue as chief of staff of the IRA. Rory O'Connor and a number of his supporters who had voted for Barry's resolution for war walked out of the convention, and later, in the Four Courts, Joseph McKelvey was elected as the new chief of staff in Lynch's place.

The annual commemoration of the Irish revolutionary Wolfe Tone had been held by the Irish Republican Brotherhood on the Sunday nearest 20 June every year since the late nineteenth century. Rory O'Connor decided that the IRA executive would have its own commemoration that day, and on a cloudy, humid morning a convoy of army tenders took the senior IRA officers from the Four Courts out to Bodenstown, Co. Kildare. Liam Mellows gave an impassioned and defiant address over Tone's grave about the republic being subverted by the pro-Treaty government.

There was a concert in the Four Courts that night, but Todd Andrews remembered that the prevailing atmosphere was one of approaching doom.

Michael Collins had hoped that, if the pro-Treaty faction won a majority in the general election, democracy would be respected and the IRA would leave the Four Courts and other buildings, such as the Masonic Hall, Fowler Hall and Kilmainham Gaol, that they had occupied in Dublin. It was becoming clear now that this would not be the case, and Rory O'Connor's comments on 22 March about dictatorship were looking more ominous.

On Thursday, 22 June, Field Marshal Sir Henry Wilson, security advisor to Sir James Craig, prime minister of the newly created Northern Ireland, who had spoken out strongly against the IRA and was vehemently anti-truce, was gunned down on the doorstep of his home in Eaton Square, London. After an illustrious army career, in December 1921 Wilson had been invited by Craig to advise his government on security. He had recommended that the Special Constabulary be enlarged, and that Catholics be encouraged to join the force. One historian claimed that Wilson proposed the organization of a strong military force in Northern Ireland which would be sufficient to conquer the south![3] During the Irish War of Independence, although he spoke out against the unofficial killing of republicans, Wilson had suggested that 'a little blood-letting' was needed and recommended that 30,000 troops be sent into Ireland to carry out a robust military campaign. Later, in 1920, he wanted the names of known IRA men to be published, and because of the difficulty of obtaining evidence or witnesses when a member of the Crown forces was murdered, he suggested that, for each murder, five IRA men from a roster should be executed. When de Valera was due in London for the truce talks with Lloyd George, Wilson had told the prime minister that he would not talk to murderers, and if it were up to him, he would hand de Valera over to the police as soon as he appeared. He referred to the establishment of the Truce on 11 July 1921 as 'rank, filthy cowardice'.[4]

Wilson was born at Currygrane, Edgeworthstown, Co. Longford, in 1864; in 1882, after a number of unsuccessful attempts to gain entry to Sandhurst and the Royal Military Academy, he was commissioned as a lieutenant in the Longford Militia. He went on to serve with distinction in India, Burma and the Boer War, becoming a protégé of Field Marshal Lord

Sir Henry Wilson.

Roberts VC. In 1907 he was appointed Commandant of the British army staff college at Camberley, with the rank of brigadier-general, and in 1910 he was made director of military operations in the War Office. In that capacity, foreseeing that war with Germany was inevitable, he had his staff carry out 'war games', attempting to predict what would occur if war did break out. When war did come, Wilson played a significant role on the army general staff and in the War Office, and he fought as a commander in the field from 1916 onwards. It had been suggested that he would be the ideal man to put down the Easter Rebellion in Dublin in 1916, but subsequently it was felt

Wilson's assassination featured on the cover
of the French magazine *Le Petit Journal*.

that his northern allegiances disqualified him. He had ended the war as chief of the imperial general staff.

In its obituary, *The Times* called Wilson 'a warrior Irishman'. The *Irish Times* said 'the assassination of Wilson has horrified the whole civilized world', but the *Daily News* suggested that he must bear some responsibility for stirring up the bloodshed in Belfast. Wilson was buried, with great ceremony, in the crypt of St Paul's Cathedral, between Field Marshal Lord Roberts and Lord Wolseley.

Wilson's assassins were Commandant Reggie Dunne and Volunteer Joseph O'Sullivan of the London Battalion of the IRA, and they were quickly apprehended. O'Sullivan had served in the British army in the First World War, and had lost a leg at Ypres, which slowed up his escape after the shooting. Another member of the London Battalion, Frank Martin, claimed in a written statement that Dunne had come to him and asked him if he would take part in a 'big job'. He claimed he told him that the 'Four Courts people' had decided to shoot Sir Henry Wilson, an act that would precipitate an attack on the Four Courts by the British military. If this happened, the 'Portobello people' (the National Army) could not stand by and watch their old comrades attacked but would come to their assistance, healing the split once and for all. Martin declined Dunne's request, and Dunne 'got Sullivan to assist him in the job.'[5] Rory O'Connor stated that the anti-Treaty IRA had nothing to do with the assassination, and that, 'if we had, we would admit it'. Although there is some evidence that Michael Collins issued the order for Wilson to be shot, the British government took the line, in spite of denials from the Four Courts, that the anti-Treaty Republicans were behind the assassination.

Lloyd George cabled Michael Collins, stating that evidence had been found 'upon the murderers... connecting them with the Irish Republican Army.' He went on to say that his government was aware that active preparations were being made by the Irregular elements of the IRA to resume attacks upon the lives and property of British subjects both in England and in Ulster. 'The ambiguous position of the Irish Republican Army can no longer be ignored by the British government. Still less can Mr Rory O'Connor be permitted to remain with his followers an arsenal in open rebellion in the heart of Dublin... His Majesty's Government cannot consent to a continuance of this state of things, and they feel entitled to ask you formally to bring it to an end forthwith.'[6]

Within hours of Wilson's murder, Gen. Macready was summoned to Downing Street from his headquarters at the Royal Hospital, Kilmainham, in Dublin. Lloyd George asked him if the army would be in a position to capture the Four Courts. Macready strongly opposed the idea, telling Lloyd George that such action would immediately unite the two sides in Ireland and restart the war. He wrote later in his memoir *Annals of an Active Life*: 'I must confess that I was somewhat taken aback when asked if the Dublin Four Courts... could be captured at once by British troops. From the military point of view the operation was comparatively simple; indeed, plans for such a contingency had been long prepared in case the Republicans in the Four Courts at any time molest the troops.' He was clear, however, that such an operation would unite the pro- and anti-Treaty factions, and lead to loss of life among civilians.

By the end of Thursday, 22 June, the *Irish Independent* reported, casualties in the Dublin area from sporadic clashes between the National Army and the Irregulars amounted to nine dead and twenty-one injured, and civilian casualties outnumbered those of the belligerents.

The next day, Arthur Griffith had a meeting with Sir Alfred Cope, the British under-secretary for Ireland, during which the Four Courts situation was raised. Maj.-Gen. Emmet Dalton, National Army director of military operations, and two British officers also attended the meeting. It seems that one of the points discussed was the possibility of the provision, by Britain,

During the Treaty negotiations in London in 1921, Major General Emmet Dalton, seen here on the left, watches Arthur Griffith, Harry Boland and Michael Collins enter a car.

of additional military equipment, if the Provisional Government forces were to move to bring an end to the Four Courts occupation. Arthur Griffith had previously told Ernest Blythe, Provisional Government Minister for Trade, 'if we are not prepared to fight and preserve the democratic rights of the ordinary people and the fruit of national victory, we should be looked upon as the greatest poltroons who had ever had the fate of Ireland in their hands'.[7] His colleague, Kevin O'Higgins, Minister for Justice, was concerned that the continual failure to move on the garrison was giving the impression that the new government was weak-willed.

An t-Óglach, the official newspaper of the Irish Volunteers, had sided with the pro-Treaty faction since the truce, and its optimistic editorials had assured its readers that the problems in the army would be resolved. By June 1922, however, the tone had changed, and in the issue of 24 June the paper hit out hard at the general lawlessness in the country, hinting that this was the responsibility of the anti-Treaty IRA and commenting that, 'For some months past armed gangs have been taking advantage of the transition stage in Irish affairs to enrich themselves at the expense of their country.'

On that Saturday, the British government, still furious at Wilson's murder, decided, against Gen. Macready's advice, to use British forces to bring a forcible end to the occupation of the Four Courts. The Admiralty was ordered to send ships to Dublin with reinforcements, and the same ships would then take back to England prisoners arrested during the action. A proclamation was drawn up by the Secretary of State for the

Colonies, Winston Churchill, stating the British government's case, and pointing to Irish breaches of the Treaty as the reason for the military action. It was to be published widely throughout Ireland as soon as the operation was completed.

Gen. Macready was sent back to Dublin to put plans in place for the attack on the Four Courts. On his arrival back at his headquarters at the Royal Hospital, Kilmainham, he resurrected the contingency plans for military action against the Four Courts which had already been drawn up, and went through them with his staff, including Gen. Boyd, whom he designated to command the attack. As they were working out the details, a telegram arrived from Downing Street ordering that the attack should be put into effect the following day, Sunday, 25 June.

The Royal Hospital, Kilmainham.

'Whilst every soldier in Dublin would have been overjoyed at the opportunity of dealing with Rory O'Connor and his scally-wags,' Macready wrote later in his memoir, he and his officers knew that their action would, without doubt, reopen hostilities throughout the island of Ireland. He felt so strongly about this that he sent one of his staff, Col. Brind, to London, in a last-ditch attempt to persuade the cabinet to change its mind.

On the same day, the results of the Irish general election were published. The pro-Treaty members won 239,195 votes or 58 seats, against 135,310 votes or 36 seats for the anti-Treaty side. The Labour Party, the Farmers' Party and Independents cumulatively won a total of 247,080 votes, over 40 per cent of the overall total, a sure sign that a large proportion of the population of Ireland was moving on from revolution. It is calculated that 28 per cent of the electorate specifically voted against the Treaty. In the event of a vote in the new Dáil, the first meeting of which was set for 1 July, it is thought that the Unionists and Independents would vote with the Treaty party, and even if Labour and the Farmers voted with the anti-Treaty party, the government would still win a division by sixty-eight votes to sixty.

On Sunday, 25 June, much to Macready's relief, word came from London to cancel the Four Courts attack. 'I have never ceased to congratulate myself', he wrote in his memoir *Annals of an Active Life*, 'on having been an instrument in staving off what would have been a disaster.' He believed that it was Churchill's 'feverish impetuosity' that had brought the situation to the brink. Indeed, Churchill came to the realization later that if his urgings to send in the British army had succeeded, there would have been catastrophic results. The personal reputational damage would be severe, and to bury those few aberrant hours of panic and bad judgement he tried to have copies of his drafted proclamation destroyed.

In the Four Courts, unaware of the momentous events that were happening in Whitehall and at the British headquarters in the Royal Hospital, Kilmainham, the leaders had come to the decision to send their first military force into Northern Ireland, and appointed Peadar O'Donnell to command it. O'Donnell had commanded the 2nd Brigade of the Northern Division of the IRA in many actions during the War of Independence. The executive members in the Four Courts were anxious that the rift with Liam Lynch which had occurred at the last convention would be mended, and there were discussions about how they might go about it.

Late in the afternoon, Liam Mellows called in at the Clarence Hotel, where Lynch, no longer welcome in the Four Courts, had set up his headquarters, and the two men had a long and productive meeting.

Around the country, the depredations of individual units of the anti-Treaty IRA continued. On this Sunday, the train from Derry to Belfast was stopped and all the Northern Sunday news-papers were taken off and burnt. Fruit, groceries and forty-two boxes of butter were also seized. During the robbery of another train, 1,000 bags of potatoes were taken.

On Monday, 26 June Commandant-Gen. Leo Henderson, the Four Courts-based IRA officer in charge of enforcing the

Belfast Boycott, led a raid on the car showrooms of Belfast man Harry Ferguson in Baggot Street in Dublin, to obtain more vehicles for use in offensive operations in Northern Ireland.

National Army troops arrive at the Harry Ferguson garage in Baggot Street in Dublin to surprise a Belfast Boycott raid being carried out by members of the Four Courts garrison.

The Provisional Government was in session when news that the raid was in progress was received. The administration had already suffered the embarrassment of the British lord lieutenant's car being spirited away from a race meeting at Punchestown under the noses of a National Army guard, British army lorries being taken in the same way and ending up in the Four Courts, and Michael Collins even having had his car taken from him, at gunpoint, in the street. The Baggot Street raid was a last straw:

the cabinet could not continue to be seen to turn a blind eye to these activities, and a call was made to Beggars Bush barracks, only minutes from Baggot Street, to put a stop to the raid. Henderson and his men were in the process of removing sixteen cars and various machinery, worth £9,000, when a National Army unit under Frank Thornton, a former member of the Collins squad, arrived in lorries and surrounded the Ferguson premises. Henderson and his men had been in no hurry; they had been carrying out similar raids for some time now without any interruptions, and had expected this operation to be no different. They were surprised to be challenged. No shots were fired, but Henderson was arrested and taken to Mountjoy Prison, where he was guarded by a detachment of the Dublin Guards in case a rescue attempt were made, while the authorities considered what to do with him. One of the onlookers in Baggot Street was Clare Sheridan,* a roving European correspondent of the *New York World* newspaper. She wrote later that a fellow in the crowd had said to her, 'Something'll sure happen soon; it's working up for a scrap!'[8]

The reaction of some of the leaders in the Four Courts at Henderson's arrest was disbelief; he had been engaged, after

---

* Clare Sheridan (1885–1970) was born Clare Consuelo Frewen in London, to an Irish father and an American mother who was the elder sister of Lady Randolph Churchill, Winston Churchill's mother. She spent her childhood and youth in Inishannon, Co. Donegal, and was educated in England, Ireland, France and Germany. She became a writer, encouraged by family friends Henry James and Rudyard Kipling, and later took up sculpting. In 1920 she was invited to Moscow to sculpt busts of Lenin and Trotsky.

Clare Sheridan.

all, in commandeering transport for the removal of supplies to the north – a project on which, they believed, both sides were still, at least nominally, co-operating.[9]

On that same Monday an angry House of Commons met, and Winston Churchill, still convinced that the murder of Sir Henry Wilson and other outrages had been planned in the Four Courts, stated, regarding their occupation:

If it does not come to an end, if through weakness, want of courage or some other even less creditable reason it is not brought to an end, and a speedy end, then it is my duty to say, on behalf of His Majesty's Government, that we shall regard the Treaty as having been formally violated, and we shall take no steps to carry out or legalize its further stages, and that we shall resume full liberty of action in any direction that may seem proper...[10]

The House of Commons, according to the veteran Nationalist MP William O'Brien, was 'hungry with anti-Irish fury'.

The editorial in the *Irish Times* that day could have been written by Churchill: it made clear that 'the duty of Messrs Griffith and Collins – if they are still resolved to save the Treaty, and with it, the last hope of Irish unity – is plain and urgent. They must begin to govern now or they must make room for better men.'

Lloyd George again cabled Collins, stating that unless he took strong and prompt action against the Four Courts garrison, the Treaty would be held to have been violated, and grave consequences would ensue.

Also on that Monday morning Emmet Dalton, who had attended with Griffith the meeting with Alfred Cope the previous Friday, wrote a letter, as Irish evacuations officer, to his counterpart at British headquarters. He stated that he was authorizing Capt. Matthews of his staff to sign any documents affecting his department on his behalf, indicating that he would not be available for some time. This seems to suggest that he knew at this time that the government was going to order a military intervention in the Four Courts.

Without a lot of consideration of the consequences and perhaps not realizing the seriousness of such a move, some of the Four Courts leaders decided to retaliate for the detention of Leo Henderson by capturing a National Army officer of equal rank, and to hold him in the Four Courts until Henderson was released. Gen. J. J. 'Ginger' O'Connell,* the deputy chief of staff of the National Army, and known for his hardline attitude towards the anti-Treaty faction, was selected as the appropriate person to take hostage. That same evening, an armed party which included Seán MacBride and Ernie O'Malley, set out to where they were told they would find O'Connell. As he left a colleague's house in Leeson Street at 11 p.m. and proceeded on foot towards Beggars Bush barracks, unarmed and in uniform, O'Connell was stopped on the street at gunpoint, forced into a car and taken to the Four Courts.

Ernie O'Malley made a phone call from the Four Courts to Eoin O'Duffy in Beggars Bush barracks a little later, confirming that O'Connell was in custody at Republican headquarters, and blithely announced that he would be exchanged for Leo

---

* J. J. O'Connell (1887–1944) was born in Co. Mayo and educated at Clongowes Wood and at University College of Dublin, where he received a first-class MA. He emigrated to the US in 1912 and joined the US army. In 1914 he returned to Ireland and joined the Irish Volunteers, and with his short but useful experience in the US, was made Chief of Inspection of the Irish Volunteers. In this capacity he travelled throughout the country lecturing Volunteers on military tactics. Sent by Eoin MacNeill, a key figure in establishing the Irish Volunteers and editor of the *Irish Volunteer* newspaper, to Cork in 1916 to issue a countermanding order to stop the Rising, he missed the action, but was arrested anyway and spent time in Frongoch Camp. From 1917 to 1921 he was involved in training the IRA, and he took part in meetings on military matters in London during the Treaty negotiations. He was appointed deputy chief of staff of the National Army in 1922.

Henderson. Desmond Greaves, biographer of Liam Mellows, wrote of this matter: 'Anti-Treaty parochialism, uninventiveness and insensitivity to political mutation soon cost the Republicans dearly.'[11]

Just before midnight those members of the Provisional Government still working in City Hall were informed of the hostage-taking. Since the murder of Sir Henry Wilson and the subsequent reaction of the British government, the midnight oil had been burning in the offices of the Provisional Government. There was no doubt in anyone's mind that the Four Courts situation violated the Treaty, and while the repeated urgings from London would have not been without effect, the taking of 'Ginger' O'Connell was the last straw. In his report to the British cabinet for the week ending 1 July 1922, Gen. Macready does not mention pressure from London, but states that 'this open flouting of their authority was too much for the Provisional Government', and it precipitated the surrounding of the Four Courts and a demand for surrender. O'Connell was highly respected and popular among his fellow officers and men, and they were angered by his kidnapping. It was a turning point for many in the new army who had been unsure up until then about where their loyalties lay.

At a cabinet meeting early on the morning of Tuesday, 27 June, attended by Collins, Griffith, Mulcahy, Cosgrave, Higgins, Duggan, Lynch, Hogan and Walsh, Richard Mulcahy, as Minister for Defence, reported on the kidnapping of 'Ginger' O'Connell. It was decided that the occupants of the Four Courts would be ordered to evacuate the premises, and that if they did not do so, military action would be taken at once. The decision to take military action against former colleagues was made with, for some, great reluctance, and when the cabinet received details of Churchill's threatening speech in the Commons the previous day, some members began to waver. No one wanted to seem to be bowing to the British under Churchill's threats. Some ministers wished to cancel the attack because of Churchill's remarks, but after much discussion a decision was eventually made to proceed as planned.[12] The general election results had given the government a mandate from the people, and they had been assured by the headquarters staff of the army that, particularly after 'Ginger' O'Connell's kidnapping, the men would be prepared to confront their former comrades in the Four Courts. Ernest Blythe, Minister for Trade, recalled that Gavan Duffy, Minister for Foreign Affairs, 'who was a strange bird among us', was hesitant, and asked how long the fighting would take. Gearóid O'Sullivan, the National Army adjutant-general, who attended the cabinet meeting, replied optimistically that the Irregulars all over the country would be 'disposed of' within a week or ten days, and this seemed to satisfy Duffy.[13]

Apart from the immediate events, the cabinet, aware of the split that had occurred the previous week between Liam Lynch and members of the executive in the Four Courts, believed that the time was right to strike. It was possible that the republican rift might allow the Four Courts to be dealt with without the rest of the anti-Treaty forces in Dublin, or the southern divisions, becoming involved. They were not to know, however, that unity was to be re-established only hours before the attack was launched.

Little is reported of any significant contribution to these discussions by Michael Collins himself; most historians repeat that the kidnapping of 'Ginger' O'Connell was 'the last straw' for him. Before he left at the end of the meeting, Collins advised his fellow ministers not to sleep at home in case 'any whisper of what was intended got out'. He was concerned about further kidnappings.[14] Subsequently, some ministers 'camped out' in their offices for the first period of the Civil War. They slept on mattresses on the floor at night and rolled them up, together with the bedclothes, in the morning and piled them in a corner.

Tuesday, 27 June dawned to a lot of activity in the Four Courts. Final arrangements were being put in place for a military expedition to Northern Ireland, and there was a continual stream of visitors throughout the day. Rumours circulated about a possible impending attack by the National Army. There was always a gathering of people around the Chancery Street gate, often including off-duty National Army soldiers, chatting with old comrades who were members of the garrison. There is little doubt that there was a free flow, both ways, of rumour and information, about movements of the National Army and what was happening in the Four Courts.

While many members of the garrison seemed to be unaware of the seriousness of the events of the past ten days, there are indications that at least some of the leaders knew that an assault was imminent. Mellows is said to have told Liam Lynch that he had received indications from 'the higher echelons of the Provisional Government that there would be an attack'.[15] Other members of the garrison, including Ernie O'Malley, also sensed that the situation had worsened in the past couple of days: he arranged for considerable defensive work to be carried out during Tuesday, erecting additional barbed wire and laying more defensive mines.

That morning, Patrick Little, who worked with Erskine Childers* in Éamon de Valera's publicity office in Suffolk Street, late into work because of a visit to the dentist, was told by one of the staff that he had just missed 'the most beautiful sight' of his life, because 'a gorgeous girl' had come to see him. She came back again later, and he gave her an interview.[16] It was Clare Sheridan, the visiting American journalist. Sheridan told Little that she was the European correspondent of the newspaper *New York World*, and that she had been sent to Europe to write about conditions there following the First World War. Happy to do some name-dropping, she mentioned that both Winston Churchill and Rudyard Kipling had advised her not

---

* Erskine Childers was born in London, but was brought up in County Wicklow. Critical of British policy in Ireland, he smuggled guns and ammunition on his yacht *Asgard* from Holland to the Irish Volunteers in the late summer of 1914, before joining the Royal Navy at the outbreak of the First World War. He returned to Ireland in 1919, and began to work for the first Irish Dáil as director of publicity. He was secretary-general of the Irish delegation that negotiated the Anglo-Irish Treaty in late 1921, but was vehemently opposed to the Treaty, and aligned himself with the anti-Treaty faction during the Civil War. Captured in possession of a firearm on 10 November 1922, he was sentenced to death and was executed fourteen days later.

to miss the exciting happenings in Dublin. A few days before, she had travelled by rail to Cork as a guest in Michael Collins's private carriage, and had spent the time talking with him and the Deputy Mayor of Cork city, Barry Egan. She described Collins as having the look of a very young Caligula. She told Little that it was very important for her to report about the anti-Treaty side as well as the Free State side, and that she wanted in particular to interview Rory O'Connor, and asked if he could arrange this. Little knew O'Connor well, and was aware that he had taken over the office of Sir John Ross, the Lord Chancellor, in the Four Courts. He opened the telephone book, found the number for the Lord Chancellor, and rang it. The phone was answered by Rory O'Connor, and he agreed to talk to Sheridan. While she was speaking with Patrick Little, everyone in the office made an excuse to pass by his desk to get a look at this exotic visitor.

Little brought Mrs Sheridan down the quays to the Four Courts, where he told the guards on the Chancery Street gate that the journalist had an appointment with Gen. O'Connor. While she waited to be called, the guards gave her a chair to sit in, in the courtyard inside the gate.

She wrote later:

The place swarmed with very young boys, some as young as fifteen. They had no uniforms, but were heavily armed. Cartridge belts over serge suits seemed the dominant note. Rifles were clicked and rattled while everyone laughed and joked and made merry... It seemed as though a whole college of boys were being allowed to play with loaded rifles. Synge's *Playboy of the Western World* is no longer allowed to be acted in Dublin. The Irish have grown supersensitive. But here they were, armies of playboys, playing with fire, the real Playboys of the Western World.

After a long wait, Clare Sheridan was led with Little through two courtyards full of lorries and past the armoured car called 'The Mutineer'. They climbed a wide stone staircase and, passing through an office where men and women sat at desks, were shown into the office of Rory O'Connor. O'Connor gave them chairs, and sat the journalist in front of his desk. He said that he would prefer to give a written statement, because he always liked to have time to consider answers, but they chatted on easily about the future of Ireland. There was a large revolver on the desk beside her, while O'Connor had an even larger revolver next to him. She described him as:

typically the Irish patriot, thin and ascetic, his white face sunken, revealing the bone formation. His eyes are deep set. He was clean shaven and dressed plainly, in dark clothes. His speech was that of a scholarly man and he seemed imbued with the spirituality of a fanatic... He talked in a very deep voice, and very slowly and deliberately, and as he talked he played abstractedly with revolver bullets on the desk top, lining them up in 'military formations'... Now and then he would look up from his regiment of bullets with a smile so sad it seemed full of foreboding.

O'Connor told her that Irishmen would walk into English jails with their heads held high, but they never could hold their heads high as subjects of a British colony. The Treaty making Ireland a Free State had lost them their strategic position and everything Ireland had fought for. He said that if Ireland was a republic, the country would be a friendly neighbour to Britain, but so long as it was forcibly attached, it would be a menace. Collins, whom he knew 'pretty well', was not a leader, but an opportunist and a bully, but he assured Sheridan that he did not use the word 'bully' in a derogatory sense: sometimes it was useful and important to be a bully.

O'Connor did not think that industrialization brought happiness, and instead saw in Ireland a prosperous agricultural nation, exporting its products by its own merchant navy. Sheridan reported that the telephone rang, and O'Connor had a short conversation with someone she thought was a press representative, but Patrick Little thought the caller was Gen. Mulcahy, the Minister for Defence, who was urging O'Connor to evacuate the Four Courts. Whoever it was, Sheridan was impressed by O'Connor's stated determination not to leave.

As they took their leave, Sheridan said to O'Connor, 'Surely you will not stay here? They will blow the walls and roof down on your head. You haven't an earthly chance.' She said that he shrugged with a fatalistic indifference and said, 'Then I'll go down in the ruins, or in the flames.'

When she got back to Suffolk Street, Sheridan reported that she interviewed Éamon de Valera, whom she described as 'like a gigantic bird of prey' with 'a great flow of rapid talk'. He told her that the signing of the Treaty was like sending a trusted farmhand to the market to buy a cow, and for him to bring back a donkey.[17] De Valera, however, was not in Dublin on that day, so she must have met him on another occasion.

In the anti-Treaty camp, there were some who fully expected that the bullying threats from the British would drive the Provisional Government to call for unity in the army, and set up a coalition government, standing firm against England. It is said that Éamon de Valera and his loyal supporter, Harry Boland, were waiting for the call they expected from Collins or Griffith for them to nominate the members to sit in the new administration – but they waited in vain.[18] Far from reacting to the rumblings from Westminster the way the anti-Treaty camp expected, the Provisional Government had already decided to take military action and forcibly evict the Four Courts garrison.

One wonders if the taking of 'Ginger' O'Connell had the approval of those members of the executive who were based in the Four Courts. At 5 p.m. on that Tuesday, 27 June, there was a meeting there of the executive, but the kidnapping was not mentioned. Many of those attending, such as Commandant Joseph O'Connor,* were unaware of the changing situation

---

* Joseph O'Connor (1880–1941) joined the Irish Volunteers in 1913, and fought in the Rebellion as Éamon de Valera's second-in-command. During the War of Independence he was a member of Michael Collins's 'squad' and commanded the 3rd Battalion 'Dev's Own' of the IRA.

and that 'Ginger' O'Connell was being held in the building. As O'Connor was leaving, however, his adjutant told him that he had received information that Free State troops had been confined to their barracks, a sure indication that something was about to happen. It was only when he mentioned this to Liam Lynch that he learned about 'Ginger' O'Connell's arrest.

Once the cabinet had decided to expel the garrison of the Four Courts, a statement was drafted to be issued to the press, preparing the Irish people for what was about to happen. The carefully worded piece, much of which appears in notes written by Collins, was completed and issued on the Tuesday night:

> Since the close of the general election, at which the will of the people was ascertained, further grave acts against the security of person and property have been committed in Dublin and some other parts of Ireland by persons pretending to act with authority.
>
> It is the duty of the government, to which the people have entrusted their defence and the conduct of their affairs, to protect and secure all law-abiding citizens without distinction, and that duty the government will resolutely perform.
>
> Yesterday one of the principal garages in the metropolis was raided and plundered under the pretext of a Belfast boycott. No such boycott has any legal existence, and, if it had, it would not authorize or condone the action of irresponsible persons in seizing private property.

Later in the same evening Lieutenant-General O'Connell, deputy chief of staff, was seized by some of the persons responsible for the plundering of the garage, and is still in their hands. Outrages such as these against the nation and the government must cease at once, and cease for ever.

For some months past all classes of business in Ireland have suffered severely through the feeling of insecurity engendered by reckless and wicket [*sic*] acts, which have tarnished the reputation of Ireland abroad. As one disastrous consequence, unemployment and distress are prevalent in the country, at a time when, but for such acts, Ireland would be humming with prosperity.

The government is determined that the country shall no longer be held up from the pursuit of its normal life and the re-establishment of its free national institutions. It calls, therefore, on the citizens to co-operate actively with it in the measures it is taking to ensure the public safety and to secure Ireland for the Irish people.[19]

On receiving orders to remove the Four Courts garrison, National Army staff met to plan the operation and to discuss the tactics that would be used. Other than the Custom House debacle of the previous year, the army, having had most of its success in the past by using guerrilla tactics, was unfamiliar with organized urban warfare on a large scale. A number of senior officers, however, had fought in the British army in the First World War, and one of these, twenty-four-year-old Maj.-Gen. Emmet Dalton, was selected to take command of the action.

The army's director of military operations, Dalton was close to Michael Collins, who was aware that his extensive military experience would be very important now that conventional military operations were to be undertaken.

Various methods to bring about the end of the occupation were discussed, including putting a tight cordon around the courts and turning off the water supply, effectively starving out the IRA. From the beginning, Dalton disagreed with this: he believed that a brief 'shock and awe' bombardment by light artillery would have a demoralizing effect on men unused to being on the receiving end of such shelling, and would swiftly flush out the garrison, leading to an early surrender. He had already discussed the idea of borrowing 18-pounder field guns from the British to achieve this result, and now the official request was made to British army headquarters in the Royal Hospital. There did not seem to be any intention at this stage to cause major damage to the buildings or indeed physical injuries to members of the garrison; indeed, Dalton assured those concerned that the employment of artillery 'as a destructive agent on the Four Courts buildings would be quite insignificant'.[20]

At least some of those involved in the hasty planning of the attack on the courts must have been aware that six years previously – during Easter Week 1916, when the Four Courts had been occupied by a party of rebels under Edward Daly – the eastern wing had briefly come under fire from a British army 18-pounder. Under cover of an ambulance, the gun had been placed on the south side of the river, but the rebels in the east wing had grown suspicious when they heard a noise coming from behind the ambulance that they 'identified as crow-bars lifting paving stones'. They had opened fire on the ambulance, and it had been quickly driven away, exposing the gun.[21] The soldiers had started firing the 18-pounder soon afterwards; at least four shells hit the corner of the east wing, causing the occupants to vacate that part of the building, before the gun was withdrawn. The repairs to the damage inflicted then had been completed only in late 1921. In 1916, however, Daly and his men, unlike the 1922 garrison, had established a wide, defended perimeter in the buildings around the Four Courts and had successfully resisted repeated British infantry attacks.

This photograph, taken after the Battle of the Four Courts, shows artillery damage to the east wing of June 1922: the light-coloured stonework is where repairs had been carried out a short while before to repair the damage done by similar shelling in 1916.

Daly and his men remained undefeated, and his unit was perhaps the most successful, militarily, of the entire Rebellion.

While Dalton concerned himself, initially at least, with the matter of procuring the artillery from the British, Maj.-Gen. Tom Ennis was appointed as Dalton's second-in-command, with overall responsibility for the infantry. He had been in the GPO in 1916, and during the War of Independence had been a member of Collins's assassination squad, taking part in the Bloody Sunday killings. Although he had been the officer in charge of the Custom House attack the previous year, he had no conventional battle experience. He did, however, have a number of experienced officers at his disposal, including Commandant-Gen. Dermot MacManus, who had fought in Gallipoli, and was a close friend of 'Ginger' O'Connell.* He also had Brig.-Gen. Paddy O'Daly of the Dublin Guard, who, as a captain four months before, had marched past the Four Courts, leading the new National Army contingent taking over Beggars Bush barracks from the British. O'Daly was also useful because he was familiar with the Four Courts, having been a member of

---

* Commandant-Gen. Dermot MacManus (1892–1990) was born in Co. Mayo and enjoyed a long and colourful career as a soldier, journalist and author. He was Captain of the 10th (Irish) Division (1914–18); director of training, Dublin Guard, IRA (1922); General Officer Commanding Limerick, NA (1922); and Provost Marshal, Southern Command, NA (1922–3). Like many Home-Rulers, Dermot MacManus joined the British army in 1914 where he rose to the rank of captain, and fought at Gallipoli (1915). After the war he studied at Trinity College Dublin, where he joined Sinn Féin. By 1922 he was director of training in the Dublin Guard, IRA, and, because of his valuable combat experience, was promoted to Commandant-General. He became Assistant-Governor of Mountjoy Prison in 1923.

the occupying force there in 1916, during which he received a gunshot wound. He had fought with Dan Breen during the War of Independence and, as a member of Michael Collins's assassination 'squad', had been involved in a number of actions, including killings of British Intelligence officers and of Frank Brooke, director of Great Southern and Eastern Railways.

It seems that the British army had at least two types of artillery available in Ireland, awaiting evacuation to England, the 18-pounder QF (quick-firing) gun and the 60-pounder QF howitzer. The latter was the mainstay of the British army medium artillery during the First World War; with a 5-inch (127-mm) diameter barrel, it could fire a 57-pound (25.8-kg) shell over 8 miles (12.8 km), and was used primarily as a counter-battery weapon to destroy enemy artillery. It was a massive piece of equipment with great destructive potential, and needed up to ten horses to pull it. Winston Churchill was so enthusiastic about clearing the Four Courts that he urged Collins to make use of this gun.

The 18-pounder QF was a very mobile, versatile and successful weapon, introduced in 1904, but remaining in service well into the Second World War. Although the gun was primarily an anti-personnel weapon, designed to kill advancing infantry by firing shells that would explode over their heads and shower them with lethal shrapnel, high explosive shells were developed for it early in the First World War. Probably for its mobility and ease of use, the 18-pounder was the weapon

Dalton selected, and the Provisional Government requested the British to make two available. The British commander, Gen. Macready, was understandably reluctant to provide artillery to the National Army for the attack on the Four Courts, and when first approached about handing over big guns, he refused. Sir Alfred Cope, the assistant under-secretary for Ireland, had to give him an official order to hand over whatever the National Army required. Most of the 18-pounder munitions had already been shipped to England, and Macready had only a small stock of shells remaining, but he indicated that he could let the National Army have the two 18-pounders with a reasonable supply of ammunition. This 'reasonable supply' is variously quoted by historians as ten or twenty rounds per gun, but it is likely that it was more.

Macready's relief at not having to launch an attack himself on the Four Courts must have been tempered by the realization that he was being ordered to make a gift of powerful armaments to a force with which he had been at war the previous year, and which, before many days had elapsed, he might be at war with again. He had little faith in, or respect for, the politicians in London. He believed that they were out of touch with the situation in Ireland, particularly after their panicked, but fortunately short-lived, orders for him to attack the Four Courts. 'Few, and none connected with the inner circle of government, had set foot in Ireland to examine the problem on the spot, where alone a true perspective of the situation could be obtained', he later wrote.[22] It seems that Macready was a little out of touch himself, particularly in relation to the complexities of the political situation current in Ireland at the time. In spite of subsequent events, in his memoirs he refers to 'de Valera and his henchman, Rory O'Connor.' While the two men had, for a while, offices in the same building in Suffolk Street, at the time Macready refers to they had little more in common, and O'Connor was clearly no 'henchman' of Éamon de Valera.

The new commanding officer of the artillery barracks at Athlone, twenty-four-year-old Commandant-Gen. Tony Lawlor, was summoned to Dublin with a squad of his men to assist with the 18-pounders. He and Emmet Dalton knew each other well; they had been students together at the Royal College of Science for Ireland. Five days before, on 22 June, Lawlor had commanded an impressive guard of honour of National Army troops that had lined the streets of Longford town for the wedding of Gen. Seán MacEoin to Mary Cooney. Lawlor had joined the Royal Flying Corps at the age of eighteen and seen two years' service during the First World War, and on his return to Ireland at the end of the war had joined the IRA. It seems that Lawlor had some knowledge of artillery, and a few months before he had begun training the men at Athlone barracks in the operation of an obsolete 15-pounder gun left behind there by the British.

At 9 p.m. on the evening of Tuesday, 27 June Emmet Dalton travelled with Lawlor and two other officers in two lorries to the Phoenix Park by way of the Islandbridge gate, and, after passing the zoological gardens, reached the park gate of Marlborough barracks (McKee barracks today).[23] There they received from the 17th Battery, Royal Field Artillery, two standard British army

18-pounder QF Mark II.

18-pounder QFs and a supply of ammunition. The handover was overseen by a British army intelligence officer, Maj. Colin Gubbins, who had fought in some of the key battles of the First World War and the north Russia campaign before being posted at the war's end to the Curragh in Ireland where he served as an intelligence officer.*

British army records show that the guns were handed over at '11.59 a.m.'.[24] This is most likely a mistake by the person

---

* Gubbins's life reads like an adventure story. Barely escaping from Germany at the beginning of the First World War, he fought as an artillery officer in the second battle of Ypres, and in the battles of the Somme, Arras and St Quentin. He was gassed on one occasion and wounded on another. During the Second World War, in 1939 he was in charge of the British military mission to Poland, and saw the effectiveness of the German panzer *blitzkrieg* before escaping back to Britain. There he joined the Special Operations Executive (SOE) and saw considerable action in north Africa against the Afrika Korps. He eventually took command of SOE and was involved in co-ordinating resistance activities worldwide. He died at his home in the Hebrides in 1976.

writing the note, and should probably have been noted as 11.59 p.m. It seems reasonable to suggest that the three hours between Dalton setting out to get the guns and the official handover gave sufficient time for the British artillery officers concerned to instruct the Irish officers in the operation of the guns. (A retired Irish army artillery officer, Lt.-Col. Cormac Lalor, assisted greatly in my understanding of artillery, shells and fuses and associated matters, and assured me that the 18-pounder was a very straightforward weapon that could be easily operated by experienced soldiers after even perfunctory instruction.) It is likely that the guns came with the 96-page manual, *Gun Drill for 18-pounder Q.F. Gun*, of 1920, which describes, comprehensively and in the simplest terms, the duties of each member of the six-man crew.

I have found no documentary evidence as to what type of shells were provided with the guns at this time, but it seems likely, from some of the initial damage they inflicted on the Four Courts, that they were of the HE type. There is no record of Dalton objecting to either the type or the small number of shells that were handed over; presumably, he believed that what he had received was sufficient to force a quick surrender of the Four Courts garrison. In the Irish army archives I found the record sheet of the rounds fired by 18-pounder Mark II, serial number 10756. Prior to the handover, it was recorded that it had only fired seven shells, probably practice firings, in July 1918.

Commandant Padraig O'Connor of the Dublin Guard, stationed in Portobello barracks, was one of the officers in the

National Army who received orders to prepare their men to take part in the Four Courts attack. His account of the siege, written not long after the event, is the only extensive description of the action from the National Army side. His notes, edited by his nephew Diarmuid O'Connor and Frank Connolly, form the basis of *Sleep Soldier Sleep*, published in 2011. In spite of being only twenty-one years of age in 1922, O'Connor was an experienced IRA officer, having joined the Volunteers as a young teenager in 1914, and taken part since 1920 in many urban guerrilla actions against British forces as a member of the Active Service Unit of the Dublin Brigade, under Oscar Traynor. One of these involved an attempt to break Ernie O'Malley out of jail. Other officers who were to participate in the siege, such as Maj.-Gen. Paddy O'Daly and Commandant Joe Leonard, were O'Connor's comrades-in-arms during a number of these actions, and the three had been involved in the taking over of Beggars Bush barracks from the British five months before. Years later O'Connor told Ernie O'Malley that, like many others, he had not fully made up his mind whether to remain in the National Army or to join with the anti-Treaty IRA until that Tuesday, when they received their orders for the attack on the Four Courts. Many of his friends were with the anti-Treaty faction, but, with some reluctance at first, he threw in his lot with the Provisional Government.

Many others wavered at this stage: unwilling to open fire on their erstwhile comrades, they began to have second thoughts. Others would have felt the same had it not been for the kidnapping of 'Ginger' O'Connell, a popular officer and one of their

Commandant Padraig O'Connor.

own. Before the night was out, however, as many as twenty men in Portobello barracks alone had refused to take part in the attack; they were arrested and imprisoned for refusing to obey orders.[25]

At 'about teatime' that Tuesday evening, according to O'Connor, officers were summoned to a briefing on the Four Courts operation. The idea of the attack may have been discussed informally many times by senior officers in the army, but relatively little in the way of planning for such an enterprise seems to have been carried out. While there was still hope that Dalton's bombardment would quickly bring an end to the occupation, they had to be prepared for a concerted infantry assault on the courts. For this they would have to have at their disposal ordnance maps of the surrounding area to assist in deciding on the disposition of troops and, ideally, floor plans of the buildings in the Four Courts complex so that they could plan the best way to gain entry and drive out the garrison.

After O'Connor had received his orders, his men were fed before being briefed and equipped, and selected men, presumably those who had some experience of machine-guns, were issued with Lewis guns. The Lewis was a light machine-gun invented by US army Col. Isaac Lewis in 1911, and it had been manufactured in Birmingham from 1914. It was extensively used in the First World War, and was still in use during the Korean War in the early 1950s. Weighing 12.7 kilograms (28 lbs), it was usually set on a bipod; gas-operated, it fired standard issue .303-inch bullets from a drum that contained either forty-seven or ninety-seven rounds, at a rate of 500 rounds per minute. O'Connor's

The Lewis automatic light machine-gun, used by both sides in the battle.

men had not handled this particular type of gun before, and they had to have a crash course in its operation.

O'Connor discussed the coming action with his second-in-command, Commandant Jimmy McGuinness, whom he described as 'a solid, imperturbable and efficient officer'. O'Connor believed that the new National Army was outnumbered by the anti-Treaty IRA: they had only 1,000 men in Dublin, against what he thought were 3,000 anti-Treaty combatants, and he did not believe that the Republican leaders would remain in the Four Courts, but thought they would attempt to break out and gain control of the city. McGuinness disagreed and made a bet with O'Connor that the Irregulars would be beaten in Dublin within a fortnight. O'Connor noted later that McGuinness never collected his winnings.

In the Four Courts, as the evening hours passed, defensive positions were manned and arms and ammunition checked. The scene Ernie O'Malley conjures up in his description of activities at this time in the grand Central Hall is surreal: in a place usually bustling with solicitors, barristers, clients and witnesses, members of the IRA executive gathered together under the dome, sitting in a circle on the marble floor, discussing their options. These moments were crucial. They must have been aware, through their contacts outside, that if they now voluntarily vacated the Four Courts and then released 'Ginger' O'Connell, it would take the wind out of the sails of the Provisional Government. They might also have been able to walk away unhindered. There was, indeed, some discussion about leaving and heading for country areas where they had plenty of support. Paddy O'Brien, in particular, tried to persuade members of the executive that they should indeed leave, and organize a more powerful and cohesive anti-Treaty IRA in the provinces. The majority of the executive, however, wanted to stay and face whatever was thrown at them. They discussed the possibility of artillery being used, and Seoirse Plunkett who, like a number of the men in the garrison, had been in the GPO in Easter week 1916 said, 'You get used to it; it's not bad.' Anticipating some kind of attack, Rory O'Connor

One of the statues in the Central Hall of the Four Courts that overlooked the meetings of the executive. It depicts Lord Chancellor O'Hagan (1812–85), the first Roman Catholic to hold the chancellorship for Ireland since the reign of James II.

and Joseph McKelvey worked together drafting a 'Proclamation to the Citizens of Dublin'.[26]

It was a busy time in the Four Courts. Oscar Traynor, commandant of the Dublin Brigade, arrived, and, backing up Paddy O'Brien's pleas with the members of the executive, also tried to persuade O'Connor and the others to evacuate the complex, but without success. When he left, he took away O'Connor and McKelvey's proclamation to have it printed and distributed. Commandant Padraig O'Connor claimed that a large amount of cash, up to £500,000, was spirited out of the Four Courts at the last minute; if this is so, perhaps it was Traynor who took it with him.

Late in the evening it is said that a National Army officer with the unusual name of Petit de Mange, who was a son of the former

Two Capuchin friars who gave support to the Four Courts garrison, Fr. Albert Bibby, on the left, and Fr. Dominic O'Connor.

Chef de Cuisine of the Gresham Hotel, brought a message to the Chancery Street gate addressed to Joseph McKelvey, demanding that the courts be evacuated, but after a short time de Mange was told there was no reply.[27]

At about 10 p.m., a Capuchin friar sympathetic to the Republican cause, probably Father Albert Bibby,* told some of the Four Courts occupants that he had information that an attack by the National Army was imminent. There had been no reason until then to build up a store of provisions for the garrison, and since food stocks were low, Ernie O'Malley went out with some men in a Crossley Tender to requisition some. Owners were 'persuaded' to open their shops and a substantial supply of food was brought back to the Four Courts without incident.[28]

Gen. J. J. 'Ginger' O'Connell whiled away Tuesday evening playing bridge with a few of his captors. Later, possibly at about 10 p.m., Liam Lynch, following up on his earlier discussions with Liam Mellows, arrived at the courts for further discussions with the executive about mending the rift that had

---

* Father Albert Bibby (1877–1925) was born in Bagenalstown, Co. Carlow, and was ordained a Capuchin priest in 1902. A Gaelic speaker, he was a member of Conradh na Gaeilge and one of the first Capuchins to receive a BA degree from the Royal University, Dublin, which in 1909 became the National University of Ireland. Based in the Capuchin monastery in nearby Church Street, he and another priest, Father Augustine Hayden, were summoned to Kilmainham Gaol in the aftermath of the 1916 Rebellion to provide spiritual comfort to some of the rebel prisoners there who had been sentenced to death. He and Father Augustine ministered to Seán Heuston, Michael Mallin, Con Colbert and Eamon Ceannt before their executions, and Father Albert was present at Heuston's execution.

occurred. James Cunningham, who was the IRA's Birmingham-based procurer of arms, finished a meeting with Liam Mellows at about 11 p.m. and left the Four Courts. He wrote afterwards that he had worked with Mellows for about two years, and that this was the last time he saw him. He described Mellows as a kind and generous man, who had shared his bed with him many times when Cunningham was in Dublin on arms-purchasing business.[29] His high opinion of Mellows was echoed by Todd Andrews, who worked in O'Malley's office. He described Mellows as 'a low-sized man with thinning sandy hair and merry blue lively eyes... the man's whole personality radiated kindness'.[30]

CHAPTER 4

WEDNESDAY, 28 JUNE: THE FIRST DAY OF THE SIEGE

It seems that it may have been around midnight when the crucial meeting involving Liam Lynch, the officer commanding Southern Command, his adjutant, Liam Deasy, and the Four Courts members of the IRA executive came to an end. As a result of their discussions, the rift that had occurred during the IRA convention of 18 June was healed, and although little was agreed on future actions, it was decided that Lynch would resume his position as IRA chief of staff. Liam Mellows escorted Lynch and Deasy to the Chancery Street gate of the Four Courts, and their parting was good-humoured and relaxed. In spite of the rumours that were circulating among the garrison, there is no indication that either of the two parties were concerned about the imminence of an attack. Returning on foot to the Clarence

Hotel, on the south side of the Liffey, Lynch and Deasy probably went by way of the North Quays before crossing the river at Capel Street Bridge. Whichever way they made their way to the hotel, they would have missed, probably by mere minutes, the sight, by gaslight, of one of Emmet Dalton's 18-pounders, collected at the Marlborough barracks a short time before, being wheeled down Winetavern Street towards the quays.[1]

There is evidence that the other 18-pounder was placed, at about the same time, at the junction of Bridge Street and Merchants Quay, to face the west wing of the Four Courts. The Bridge Street gun was commanded by Commandant-Gen. Tony Lawlor, and the gunners were mainly from his trainee group at Athlone barracks, the Curragh Camp and the Midland Division. None of these men had any experience of firing an 18-pounder field piece, and they must have been nervous, particularly in drizzling rain in the half-light of an early summer morning, as they made their preparations, setting up unfamiliar lethal equipment with considerable urgency. Some accounts suggest that British gunnery officers came with the guns and advised on their use, but while it is on record that British soldiers in a lorry made a delivery of shells to the quayside guns at one stage during the siege, I could find no evidence that any British personnel were involved at any time in the firing of the guns. The photographic evidence shows that all the men working on the guns wore the leather gaiters newly issued to the National Army, rather than the puttees still being worn by the British army at that time. In the circumstances, to borrow such artillery from the British was provocation enough to the anti-Treaty side;

and the Provisional Government did not want there to be even a suggestion of British 'boots on the ground' participation. As for the British military, having handed over, very reluctantly, this powerful weaponry, it is very unlikely that they would do any more than they were ordered to do.

As soon as Lynch and Deasy arrived back in the Clarence Hotel in the early hours of the morning, they gathered together the other officers of the 1st Southern Division who were staying in the hotel and told them that they had managed to work things out with those in the Four Courts, and that Lynch had resumed his role as chief of staff of the anti-Treaty IRA. Dick Barrett, one of Lynch's brigade commandants, was particularly relieved about this. He had been with Rory O'Connor when the Four Courts had been occupied but, loyal to Lynch, had left and stayed at Lynch's side during the rift. He now decided to return to the courts, a decision that subsequently led to his capture and, six months later, his execution, in Mountjoy Prison.

At the same time, vigilant members of the Four Courts garrison detected increased activity in the streets around the complex and across the river, as the 18-pounders were dug in and National Army troops began to move into position in the surrounding buildings. Lights went on in the Bridewell police station across Chancery Street from the Record Treasury, and troops could be seen entering and fortifying the windows with sandbags. One of the Four Courts garrison, Seán Prendergast, says in his Witness Statement that he and his comrades were now sure that something was going to happen, and that whatever doubts anyone had had about the imminence of fighting had long since been dispelled. Scouts who had been sent out were returning to report extraordinary military movements around the city centre, including the moving about of many armoured cars and lorries.[2]

An anonymous *Irish Times* correspondent watched the events of that early morning from the window of his office in D'Olier Street:

> A dreary drizzle blurred the yellow lights on the tramway standards and Dublin was looking grey and careworn in the half-light of a dismal dawn. An hour or so before, the tramp of many marching men had attracted the curious from their sleeplessness, and all the windows in the vicinity were garlanded with tousled heads. Irish troops were on the move. Down the street they tramped in the misting rain, two long files of them on either side of the road, strapping men and whistling boys, equipped with all the cruel paraphernalia of modern war. One could not see where they were going; all we knew was that they were marching towards the north side of the city, and as they passed across O'Connell Bridge they were swallowed up in a blanket of steadily falling rain. Then came the ambulances, with their scarlet emblems of human mercy, to which the bare poles of empty stretchers lent an air of grim realism. More soldiers followed, and still more. Dire events were toward in the Irish capital.

Over 1,000 troops were moving into central Dublin: the inner ring around the Four Courts was to be made up of about

500 men of the Dublin Guard, while a further, defensive ring of 600 men of the 2nd Eastern Division formed an outer cordon.

A light rain was falling when Padraig O'Connor marched his men out of Portobello barracks after midnight. He was cautious, and expected that they might be ambushed on their way to the Four Courts, so he went ahead at each junction with an advance party to flush out potential snipers, while his second-in-command, Commandant McGuinness, followed with the main force. As they converged on the Four Courts half an hour later, they merged with troops moving across the city from other barracks. O'Connor's orders were to occupy houses in Church Street, to the west of the Four Courts complex, opposite the Public Record Office, and the Bridewell police station, to the north and opposite the Land Registry Office.

At about 2 a.m., the residents of the Four Courts Hotel, a short distance from the Four Courts, were awakened by National Army troops and, together with the night staff, were evacuated.[3] They were escorted to the nearby Rosses Hotel; when the guests and staff had left the Four Courts Hotel, the National Army occupied it. There is no record of any such temporary arrangements being made for the occupiers of the many commandeered tenement houses that were also evacuated that night. It had been decided that, in spite of the Four Courts Hotel's proximity to the Public Record Office, the hotel would be established as brigade headquarters for the pending assault. The men of Commandant Joe Leonard's battalion took up positions in the windows at the back of the hotel and the other buildings on the block, only a short distance from the

front door of the Record House, and fortified them with whatever furniture and mattresses were available.

This contemporary photograph shows the proximity of the south façade
of the Record House to the back of the Four Courts Hotel block, which
stood, in 1922, where the red-brick building on the left is today.

Commandant-Gen. Dermot MacManus arrived at brigade
headquarters in the Four Courts Hotel in his old Volunteer uniform, which he had not worn since 1914. Even though he was
the Dublin Guard director of training, he had somehow been
left without any specific command in the operation, and so he
approached Padraig O'Connor wondering if he could be of
use. O'Connor gave him twenty of his men and asked him to
occupy a terrace of tenement houses on the west side of Church
Street, opposite the Public Record Office. His old Volunteer
uniform got MacManus into trouble, briefly, later on, when he
was mistaken for an anti-Treaty man and arrested.

Padraig O'Connor wrote that he established a battalion base in Roe's Distillery, adjacent to Hammond Lane, but he probably meant Jameson's Distillery, which at the time was sited between Bow Street and Smithfield, behind Church Street. Roe's Distillery was located between Thomas Street and the river, on the south side of the Liffey. South of Hammond Lane another National Army company, under Commandant Billy McClean, occupied the Maguire & Patterson match factory, the east façade of which was opposite the Public Record Office.

The tallest building on Church Street, the late-seventeenth-century St Michan's Church, where George Frideric Handel is said to have played the organ during his stay in Dublin in the winter of 1741/42, stood on the west side of the street. The church tower was nearly 30 metres (98.5 ft) high, and less than

St Michan's graveyard and tower today, seen from the west.

100 metres (109 yds) from the north-west corner of the Public Record Office. O'Connor may not have been familiar with the area around Church Street, but he could not have failed to recognize, in the dim pre-dawn light, that the top of St Michan's tower would make an ideal machine-gun post. Circling the church in the dark, he found a door at the base of the tower, and, after breaking in, he and four of his men climbed the narrow stone spiral staircase to the top. The 125 steep steps were covered with years of pigeons' nests and droppings, and one can imagine the difficulties they had lugging a Lewis gun and ammunition up the high tower in the dark.

From the top they had a bird's-eye view of the roofs of the Public Record Office, the Land Registry Office, the Headquarters Block and the western wing of the Four Courts.

The view that Padraig O'Connor's Lewis gun operators
in St Michan's tower had of the Public Record Office,
seen as it is today, in the middle of the photograph.

As the darkness receded, they found that they could see clear over the top of the fortification of sandbags that the garrison of the Public Record Office had constructed on the roof of the Record House. Having established the Lewis gun's position, O'Connor left his men and descended the stairs, though he lost his balance and fell a couple of times because it was so slippery and treacherous. He decided to take a short cut back to his battalion base, and made his way in the dim light west across St Michan's graveyard to Bow Street, and vaulted the low boundary wall. He found out too late, however, that the ground level on the Bow Street side of the wall was much lower than that on the graveyard side: 'it felt as if I was falling for

The outside of the wall at the western end of St Michan's graveyard, over which Padraig O'Connor 'vaulted', only to find that the ground level on the other side was far lower.

a week before I hit the ground', he wrote later. It could have easily been the end of the battle for O'Connor but, apart from 'jarred ankles', he was uninjured.[4]

The soldiers of the National Army cordon being established around the Four Courts in the hours before dawn had a number of disadvantages that the garrison they were surrounding did not have. Some of the troops may have seen the Four Courts before, but as their officers distributed them into their firing locations, they would have had little idea of their general surroundings, which within hours would become a battlefield. It is easy for a layperson to assume that there is little more to firing a rifle in wartime than knowing how to load the gun, point it at your target and pull the trigger. There is a lot more to it, however. The efficient use of the Lee Enfield rifle requires a considerable amount of training, familiarization with the weapon, learning to disassemble, clean and assemble the gun and all its parts, and practise firing, which many of the soldiers now getting into position around the Four Courts had not had. Most critical in the use of the Lee Enfield, or any rifle, is being familiar with setting the sights, which have to be accurately set in relation to the distance to different targets, and with longer ranges to take into account anomalies such as cross-winds.

Normally, a rifleman would prepare a range card, estimating the distances to and the elevations of the potential targets before him, and noting these on the card. During battle, he would use the card to guide him in adjusting his sights for accurate firing at the different objectives. The members of the Four Courts garrison had had a couple of months to become

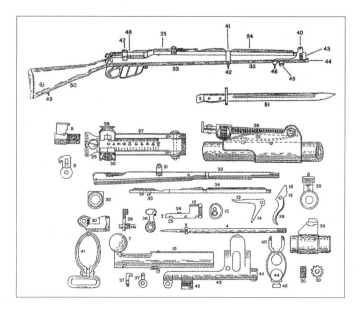

Illustrations from the National Army's manual for the
Lee Enfield .303 rifle, showing the complexity of its individual
parts, with which every soldier would have to be familiar.

familiar with their defence locations, and, noting the positions
that an attacking force were likely to occupy, had prepared their
range cards.[5] This enabled them to set their sights properly, and
so their rifle fire would have been reasonably accurate from
the beginning. The National Army soldiers, by contrast, found
themselves in unfamiliar locations in the dawn light with little
time to prepare, which for an inexperienced rifleman, and many
of these troops had little training in the use of rifles, would have
made accurate firing almost impossible to achieve.

As a cordon was set up around the Four Courts, the Provisional Government moved to impose censorship on telegraphic
communications, and to take control of the telephone system,
reserving it exclusively for military use.[6]

*

In the early hours of the morning Father Albert Bibby returned to the courts with another Capuchin priest, Father Dominic O'Connor.* During the subsequent siege, these two men were allowed to come and go as they pleased, providing spiritual comfort to the garrison and assisting in the evacuation of the wounded. They also carried messages in and out of the Four Courts for the IRA executive and for individuals wanting to assure their loved ones of their safety, and they played an important part in facilitating the surrender at the end of the siege. It is said that the executive also asked the clergy of the Pro Cathedral in Dublin to provide two diocesan chaplains for those in the Four Courts and other occupied buildings; they felt that the men needed to receive spiritual comfort and in its absence were losing morale. The Archbishop of Dublin and the Catholic hierarchy were generally pro-Treaty, and refused to provide chaplains, but undertook that spiritual comfort would be provided 'in cases of extremis'. The two Capuchin priests were well accustomed to administering to revolutionary soldiers, and were also prepared to assist in looking after some

---

* Father Dominic had been a staunch supporter of the nationalist movement throughout the War of Independence, having been chaplain to the Cork Brigade of the IRA under Tomás MacCurtain, and he was present at the death in Brixton Prison after a hunger strike of Terence MacSwiney in October 1920. Arrested by the British in January 1921, Father Dominic was sentenced to five years' penal servitude for sedition, but was released in December of that year on the signing of the Treaty.

of the temporal needs of the garrison. Although the Capuchin order was relatively independent, a few days after the siege was over, they were brought before the Catholic Archbishop of Dublin, and before long were transferred to Capuchin missions in the United States.

At 3.40 a.m. a message was handed by a National Army officer to the guard on the Chancery Street gate of the Four Courts:

To the Officer in Charge
Four Courts

I, acting under the order of the government, hereby order you to evacuate the buildings of the Four Courts and to parade your men under arrest, without arms, on that portion of the quays immediately in front of the Four Courts by 4 a.m.

Failing compliance with this order, the building will be taken by me by force, and you and all concerned with you will be held responsible for any life lost or any damage done.

By order
Thomas Ennis
O/C 2nd Eastern Division

The message was taken to Rory O'Connor and the other members of the executive. They had already made up their minds to stay in the Four Courts complex, and so the message was ignored and no reply was made. Some time later, the electricity

Major General Thomas Ennis, on right, with Richard Mulcahy
and General 'Ginger' O'Connell at Beggars Bush barracks.

supply to the Four Courts was cut off and the occupants were
left in darkness. There was a flurry of activity to find and light
candles. There would have been few among the garrison who
would not have known at this stage that what they had wondered about for so long was finally about to happen. Those
who were not on look-out duty were ordered to assemble in the
Central Hall. They gathered in the big echoing space quickly,
and, overlooked by six tall marble statues of Thomas O'Hagan,
Henry Joy and other Irish men of the law, they knelt, prayed
and were given general absolution for their sins by Father
Albert Bibby. There was no encouraging address by the man
who was in charge of the occupation, Rory O'Connor: the garrison commander, Paddy O'Brien, simply brought the men to

attention and ordered them to take up their action stations. Ammunition was scarce, and the men were warned not to waste it. Commandant Simon Donnelly was short of ammunition for his Parabellum automatic pistol, and Liam Mellows gave him some, telling him to be sparing in its use, since it was needed for the one and only ancient enemy, England, and not for 'the misguided dopes outside'.[7]

There have been a number of claims as to who fired the first shot in the action that started the Civil War. An official government news release later reported that when there was no reply to the ultimatum from Maj. Gen. Ennis, an armoured car passed up King's Inns Quay in front of the Four Courts and was fired upon by the garrison. It is doubtful that this is true, because the garrison was under strict orders not to fire until fired upon, but, as the armoured car drove quickly away down the quays, one of the 18-pounders across the river, the Winetavern Street gun operated by Emmet Dalton, opened fire. Fusillades of rifle and machine-gun fire from all the National Army posts surrounding the courts ensued. The deafening roar of the 18-pounder's opening salvo was followed immediately by the thud of a shell exploding against the 800-mm (31.5-inch) thick, granite-faced walls of the Four Courts, just 121.5 yards (120 m) from the gun.

In Winetavern Street, the detonation of the gun was followed by the sound of glass shattering as windows in the old buildings within a 30-yard (27.5-m) radius of it fell into the street, and 'razors, shaving brushes, looking glasses and the like' showered to the ground.[8] The cataclysmic noise woke those residents of the surrounding houses who had not earlier been roused by the movement of the lorries and the many soldiers in the streets, terrifying them.

Because no practice was possible, the first shells fired by the novice artillerymen from their 18-pounders were those let loose at the opening of hostilities. The gun at Winetavern Street fired first. The gun's crew narrowly escaped injury as it recoiled violently: in the frenetic preparations Dalton had forgotten to dig the 'trail' or tail of the gun into the roadway – to bed it and so absorb the recoil. One report says the first shell went careering wildly over the Four Courts, 'a happening not exactly to the surprise of the gun crew'.[9]

An 18-pounder shell discovered in recent decades at Church Street.

The only shell from this gun known to have passed over the Four Courts at this time can be seen in the Carmelite archive in Church Street: it had landed north of the complex, somewhere in the Carmelite grounds, 500 metres (547 yds) from Winetavern Street and apparently had failed to explode. The opposite also occurred when the crew were adjusting the gun to attempt to hit the south façade low down. It was aimed a little too low and scored two explosive hits on the river wall only 13 yards (12 m) away, scattering lethal shards of granite

Note the shell strikes on the riverside wall opposite
Winetavern Street at the left of this photograph.

in all directions. This also happened with the Bridge Street gun. After this shaky start, however, the guns were properly bedded into the cobbled surface of the street and the crews settled down to fire one shell about every fifteen to twenty minutes.[10]

A report written by Gen. Eoin O'Duffy the following afternoon suggests that only one gun, that based at Winetavern Street, was used in the early bombardment, and that after 6 a.m. it was moved to Bridge Street. He wrote that this gun fired five shells between the hours of 7 and 8.30 a.m., with the 'effect of shattering the entire front of the Four Courts, openings in the walls being as large as 7 ft [2.1 m] square'. O'Duffy, however, seems to have been in his office in Portobello at the time, and was basing his reports on telephone conversations with Emmet

The 18-pounder stationed at Bridge Street. The gunner is
just about to pull the lanyard to fire the gun. A row of high
explosive shells lie in straw in the middle of the street.

Dalton; it seems that there was some confusion over details. He
refers to 'the artillery piece' being transferred and 'the artillery'
being moved, suggesting that he was aware of only one gun
being involved.[11] A number of eyewitness accounts, however,
suggest that the second gun, located at Bridge Street and under
the command of Commandant Tony Lawlor, was involved from
the beginning.

Under normal circumstances, the most complex part of the
operation of an 18-pounder was perhaps the calibration of
the gunsight, to which eight pages of the official handbook *Q.F.
Gun* is devoted. It is unlikely that Dalton's men had the time or
the knowledge to properly calibrate the sights, so they probably
simply opened the breech and sighted their target through the

An early breach by artillery shells in the south façade of the main block.

interior of the barrel. Their target was so large and so near, there would not have been any significant fall in the trajectory of the shell, so this was a practical and effective method of aiming the gun.

There are a number of accounts of the use of the borrowed guns which suggest that their crews were incompetent, but evidence shows the opposite. The original reason for using 18-pounders in the siege was to frighten the occupants of the Four Courts sufficiently that they would surrender. This required the

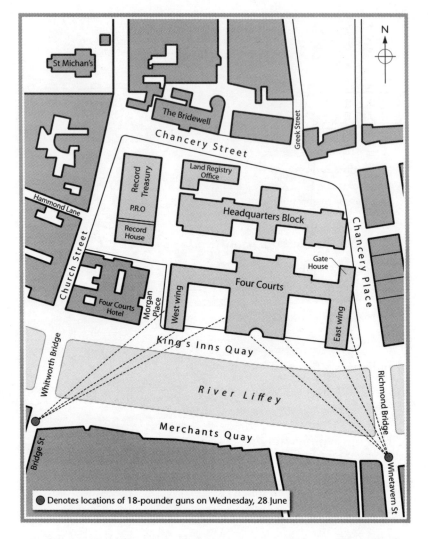

Locations of the two 18-pounders on the Wednesday morning.

crews to direct their shells at as many parts of the Four Courts as possible, so that none of the occupants was far from exploding shells. A study of the wide spread of 'hits' on the southern façade of the Four Courts, from contemporary photographs, indicates that this was successfully achieved (see elevation, right).

The dots indicate initial 18-pounder shell impacts on the south façade of the Four Courts and its wings, evidence of the intention of frightening as many of the garrison as possible.

The men in the Four Courts, relieved that the waiting had finally come to an end and that the National Army had fired first, enthusiastically returned fire with rifles, pistols and machine-guns. Snipers on the roof parapets overlooking the river concentrated their fire on the 18-pounder gun crews, and a continuous shower of bullets rang against the steel gun shields and ricocheted off the cobbled street. One of the men operating the guns was hit and wounded, whereupon a companion, shocked by the sight of his companion's plight, said he was going home and left.[12] Lancia armoured cars had to be brought in to act as shields for the guns against the hail of bullets they were attracting.

A number of pro-Treaty soldiers unofficially joined in the attack. Capt. Tommy Ryan was one of them; he had not yet been issued with a National Army uniform, but, armed with a Thompson sub-machine-gun, he went into one of the tenement houses overlooking the Four Courts, and climbed to the top floor from where he had a good field of fire. The flat was occupied by a young girl and an old woman, who offered to make Ryan a cup of tea and give him eggs on toast. When the firing started, however, and he joined in, shooting a burst of sub-machine-gun fire out of the window, the old woman, seeing that he had no uniform and thinking that he was perhaps an anti-Treaty man, changed her mind about hospitality and smashed the teapot over Ryan's head.[13]

Commandant-Gen. Dermot MacManus claimed that he had fired the first shot. He had taken the twenty men Padraig O'Connor had given him and spread them through the ramshackle and semi-ruined tenement houses on the west side of Church Street. The residents of occupied flats were turned out while MacManus and his men occupied the top-floor rooms, the windows of which gave a good view of the Record Treasury and the Record House across the narrow street. Members of the garrison could be seen manning sandbagged fortifications on the roof, and, in the excitement of the moment, MacManus claimed to have smashed a window and fired what he believed was the first shot of the attack. He had to immediately dive for the floor, however, when his shot was accurately returned by a fusillade from the other side, five bullets coming through the window and striking the wall behind him.[14]

There were thirty-three men, under Tom Morrissey, defending the Public Record Office. Most of them were what Ernie O'Malley referred to as 'young lads' of the Republican youth movement, Na Fianna. Not long after the attack began it became clear that, of the four buildings in the Four Courts complex, the Public Record Office was the most vulnerable, taking intense fire from the Four Courts Hotel to the south, the Bridewell police station to the north and the row of tenements across Church Street to the west, in addition to the Lewis gun in St Michan's tower. The planning for the defence of the building had been, at best, naïve. While the sandbagged roof parapets overlooking Church Street might have seemed, to an inexperienced soldier, to be an ideal, protected sniper position, they provided no protection against the elevated position of the St Michan's Lewis gun, little more than 100 yards (91.5 m) away. It must have been a terrifying baptism of fire for the young Fianna members; after their first brave fusillade that disconcerted Dermot MacManus on the other side of Church Street, the rooftop of the Public Record Office had been raked with machine-gun fire, and most of the young men cowering in the inadequate cover of their sandbag fortifications had to make a panicked withdrawal, scurrying downstairs into the safety of the Record House. Five of them were wounded in the early minutes of the action. A few of them had to stay put on the roof, under sparse cover, through the rest of the day, until they could make their escape when darkness fell.

A British officer in plain clothes, possibly sent to observe the battle, managed to get into the Bridewell, opposite the Record Treasury, where he watched a National Army man exchanging shots with 'a rebel' not more than 150 yards (137 m) away. The soldier was clearly having no success with his rifle, and the officer, wishing to show him how to fire it properly, said, 'Here, give me your rifle.' 'Indeed I will not,' the man replied; 'you might kill the boy!'[15] This and other contemporary accounts suggest that, during the early part of the siege particularly, there was an almost universal disinclination, on both sides, to cause injury to their opponents. The under-secretary for Ireland, Sir Alfred Cope, sent a report to London commenting on this reluctance on both sides to draw serious blood: 'Rory is in the Four Courts. Free Staters are in the houses opposite each firing at the other hundreds of rounds with probably remarkably few hits. A hundred yards away people carry on their ordinary business.'

Before long, shards of glass were flying as the long glazed roof light and the tall windows of the Record Treasury were pulverized, with bullets thudding into storage racks of archives and ricocheting off the iron and stone structure. The tall windows made this part of the building untenable, and it was evacuated. The garrison regrouped in the marginally safer Record House at the southern end of the building, which was at least out of the danger zone from the St Michan's Lewis gun. Because most of the sandbags had been used on the roof, there were only a few left to fortify the windows in the Record House. Across Church Street, MacManus and his men had discovered that the sandbags used in the windows of the Record House had been filled with dry sand, and that when they were raked with Lewis-gun fire the sand drained out of them, making them useless. The Record House garrison then had to barricade the windows with desks, cupboards and towers of books and ledgers. Armfuls of documents and files were also brought across from the shelves in the Record Treasury to build protective barriers: these valuable records, and some that were held over for readers in the Record House before the occupation, were the only ones then stored in the Treasury which survived the fire that later destroyed the rest of the holdings.

In spite of its difficulties, the Record House garrison was conspicuously brave and tenacious. After the traumatic early minutes of the attack, the men quickly recovered and were able to make things difficult for their attackers, the men of A Company of the National Army, which occupied the Maguire & Patterson match factory across Church Street.

Under the charge of Commandant Billy McClean, like their opponents across the street they had no sandbags, and had to make do with heaps of hessian sacks piled in the windows which provided little protection against the 'stream of lead' that kept pouring through the window openings from the guns of the young Record House garrison, the bullets screeching and whining as they ricocheted off the walls. To make matters worse, the water storage tank in the roof of the building they were occupying burst in the intensive firing, and a deluge of water cascaded into the rooms below, drenching the National Army soldiers to the skin. This was the last straw, and they had to retire to the back of the premises.

The Record House garrison was also under fire from National Army men in the Four Courts Hotel and the adjacent houses only yards away. In the hotel, a visitor from Cork, who somehow had been overlooked during the evacuation a couple of hours before, woke to the thunder of guns, and a rifle bullet smashed through the window of his room and lodged in the wall. He lay shaking with fear on the floor until shortly after midday, when he finally plucked up his courage and, dragging on his clothes, made his escape.[16]

At 5 a.m., about an hour after the attack began, the shooting slackened and there was silence for a while. It is probable that Dalton and the other officers were hoping that, after an hour of bombardment, they had done enough to persuade the garrison that they meant business. The telephone line into the Four Courts was still operating, and a call was put through to Capt. Paddy O'Brien, the officer in command. He was asked if his force was going to come out. He gave 'a very definite reply' that 'we were not leaving the courts until we were beaten out of it'.[17] Shortly after, there was the thunderous roar of an 18-pounder, and the insistent rattle of machine-guns started up again, 'with terrific fury', blending with the tolling of Dublin's church bells for early mass.

Apart from Capt. Tommy Ryan's teapot injury, the first casualty in the battle seems to have been a Mrs Kelly, aged sixty, a resident of Chancery Street, who apparently died of heart failure when the guns started firing. The ambulance that took her body to Jervis Street hospital also carried the first National Army casualty, Volunteer Long, who had been wounded in the same street, where the National Army occupied the Medical Mission, just opposite the gate to the Four Courts.

Rory O'Connor and his companions were perhaps disappointed that it was not the British who had come to oust them, but the garrison settled down to resist, as Commandant Ned Daly's men had done six years before during the 1916 Rising. It was generally assumed that Oscar Traynor's anti-Treaty Dublin Brigade would soon come to their aid, and there were also hopes that their chief of staff, Liam Lynch, would bring to Dublin a large force from the Southern divisions. The incoming fire from

The Medical Mission in Chancery Place, facing the east side
of the Four Courts complex, as it is today. Note the many
bullet hole repairs in a light-coloured mortar.

all sides of the complex, however, confirmed the concerns of
some of the garrison about the lack of planning for a possible
attack, because leaders such as Lynch had not been prepared
to adopt the necessary defensive measures while this was still
possible. Lynch and some other leaders of the anti-Treaty IRA
had had their minds on other matters, and had been confident
that, ultimately, negotiations with the Provisional Government
would succeed, and that there would be no further need for
military action.

The men who had been in the Four Courts in 1916 remembered how, with an organized perimeter of defence posts
around the complex, they had held out against British attacks.

Although Ernie O'Malley and others had recommended a range of measures to be put in place which would allow them to offer a strong defence, they were ignored.[18] Instead, a rather hare-brained attempt, fraught with difficulties, had been started three weeks before to dig an escape tunnel from the Public Record Office under Church Street to the Maguire & Patterson factory on the other side of the road, but the project had been abandoned because of flooding.[19] Three of the men who had worked on the tunnel had afterwards left to join the National Army, so even if the tunnel had worked, it would no longer have been a secret escape route.

When the assault finally came, it was clear, in particular, that failing to occupy the block at the south-east corner of the complex containing the Four Courts Hotel was a serious mistake. These buildings constituted a physical penetration into the Four Courts complex, an advanced and secure spearhead from which the National Army men had a clear field of fire into the heart of the defenders' positions.

While Ernie O'Malley had reckoned that at least 250 men would be needed to defend the Four Courts properly, there were probably fewer than 180 men in occupation at the time of the attack, and because of the size of the complex – the defensive perimeter of the buildings was nearly 2,000 feet (610 m) – they were very thinly spread. There were no reserves on standby: every man was in the front line, manning the defence points, so there was little rest for any of them.

Nurse Geraldine O'Donel arrived in an ambulance at the Four Courts at 9 a.m., five hours after the shooting started, with Dr James Ryan* and Surgeon Charlie McAuley. They were allowed through National Army lines, and brought with them a number of nurses and some members of Cumann na mBan, the women's auxiliary force of the Irish Volunteers.† They quickly set about fitting out a temporary hospital in the Headquarters Block, possibly in what had been the dining hall at the north side of the building, although this room was overlooked by the Bridewell, which was occupied by the National Army. As an example of how matters had changed since the Treaty, McAuley had operated on Major General Tom Ennis, one of the commanders of the National Army, after he had been wounded in the Custom House battle a year before, and Ennis had been cared for by O'Donel during his three-month convalescence. Now they were on different sides.

Ernie O'Malley claimed that Dr Ryan brought supplies of hospital equipment and 'bandages, lint, gauze, bottles of iodine,

---

* Dr James Ryan (1891–1970), born in Wexford, became a member of the Volunteers in 1913 while a medical student, served in the GPO in 1916 as a medical officer, and was one of the last to leave. Elected TD for Wexford South in the first Dáil, he fought in the War of Independence. His sister Mary Josephine was married to Richard Mulcahy, Minister for Defence at the outset of the Civil War, while another sister, Mary Kate, was married to Seán T. O'Kelly. He was a co-founder of Fianna Fáil with Éamon de Valera, and had a long and distinguished political career, serving as a minister in a succession of Fianna Fáil governments.

† Cumann na mBan, or in English, The Irishwoman's Council, was a paramilitary organization formed in 1914 to work with the Irish Volunteers. They played a significant part in the Rising of 1916 and the War of Independence. The majority of the organization supported the anti-Treaty side during the Civil War, during which over 400 of its members were imprisoned by the forces of the Provisional Government.

picric and splints, which were carried in and laid on the tables'.[20]
Geraldine O'Donel, however, recalls in her Bureau of Military
History Witness Statement that she found when she arrived
that no preparations had been made to deal with casualties and
that there were 'no medical dressings or other equipment'.
A staunch republican, O'Donel was a trained nurse and no
stranger to gunshot wounds: she had opened a nursing home
in Dublin in 1920, where she clandestinely treated many members of the IRA who had been wounded in action against the
British. According to her Witness Statement,[21] she was allowed
through the National Army lines again when she left the courts
that morning to walk to Fannins in Aungier Street to obtain
medical supplies. She bought £30 worth of dressings, and
managed to arrange for a fire brigade ambulance to take her
back to the Four Courts. When she got back, she found that
two defenders had already been wounded in exchanges of fire.
Tommie Keenan had received a rifle bullet through the lung,
but with prompt treatment he survived. Another member of
the occupying garrison, Mattie MacDonald, had been felled by
a bullet wound to the ankle. Two stretcher-bearers were taking him to the makeshift hospital in the Headquarters Block
when they also came under fire. When the two men dropped
the stretcher and ran for cover, MacDonald clambered up from
the ground and managed to hobble after them. While awaiting
evacuation to hospital from the Four Courts, he calmly continued to read a cowboy book, *Curly, A Tale of the Arizona
Desert*. His foot was so badly injured, however, that it was
later amputated.

When she had heard the noise of the shelling in the early hours, Cumann na mBan member Máire Comerford had cycled from Roebuck Road, Clonskeagh, to Barry's Hotel in Great Denmark Street, which had been occupied that morning by anti-Treaty forces. Since she could drive, she was asked to take a van of medical supplies to the Four Courts. She set off towards the quays through empty streets, but was stopped by Free State troops near the Dublin markets. She explained that she was only carrying medical supplies, but when they searched the van they found cigarettes. A soldier got into the vehicle and, with his rifle 'pointed at the middle of my back', Máire was ordered to drive to the battalion headquarters at the Four Courts Hotel. She followed the soldier's instructions until the van 'bumped against the back wall of the Four Courts', and the engine stalled. Unfortunately, when Máire Comerford had learned to drive, she had not mastered how to start an engine or how to reverse. The soldier would not get out for fear of being fired on by the men in the Four Courts, so he had to shout instructions through the window telling her how to crank the engine, and to take care not to get her arm broken by the crankshaft kick-back. She got the engine going and when she jumped back in the van, he showed her how to reverse, and off they went again. When they reached the Four Courts Hotel the van was searched once more, and, while they would not release it, they allowed Comerford to take the supplies, including the cigarettes, into the Four Courts.

She took some of the cigarettes to 'poor' 'Ginger' O'Connell, whom she had known during the War of Independence. 'He was under guard in the basement and he came to the door of his room to accept them; but they did not seem to relieve his gloom', and this disappointed her a little.[22] Leaving O'Connell, she joined Nurse O'Donel and Madge Clifford, who worked as a secretary to Ernie O'Malley, in assisting with the wounded.

Unlikely as it seems, throughout that day and up until the end, young women of Cumann na mBan carried dispatches, hidden on their persons, to and from the Four Courts, often under fire. One even brought a supply of much-needed ammunition in her bicycle basket, which she said had been given her by National Army men. In the early days of the conflict at least, members of Cumann na mBan were greatly admired by the men on both sides, and the National Army troops would not have dreamt of firing at them or obstructing them. They must have been aware that the women were carrying messages and more, and it is strange that some of them were not at least stopped and detained.

The buildings in the Four Courts complex were large and solidly built, and, contrary to Emmet Dalton's idea of a shell-shocked garrison soon surrendering, there is no record of members of the garrison being in any particular awe of the artillery attack. It should be remembered that the initial barrage was not concentrated on one area, but was deliberately aimed at getting a wide spread of hits on the south-facing walls, so that as many of the garrison as possible would be affected. Simon Donnelly was one member of the Four Courts garrison who was quite unimpressed at the lack of destructive power of the shells; he remarked to Dr Jim Ryan that the guns must have been bought at Woolworths.[23] It seems that Ryan agreed; he wrote a series of notes to his wife, Máirín, on tiny scraps of paper which were taken out by Cumann na mBan women, reassuring her that all was well, and that they had, in the courts, two priests and three doctors, as well as nurses. 'The big guns are no use,' he wrote, 'and many on the opposite side are not trying to shoot to kill.' In another note he asks his wife to call in to '42', presumably 42 Beresford Street, the City of Dublin Skin and Cancer Hospital, where he worked, to tell them he would not be in for a few days! A postscript says, 'Don't mind the big guns. They are harmless to us.'[24] At least one member of the garrison, however, a man named Nugent, was said to have suffered from shell-shock.

Three men were wounded seriously enough, however, in the first hours of the attack, to be taken for treatment to the field hospital that had been set up in the Headquarters Block. While Surgeon Charlie McAuley was dealing with a patient, bullets came through the door of the room they were in, probably from the Bridewell, and they had to fortify the door with piles of books from the Law Library.

The armoured car called 'The Mutineer', which Ernie O'Malley had managed to commandeer in Tullamore a couple of weeks before and bring to the Four Courts, was proving very useful. It was driven from one courtyard to another, engaging the Four Courts Hotel, the Bridewell and the Medical Mission in Chancery Place and keeping National Army snipers under frequent fire with its Vickers machine-gun. It must have been extraordinarily uncomfortable, however, for the crew inside.

The warm June weather and the constant machine-gun fire that a moving target such as theirs attracted must have made their conditions both hot and noisy.

With most parts of the Four Courts complex well within range of rifle fire from the surrounding buildings, communications between the four buildings within the complex were hazardous. As mentioned earlier, work had begun on two connecting tunnels, one between the Headquarters Block and the Record House, and the other between the Headquarters Block and the main Four Courts building, but only the last had been completed when the National Army attack began. Ernie O'Malley wrote that in the tunnel between the Headquarters Block and the main Four Courts building there was 'a very definite aroma, as the tunnel diggers had struck a sewer on their way'. Other than at night, therefore, there was no way of safely moving from the most isolated building, the Public Record Office, to the Four Courts building or the Headquarters Block without coming under fire from the Bridewell or the Four Courts Hotel. This meant that it was difficult to get supplies of food and ammunition safely to the men defending the Public Record Office. 'A garrison without proper food, surrounded on all sides, bad communication between their inside posts, faulty defences' is how O'Malley, in *The Singing Flame*, described the situation the men in the Record House were in.

Liam Lynch cannot have been long in bed in the Clarence Hotel before he was awoken by the thunderous outbreak of gunfire around the Four Courts only a couple of blocks away, and he knew immediately what had happened. It was clear to him that further negotiations with the Provisional Government were pointless, and he decided to return to Munster to organize his men. Another meeting was called of all the available senior anti-Treaty IRA officers, including Seán Moylan, Frank Barrett and Michael Kilroy, and this time Éamon de Valera and Cathal Brugha were among those who attended. The meeting was punctuated by the sound of shellfire: the nearest 18-pounder was only 350 yards (320 m) away. Lynch made clear his resolve now to fight for the Republic, and they drew up a proclamation condemning the treachery of 'recreant Irishmen' and appealing to the Irish people to rally in support of the Republic, in what was only the continuation of the struggle against the British. They also urged the Irishmen who had joined the National Army to return to their allegiance to the Republic. Lynch then departed with his men for Limerick to organize hostilities against the National Army.

By coincidence, he was spotted as he went, just around the corner from the hotel in Parliament Street, by Emmet Dalton, who was heading for the quays in an open car after a visit to army headquarters. Dalton ordered his men to stop and arrest Lynch and his companions, and to take them to Wellington barracks on the South Circular Road.

If it was the opening of hostilities at the Dublin Four Courts that started the Irish Civil War, how Lynch was dealt with later in Wellington barracks certainly ensured that it would not end quickly. He was brought to the office of Gen. Eoin O'Duffy,

Gen. Eoin O'Duffy at his desk.

who had been appointed the army's deputy chief of staff in place of J. J. 'Ginger' O'Connell. Although the split between the Rory O'Connor faction and the Lynch faction had been healed just hours before the bombardment began, O'Duffy, like the rest of the headquarters staff of the National Army, believed the schism within the anti-Treaty IRA still existed. He assumed that Lynch was still anxious to negotiate a settlement with the Provisional Government. O'Duffy was therefore concerned to keep Lynch happy, and not to make matters worse. Lynch said afterwards that the meeting was very informal, and that O'Duffy asked him his opinion of the situation, to which Lynch replied 'Ye are all mad!' Whatever else was said, the conversation left O'Duffy satisfied that releasing Lynch was not going to be a problem.[25] For reassurance, he made a telephone call to Gen. Mulcahy, Minister for Defence, explaining the situation, and Mulcahy, also believing that Lynch would remain neutral and hostilities could be confined to Dublin, ordered that he be released.

Lynch travelled south to Limerick, where he set up his headquarters and began to plan for war. If he had been detained, it is possible that the Civil War might have ended within days.

As soon as the fighting started, Oscar Traynor, the officer commanding the Dublin Brigade of the anti-Treaty IRA, mobilized his men, and they began to occupy previously selected buildings in the city centre, somewhat remote from the Four Courts, such as Vaughan's Hotel in Parnell Square and Tara Hall, the trade union building in Gloucester Street. Snipers were spread around the city with orders to disrupt the movements of the National Army. Barry's Hotel in Great Denmark Street, near Parnell Square, was also taken over; Annie Farrington, the proprietor, was an ardent Irish nationalist. Before the truce she had managed the Crown Hotel in Sackville Street, where IRA men on the run, such as Seán MacEoin, Dan Breen, Seán Tracy and Seán Hogan, were frequent guests. After the truce, at Barry's Hotel she hosted many others, such as Liam Lynch, Joe McKelvey and Maurice (Moss) Twomey; she described them as 'lovely people to have in the house; they were so well-behaved'. During those months Barry's, and particularly the bar in the hotel, became an important meeting place for both factions in the Treaty dispute. 'There were a great variety of views and they were arguing it out. They never came to blows,' she stated.

She described the measures that Traynor's men took to fortify the hotel on the Wednesday morning, which would have been similar in all the other locations:

the first thing they did was to knock all the glass out of the doors and windows. They sandbagged the windows and stuck guns out between the bags... They cleared out all the visitors – about forty – giving them barely time to pack their bags. They cleared out the staff, but I refused to go and Miss Keogh and William the porter stayed with me... the IRA brought in oceans of food but I thought it queer that they did not want to give us any of it... I was half out of my mind thinking of all the money I owed the bank which financed the purchase of the hotel and I now saw the possibility of the whole place going up in smoke.[26]

While many believed that Traynor's Dublin Brigade would go to the aid of their comrades in the Four Courts, although a few reconnaissance attempts were made westwards from Parnell Square, no serious effort was made to move on the courts in force. When Traynor established his headquarters in the Hammam Hotel and other buildings on the east side of Sackville Street, Ernie O'Malley could not understand why he would pick a place so remote from the Four Courts, on 'the wrong side of the widest street in the capital'.

There is little evidence that any comprehensive logistical planning was carried out by National Army headquarters for the attack on the Four Courts: apart from the agreement to acquire the 18-pounder guns and ammunition which had probably been made during the previous week, it seems that what arrangements were made were last-minute efforts. Gen. Macready mentions in his memoirs how Dalton admitted to him, at the end of the first day of the siege, that there were no arrangements to feed his troops, and that they had not eaten all day. There were no plans even to temporarily house the occupants of the tenement buildings that had been taken over by the army around the Four Courts.

By 9 a.m. that day, large crowds of curious onlookers had gathered along Wellington and Ormond Quays, and later they congregated in a mass on Grattan Bridge, within a few hundred yards of the Four Courts. Rumours were rife. The word went around that Rory O'Connor had been killed, but that a legendary hero was marching on Dublin with 1,000 men. People were constantly crossing back and forth over the bridge with no appreciation of the danger they were in. Although

Crowds of sightseers gathered near Grattan Bridge
on Essex Quay to watch the battle.

civilians, and particularly a host of street children, were held well back from the fighting by soldiers and constables of the Dublin Metropolitan Police, many found alleyways through which they could make their way to positions where the siege could be observed close-up.

At 9.15 a.m. a young porter from the Ormond Hotel on Ormond Quay, who had been leaning out of a window watching what was happening, was hit in the head by a stray bullet. He was taken to Jervis Street, where he later died. Minutes later, a brief truce was agreed between the two sides to allow three seriously wounded members of the Four Courts garrison to be stretchered out by the Red Cross and transported by ambulance to hospital.

A number of last-minute emergency arrangements were made by the National Army to deal with expected casualties: during the day the Ormond Hotel was temporarily converted into a field hospital, and the proprietor, Mr P. J. O'Malley, hung a large Red Cross flag out of one of the front windows. Doctors and nurses from Dublin hospitals manned the makeshift aid station, and over the following days dealt with many wounded soldiers and civilians.

The 18-pounder guns at Bridge Street and Winetavern Street continued to be targets for the snipers high up behind the Four Courts roof parapet, and the area around the guns was constantly raked with bullets and ricochets. A glance at the photographs showing the guns being operated and revealing the men crouching behind an armoured shield in the cover of an armoured car, makes this clear. Later that day a young man named

Frazer, coming around the corner of Bridge Street, walked straight into this danger zone, and was seriously injured by a sniper's bullet. His father and mother, who lived nearby, were sent for, and when they came around the corner with their little daughter, they too were shot and wounded. A correspondent for *The Times* of London found the 'heedless recklessness' of the ordinary citizens 'almost incredible'. He described a young woman casually wheeling a baby in a pram along the quay in front of the 18-pounder guns when the firing was at its height.

In the midst of all this, as one newspaper correspondent wrote,

> the ordinary life of Dublin seemed to go on as usual. News-boys shrieked their Stop Presses a little more loudly than is their wont. Crowds on O'Connell Bridge and down the quays reminded one that the civil war was in progress a few hundred yards away, but, despite the booming of the 18-pounder and the intermittent rattle of machine-guns, the teashops and cafés were full of laughing men and women, while flannelled youths with tennis racquets made one wonder whether, after all, it was not a dream.

The reporter could have been writing about young men like Denis Johnston, the future playwright* who was home in Dublin

---

* Denis Johnston (1901–84) was a dramatist and radio and television director. Among his plays is *The Moon in the Yellow River*, set in the aftermath of the Civil War.

on holiday from the University of Cambridge. He cycled into town to witness the start of the Civil War, and watched the fire brigade attempt to put out a fire in a bullet-scarred building on Parnell Square. Returning south of the river, he went up Dame Street where National Army troops were gathered in large numbers in front of City Hall, where the Provisional Government was based. Farther up the hill (probably near Christ Church) Johnston found a vantage-point from where he could look down at the Four Courts, and noted that a field gun was firing from the quays below.

Later he cycled home to Lansdowne Road for lunch, and then spent the afternoon playing tennis with his friends, while the distant boom of guns and the crackle of rifle fire continued in the background. He later wrote in his diary:

> I can't imagine what they think they're doing – except venting their spite. I can't conceive the mentality of the man behind his sandbag in the Four Courts – what he thinks is going to be the end of it, how he imagines he's going to affect anything by hanging on there and shooting at other Irishmen.[27]

The writer and political activist Rosamund Jacob watched from the corner of Parliament Street and the quays, where a crowd, held back by soldiers, was staring at the dome of the Four Courts 'in a senseless sort of way' as the 18-pounders boomed from nearby. Like many who read the English newspapers, she believed that what was happening was at the behest of the British, and she thought that it was extraordinary that the army 'could be got to so easily attack the republicans'. Jacob felt possessed, like other onlookers, by a 'diseased sense of curiosity'.[28]

Before noon, another writer, Dr Oliver St John Gogarty,* took Clare Sheridan down to the quays in his car to see what was going on. There were crowds gathered in spite of the bullets 'whistling close and chipping bits off the wall', but when he could not get near the south side of the Four Courts, Gogarty drove around to the north side, where he and Sheridan got out and mingled with the local residents standing outside their homes. Although women in the crowd holding their babies seemed unconcerned, some of them told Sheridan that a man had been shot dead not long before just where she was standing. Gogarty laughingly told Sheridan, as they left, that his car would probably be a special target for snipers, because it was a Ford, similar to the ones the Free State generals used.[29]

They went on to Hamilton Hospital (later the Meath Hospital), where some of the first casualties of the battle were beginning to arrive, including a ten-year-old boy, dead from a gunshot. Sheridan wrote: 'his face was ivory, the colour of his fair hair. His hands were crossed upon his chest; over the heart was a small red spot where the bullet had penetrated.' The child had not been identified, and after keeping him for four days unclaimed, he was buried. There was also a 'workman' shot through the leg; a monk was listening to his confession. As Gogarty and Sheridan were leaving, a strange procession of

---

* Dr Oliver St John Gogarty (1878–1957), poet, otolaryngologist, writer and wit; his friend James Joyce caricatured him as Buck Mulligan in *Ulysses*.

men and women came in from the street, the men staggering under the weight of the limp body of a grey-haired and toothless old man in a blood-soaked sheet. The women, their heads covered with their shawls, were wailing and weeping, and calling out 'the poor old man' and 'there was no better man', and they stood over the corpse cursing the name of Rory O'Connor.[30]

Two days later, on the Friday, Gogarty wrote to Gen. Mulcahy, the Provisional Government Minister for Defence, saying he would be glad to give him any help he could. He said that he had been driving a Rolls-Royce for ten years, and offered himself as a relief driver for Mulcahy's armoured car.

There is plenty of written and photographic evidence of 18-pounders No. 1 and No. 2, located at Winetavern Street and Bridge Street respectively. It seems, however, that one of them might have been at least temporarily moved. The *Irish Independent* reported that, at about 2.30 p.m., an 18-pounder was dug in at the corner of Capel Street and Little Strand Street, facing towards the Four Courts. From that location in 1922, an area of tightly packed tenements would have blocked the view of the main court buildings, and only the dome would have been visible. At about 3.30 p.m., this gun was fired. The shell struck a lamp-post about 10 yards (9 m) away in Little Strand Street, outside Vaughan Brothers' licensed premises, and exploded with terrific force. The lamp-post was cut in two, all the windows and doors around were shattered, and Vaughan's pub was almost demolished. The gun was moved from this location a few minutes later.

By late afternoon, the tactics of the National Army gunners seem to have changed. There had been no indication that the barrage of shells exploding against the robust walls of the Four Courts had so far caused any problems for the garrison, and, since the gun crews were becoming more proficient in their aim, they thought that they might achieve more effective results by sending shells into the buildings through the windows. *Irish Life* magazine reported that shells were fired at intervals of about ten minutes and 'most of the shells were directed with great accuracy through the windows, as though it was the desire of the command to injure the walls as little as possible'. An ex-British army gunner who was watching the bombardment told an *Irish Independent* reporter that the shells being used were of the 'HE type with fuses attached'.

While there is little doubt that all the rooms along the south side of the Four Courts complex, overlooking the river, were evacuated as the bombardment developed, snipers ranged along the roofs kept up their regular pot-shots at the men operating the guns. One sniper who was particularly effective was operating from the high vantage-point of one of the windows in the drum of the Four Courts dome. The stonework around this window was pockmarked with as many as 170 bullet strikes, sure evidence of efforts to dislodge him. Commandant Padraig O'Connor's men were being fired on by snipers and he made his way across the river and asked Commandant Lawlor, commanding the Bridge Street 18-pounder, if he could put

The dome of the Four Courts viewed from the south-west, at about 5 p.m. on Wednesday, 28 June. The window the sniper has been using is the one with sandbags and with the most bullet strikes around it. Below that window on the right, partly hidden by the column, is what looks to be an 18-pound shell impact. From a photograph taken after the siege, I made a count of about 170 bullet strikes on the drum around the window, together with another, very prominent shell strike.

a shell into the window the sniper was using. The gun was traversed and the barrel elevated sufficiently, a shell loaded and fired. The two officers rushed forward from the cover of the armoured car to see its effect. They thought at first that the shot had missed, and had visions of it landing on some unsuspecting victims far beyond the Four Courts in Clontarf, but a cloud of debris and dust burst from the window, indicating that the shot had been spot on. Each time the targets for the guns were altered, members of the beseiged garrison could see where the gun was being aimed, and those in the sights had time to move themselves to safer locations. There is no record of a sniper being the victim of shellfire, so it seems that this one made himself scarce in time.

During the day a strong force of anti-Treaty troops were observed by scouts making their way west through Henry Street and into Mary Street, a few blocks from the Four Courts. Padraig O'Connor, concerned that they were attempting to link up with the Four Courts garrison, sent Jimmy McGuinness with some of his brigade reserves to confront them. When McGuinness and his men got to Mary Street, however, they found that the anti-Treaty men had retreated back towards Sackville Street.

Although hemmed in by the National Army cordon, the occupants of the Four Courts managed to get reports, messages and dispatches out and in for the whole period of the siege, using Cumann na mBan couriers and sometimes ambulance personnel. From some reports, it seems also that their telephone lines were open for at least the early part of the siege. Since the opening of hostilities, good friends had found themselves on opposing sides, and there was quite a lot of 'sharing' of tactical information between conflicted individual soldiers on both sides.

From the beginning, members of the garrison referred to the Record Treasury, where hand grenades and mines were being manufactured, as the 'Munitions Block' or the 'munitions factory'. Before long, what was going on there was known to the officers of the National Army. A scribbled note by Gen. Mulcahy at the time refers to the fact that both Dalton and Daly were worried that the 'munitions factory' was being mined so as to be blown up if Free State troops attacked, and that an attempt should be made by the 18-pounders to 'get' the 'munitions factory' before the advance of the infantry.[31]

The *Freeman's Journal* reported that an aeroplane flew over the city at about 7 o'clock that evening, bearing the letters 'DE', which it was thought in some way signified the National Army. It was also noted by the defenders of the Four Courts, who thought it was an RAF plane from Baldonnel airfield observing the results of the artillery fire and reporting to the National Army. The gunner in 'The Mutineer' armoured car tried to fire at the aircraft, but he was unable to elevate his Vickers machine-gun sufficiently.

An examination of London newspapers of the following day reveals that at least two aircraft flew over the Four Courts that evening. Neither had anything to do with either the RAF or the National Army. One of the aircraft was a De Havilland flown by Alan Cobham, the well-known aviator, who had been sent to Ireland by *The Times* of London to collect photographs of the Dublin action for publication the following morning. It was a time when sales of newspapers depended greatly on photographic 'scoops'; while text could be sent by telegraph, newspapers were using photographs more and more in their reportage, and these could normally be sent only by courier or by post. Cobham ran an 'aircraft for hire' service out of Croydon airport, south London, which was increasingly being used by British daily newspapers as a fast way to obtain news photographs from abroad. Earlier in the year, he had taken part in a hazardous flight to Belgrade in Yugoslavia to bring back photographs for the *Daily Mirror* of the royal wedding of King Alexander of Yugoslavia to Princess Marie of Romania. On his return flight, he nearly crash-landed in the dark on a French airfield, but he still got the photos to the newspaper in time for them to be published, twenty-four hours before its competitors.

Having left Croydon on the afternoon of 28 June, Cobham landed and refuelled at Chester before flying across the Irish Sea to Dublin, where he landed at the RAF base at Collinstown. There he was detained by soldiers of the regiment, but managed to have the package of photographs which had been taken by the *Times* photographer delivered to him from Dublin. The RAF personnel did not have any protocols to deal with this kind of matter, however, and Cobham was prevented from taking off while they dithered about the best course of action. 'I protested, I fumed, I raged', he wrote afterwards, and in the end it was decided to seek permission for his departure from National Army headquarters. This was received within two hours, and Cobham took off again for Chester at 8.30 p.m. Before heading out across the Irish Sea, however, he took a detour over the centre of the city and flew over the Four Courts. His description of his flight to and from Dublin was given almost as much column space in *The Times* of the following day as the reports of the outbreak of hostilities in Dublin. Reading it, one obtains a revealing insight into the average Briton's knowledge of what was going on in Ireland:

Airmen have looked down on the greatest battles of the world. But no airman, so far as I know, has ever, till yesterday afternoon, witnessed fighting on the grand scale between men of our own British race for the possession of one of the ancient capitals of the Empire.[32]

The other aircraft that flew over the Four Courts on that Wednesday evening was piloted by L. J. Randall of the *Daily Chronicle*, and he described rather imaginatively the Four Courts district as 'a scene of desolation... in one or two places were heaps of ruins'.

As darkness fell, Máire Comerford was asked to go out to the National Army headquarters to request a ceasefire in order to persuade them to stop shooting at the field hospital in the Headquarters Block. The wounded had had to be taken down to the dark basement of the building for safety. She crossed the street to the Mechanics Institute, and two of the National Army troops stationed there walked her through the narrow streets to their headquarters in the Four Courts Hotel, where she had been earlier in the day. She described the two as arguing about the rights and wrongs of the anti-Treaty position – 'fighting their own war, verbally', as they went. One of them had all the standard pro-Treaty arguments while the other had republican sympathies but did not have any good arguments, so she helped him out as they walked. Before they arrived at the Four Courts Hotel, this soldier showed his gratitude by slipping her a handful of .303 ammunition. She was taken in to see Paddy O'Daly, by which time her 'skirt pocket was overweighted to the extent I feared a breakdown in the stitching which would scatter the bullets round the floor!'

O'Daly quickly agreed to the ceasefire. He spoke to Comerford about the signals that should be made by her side, and when they went out he sent orders for the guns across the river to cease firing. After O'Daly had signalled with his torch to those watching them from the Four Courts, the pair made for the Chancery Street gate, walking past the riverside front of the building. To try to distract him so that he would not see the damage that had been done by the big guns, Máire Comerford tried all the way to engage him in conversation.

At the Chancery Street gate some members of the anti-Treaty garrison came out to talk with O'Daly. According to Comerford, the atmosphere was informal and their voices did not sound angry and none was raised: 'they had the attitude of men who had said everything that could be said many times before. Daly disclaimed all intent to hurt our hospital and told us to put it back where it had been... he said it had not been properly marked, and it was agreed that we would put out certain lantern signals.'[33]

Communication between the National Army headquarters in the Four Courts Hotel and their men in the Bridewell, however, must not have been good, because as soon as the hospital was reinstated and shooting started again, the lanterns were shot at and the wounded had to be brought back to the basement.

Like the man who had passed ammunition to Máire Comerford, there were many members of the National Army who were dismayed at how events were turning out, and at the fact that they were now expected to shoot at their former comrades. Five anti-Treaty men who had been arrested by a section of the National Army in Drogheda the previous day, while attempting to raid a train, were allowed to escape that morning, as news of the attack on the Four Courts was received, and five of their captors went with them, taking nine rifles and a large amount of ammunition.[34]

As the ammunition for the 18-pounders began to run out, Dalton, anxious to keep up the barrage, made a request to the British for additional high explosive shells for the guns. The Four Courts had been successfully raked by shellfire but with little serious damage occurring, and the only casualties were members of the occupying garrison who had been slightly injured by flying stone splinters from the impact of shells. Across the river, some members of the 18-pounder gun crews, including Commandant Tony Lawlor, had also received lacerations from stone splinters from machine-gun rounds ricocheting off the cobbled street. One account mentions that Emmet Dalton, in order to encourage the frightened gunners, strolled out into the open street with Lawlor, where they smoked and chatted a while before sauntering back to cover.[35] When one looks at the photographs of the guns in action, and how all those involved are crouching behind good cover, one wonders if two experienced officers would do such a thing, however.

That night the twenty-four-year-old Maj.-Gen. Dalton went to the British army headquarters at the Royal Hospital,

Kilmainham to see the sixty-year-old Gen. Macready. The only record we have of this meeting is from Macready's book *Annals of an Active Life*, which, written two years after the events, is laced with a patronizing attitude towards the Irish. He describes Dalton's visit: 'The poor man arrived about 9.30 p.m., thoroughly worn out, but full of fight. After he got outside a drink or two he told me his story... When the fight began, he had for three hours to work a gun himself, as well as command the whole attack, such as it was.' Dalton told him that no arrangements had been made to provide rations for his men, and they hadn't eaten all day.

General Macready arranged for a Royal Navy destroyer to sail from Dublin port to the British Army Ordnance Depot at Carrickfergus to bring back a consignment of 300 HE shells for Dalton's guns. It would be at least a day before the destroyer would return with the additional shells, but Dalton needed more ammunition because he was afraid that if the guns stopped firing, 'his men would get disheartened and clear off'.[36] Macready was in a delicate position: although he trusted Michael Collins, at this juncture it was impossible to know how the whole matter would pan out, and if, by the end of the week, his soldiers camped in the Phoenix Park might be receiving fire from his own guns. Subsequently, in what could be seen as a brave move on Macready's part, he agreed to send Dalton all the ammunition he had left – fifty rounds of shrapnel – simply to keep the Four Courts men awake. The shrapnel shells differed from the HE ones in that a simple fuse needed to be set, by rotating a numbered disc on the shell, before firing.

It was a simple operation that could be demonstrated in a matter of minutes.

Towards the end of the day, Dalton was beginning to believe that he had been wrong in his notion that the garrison would soon surrender when the Republicans heard and felt the first shells explode against the walls of their headquarters. It was beginning to look like the occupiers of the Four Courts might not be dislodged by shellfire alone. After midnight, firing almost ceased until the promised shrapnel shells arrived, and at 1 a.m., the 18-pounders began shooting again, a shrapnel round being fired roughly every fifteen minutes, keeping up the noise level.

In the Four Courts Liam Mellows insisted that Máire Comerford and another Cumann na mBan woman, Bridie Clyne, should get some rest and took them to 'a great big room where there were two beds in the corner'. They were told not to move out of their corner because the rest of the room was dangerous. The glass in one of the tall windows was shattered. At one stage the door flew open, and Seán Nolan, coming off duty, walked in, unaware that they were there. The two women had a fright when, in the darkness, he threw his rifle on top of Comerford and sat down heavily on Bridie Clyne.

The continual firing of the guns did not seem to keep the tired garrison awake. Comerford mentions seeing, later that night, the floor of the guard room covered with sleeping men, 'in every kind of attitude, some on top of the others', and she came across Rory O'Connor, curled up, fast asleep, on the marble floor. At 3 a.m. Ernie O'Malley's secretary, Madge Clifford, did the rounds of the different posts with a bucket of tea and bread that she had baked in the Four Courts ovens.[37]

CHAPTER 5

THURSDAY, 29 JUNE: THE SECOND DAY OF THE SIEGE

While most businesses in the area around the Four Courts and the North Quays had closed down on the Wednesday because of military activity, the nearby Dublin fruit and vegetable market and the fish market, in daily receipt of a substantial amount of perishables, could not do so. Early that day hundreds of farmers' carts bound for the markets had had either to turn back or to set up on the streets around the city and sell their fresh produce. By the next morning, however, a temporary market had been established in Beresford Place beside the Custom House, nearly a mile downriver from the Four Courts, and business continued as usual.

At National Army headquarters that morning, Gen. Eoin O'Duffy, acting deputy chief of staff, was perturbed to find that the artillery shells for the guns had still not arrived from Carrickfergus. He contacted Macready and protested about the delay in delivery of ammunition for the 18-pounders. He made it clear that if they did not get what they needed soon, the siege would fail.

When Winston Churchill, Britain's Secretary of State for the Colonies, received a cable from Collins which complained about the delay, he replied assuring him that 300 HE shells were on the way, and he went on enthusiastically to recommend that the National Army accept the 60-pounder QF howitzer that Macready had in Marlborough barracks. Churchill displayed his complete lack of understanding of the situation by adding that it could be fired on the Four Courts even from as far away as the Phoenix Park, if necessary, and that National Army officers could be present or, indeed, could actually fire the gun.[1]

At 8 a.m. an aeroplane passed 'fairly closely overhead', circling over Parnell Street, 'its appearance being followed by a volley of rifle shots',[2] but the plane flew off in the direction of the Phoenix Park, apparently unharmed.

Between 8 and 9 a.m., Volunteer James Walsh of the National Army, who was on an upper floor of a house on the corner of Bridge Street, was wounded by a sniper from the roof of the Four Courts. He was taken to Richmond Hospital by ambulance, but he died a few hours later, and was probably the first National Army fatality.

Maj.-Gen. Dalton had asked Macready for two additional 18-pounders and it seems that they were delivered from the British lines to the National Army that morning. One of these guns was located, temporarily at least, opposite the northern side of the Four Courts complex at the corner of Greek Street and Chancery Street, where it could target the eastern end of the Headquarters Block. According to the *Irish Times*, the gun succeeded in blowing 'several holes' in the wing projecting north from the Headquarters Block, before it came under attack from a sniper.[3] Rifle fire from somewhere high up in the Four Courts, probably one of the windows in the drum of the dome, had struck the ground under the armoured shield of the gun and bullets had ricocheted upwards, wounding three of the gunners. The officer with responsibility for the gun, Phil Hyde, withdrew the gun, and refused to expose his crew again until he was provided with adequate cover. Greek Street was in Commandant Padraig O'Connor's area, so he went off to Portobello barracks to requisition a lorry-load of sandbags with which to build a fortified wall in front of the gun.

On his arrival at Portobello, O'Connor was questioned by National Army headquarters staff, who were anxious to receive a first-hand account of the progress of the battle. It seems to have been generally accepted at this stage that raking the buildings with 18-pound ordnance was not going to force a surrender. During the discussions, Capt. Johnny Doyle, one of the party that had collected the first two 18-pounders from Marlborough barracks, arrived. He was asked by headquarters staff if he could hit the Four Courts with a 60-pounder, the gun that Churchill had offered. To this he replied that if he did not hit it, he would go 'bloody near it'. This horrified O'Connor: he made it clear that his men in Church Street were 'bloody near', with only a narrow street between them and the Four Courts.[4] His comments were persuasive, and the headquarters staff sent word to the Provisional Government that the offer of the 60-pounders should not be accepted because of the danger of casualties, not only among civilians in this densely populated central city area, but among the National Army men surrounding the courts.

What is rarely mentioned in contemporary accounts is a request to the British by the Provisional Government for the supply of 'some form of gas grenades', which would make the task of clearing the rebels out of their strongholds much easier. Grenades of this kind were in stock in England, but, paying heed to the discussions of the Washington Disarmament Conference, which sought to control the use of poison gas,* the British government felt that it would be 'improper' to supply the Provisional Government with 'gas of a lethal or permanently injurious character'. Provided the Washington resolution did not forbid the use of lachrymatory or other similar gas (tear gas), it would be prepared to supply this for use against the rebels.[5] This offer was not taken up.

O'Connor brought a lorry-load of sandbags back to Chancery Street, and soon Phil Hyde's 18-pounder, with a low wall of sandbags in front of it, went into action again.

Whether it was simply bad planning, or because army headquarters believed the Four Courts would fall within hours, no

---

* The US sought to insert a clause into the Washington Treaty on Submarines and Noxious Gases (1922), but, opposed by the French, the Treaty was never ratified.

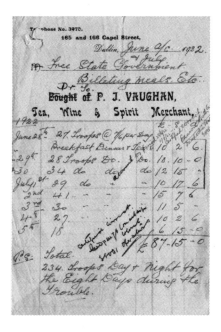

P. J. Vaughan's bill for supplying Padraig O'Connor's National Army company with food and drink for the 'Eight Days during the Trouble'.

arrangements had been made to feed the troops during the course of the attack. By the second day, however, food kitchens were established in the streets by Cumann na Saoirse, the pro-Treaty version of Cumann na mBan founded by the political activist and feminist Jenny Wyse-Power in March 1922.* It was often, however, left to individual commandants to look after their men, and, apart from the other tasks that Padraig O'Connor was dealing with, he made arrangements with

---

* Jenny Wyse-Power (1856–1941), a vehement nationalist who married a member of the Irish Republican Brotherhood, was a veteran of the Ladies' Land League and had been involved with the Home Rule party. A prominent supporter of women's rights, she was the first president of Cumann na mBan. In December 1922, she would be appointed to the Irish Free State's Seanad Éireann.

P. J. Vaughan's of Capel Street to provide breakfast, dinner and tea for his men, at 7s 6d (37½p) each, which was invoiced as £87 15s for '234 Troops, Day and Night for the Eight Days during the Trouble'.

It appears that the third 18-pounder was not always manned by a crew under Phil Hyde. Ignatius O'Neill, who was described by Emmet Dalton as 'a great character from County Clare', commanded the gun at one stage and nearly drew the British army into the battle. Although it would have been difficult to achieve the required elevation of the barrel, his gun is said to have fired at least a couple of shells over the Four Courts, apparently in an attempt to hit another sniper in the dome. O'Neill's aim was poor. Probably firing the 18-pounder from Mountrath Street (now gone) off Chancery Place, he missed the dome by a wide margin, and the shells sailed on across the Liffey for just over 1.8 km (1 mile) to land in the grounds of the Royal Hospital in Kilmainham, Gen. Macready's headquarters. Dalton was summoned by telephone to the Royal Hospital by an angry Macready, and as he arrived a shell exploded in the saddling paddock. Macready, furious, wanted to know why he was now under fire from his own guns.[6] In his memoirs, however, he underplays this incident, commenting with regard to the shells he had sent the previous night to Dalton, 'one of these shrapnel burst over the Royal Hospital. Shortly afterwards an apology arrived, from which it appeared that the gun had gone off by mistake!'[7] Fortunately, there were no casualties, and Dalton returned hotfoot to the Four Courts to find O'Neill still trying to pick off the dome sniper. Not only had he shelled the British, but ammunition was scarce, and Dalton had the gun in question removed from the Chancery Street area and held in reserve. With Oscar Traynor's force encamped not far away, east of Sackville Street, this gun may also have been seen as vulnerable to capture, which was another good reason to withdraw it.

During the morning, anti-Treaty troops began to take over more buildings in Dublin, and to commandeer substantial supplies, including foodstuffs, pots and pans, bedding and medical appliances, from Dublin businesses. When word of these activities got around, city centre shops began to close, and by the middle of the afternoon almost every shop in Dublin had shut its doors. Rooftop sniping had been going on sporadically since the previous morning, but on Thursday there were more intensive exchanges of fire in different parts of the city as attempts were made by the anti-Treaty IRA to harass passing army lorries and armoured cars carrying National Army reinforcements for the troops surrounding the Four Courts. These rooftop snipers caused considerable disruption, and civilian casualties began to rise as passers-by accidentally got in the way. People leaving mass in the Pro Cathedral, off Sackville Street, were caught in crossfire, and had to make their way slowly along the streets from doorway to doorway. In the middle of the day one woman was killed on O'Connell Bridge, and another in Cavendish Row, and the hospitals began to fill with the wounded. The soldiers of the National Army were learning, as the British army in Ireland had over the past few years, the frustrations of trying to fight an army of soldiers dressed in civilian clothes. One National Army patrol in Liffey Street engaged a group of anti-Treaty men in their usual uniform of civilian clothes but wearing bandoliers of ammunition, and a firefight ensued. During the exchange of shots, a woman came out of her house and sprinkled holy water on one of the young men who had been kneeling and shooting outside her door. The man removed his hat and, taking a cigarette from his mouth, blessed himself.

During the day, two women, one a nurse, turned up at the army cordon around the Four Courts and asked to be allowed through into the courts. Nurses and Cumann na mBan members who had been coming and going during the week were usually let through, but in this case the officer in charge became suspicious. Accounts are not explicit about how his suspicions were confirmed, but the 'nurse' was found to be the Cork IRA leader Tom Barry in disguise, wearing a nurse's dress that he had borrowed from his wife. Barry was arrested, and taken away; he claimed to have been the first prisoner of the Civil War.[8]

In St Andrew's Church in St Andrew's Street, one of Dublin's leading furriers, Wilfred Barnardo, was marrying Peggy McDonald to the chorus of rifle fire in the streets outside. During the ceremony the wedding cars, parked outside the church, were commandeered by anti-Treaty men.

Newspaper correspondents noted a significant increase in passengers, particularly 'very nervous elderly women, alone or in pairs, with much luggage', travelling on the mailboat *Hibernian* from Kingstown to Holyhead that evening. The *Irish*

Independent commented that there were more passengers on board than there had been during the height of the Rebellion of 1916. The *Freeman's Journal* stated: 'Human nature is common all the world over, and those who are seeking a healthier air than that of Dublin were very similar to the people who bolted precipitately from London after the first German air-raid in 1915.'

That afternoon Gen. Macready went to see Michael Collins in his office in Portobello to discuss the matter of the 18-pounders and their ammunition. He gave his opinion that no amount of bombardment was going to get 'the rebels out of the Four Courts, as they were probably smoking and drinking in safety in the cellars', and unless an infantry assault was made, they might go on doing that for ever. Collins complained to Macready about an incident involving British troops delivering ammunition to the National Army opposite the Four Courts, probably after Dalton's Wednesday night visit to Macready. On seeing a shell bursting against the walls of the courts, the British soldiers had given a rousing cheer. In the circumstances, Collins warned, this kind of ostentatious activity was dangerous, but Macready, although aware of how delicate the situation was, did not seem to appreciate this, and regarded the cheering as an effort by the British to encourage the National Army.

On his way back to the Royal Hospital, the general's car came under sniper fire from a house on the South Circular Road. On arriving safely at his headquarters, he rang Collins to tell him about it. Collins had the snipers arrested and the house was set on fire.

The 18-pounder gun that was located in Hammond Lane: the legend 'Hammond Lane No. 4' is painted on the shield.

National Army headquarters had already come to the conclusion that an infantry assault would be required to oust the garrison, and the previous night how and when this might be carried out had been discussed. That afternoon a conference was held at the brigade headquarters in the Four Courts Hotel during which the final details were worked out with the officers who would be leading the attack. It was decided that there would be two simultaneous infantry assaults, both on the west side of the complex. There may have been some concern that if they struck on the east side, Oscar Traynor's IRA force in the O'Connell Street area, some members of which had already been making sorties towards the Four Courts, might move in force and advance against the rear of the National Army men. It was clear from the experience of the previous day that the 18-pounders were capable of punching holes in the walls of the Four Courts, and they were now ordered to create breaches in two places, sufficient in size to allow the infantry to enter the buildings. The Bridge Street gun would aim to take out a section of the Morgan Place wall of the west wing. The fourth 18-pounder was brought to Phoenix Street, and placed at the junction between the western end of Hammond Lane and Lincoln Lane. It was put under the command of Commandant Peadar McMahon, and was to be used to make a breach in the

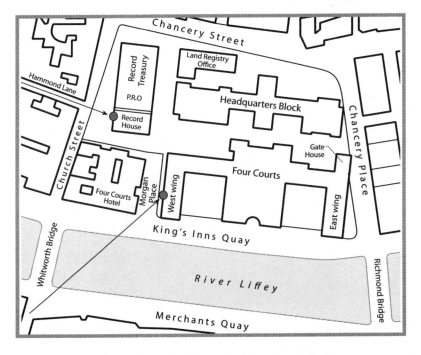

The two breaches blown by the 18-pounders located at Bridge Street and Hammond Lane.

west wall of the Record House. This gun is easily identified in later photographs because someone has painted in white on the armoured shield the legend 'Hammond Lane No. 4'.

Once the two breaches had been made, one battalion, led by Commandant Joe Leonard, was to rush across Morgan Place from the block of buildings that included the Four Courts Hotel, enter the breach, and secure the west wing. Another battalion, under Commandant Padraig O'Connor, would advance swiftly down Hammond Lane and into the Public Record Office. O'Connor and his superiors were aware that the Record Treasury part of the Public Record Office was being used as a munitions factory, and that it might have been mined by the

The view eastwards towards the four-bay Record House, from the Hammond Lane gun position. The lane was narrower in 1922, but the hoarding shown here on the left replicates the buildings of the Eagle Foundry which blocked the view of the Record Treasury at the time.

garrison in case of attack.[9] It had been suggested that the 18-pounders would target it to attempt to blow up the munitions before the infantry assault began, but this was not possible. The Record Treasury was not visible from the No. 4 gun position in Hammond Lane: it could target only the Record House section of the Public Record Office, and no other gun was in a position to land shells in the Treasury without putting their own troops surrounding the complex in danger. O'Connor knew, therefore, that his attack could be extremely hazardous, and occupation of the building would have to be carried out quickly, to secure the munitions and to attempt to prevent mines from being detonated. Viewed from the calm remove of almost a hundred years later, this particular assault looks as if it could have ended up as a suicide mission.

Later, Collins was again urged, in a cable from Churchill, to accept the heavy 60-pounder artillery, and experienced gunners and ammunition. Churchill, in a gung-ho mood, also suggested that he could provide aircraft to carry out any action that was necessary, and that they could be painted in Free State colours for the purpose. These offers were turned down.

Around the city, broadsheet songs about the attack on the courts were already circulating, including one that started as follows:

I came to Dublin one summer morning,
And what do you think of my surprise,
Along the quays was a battle raging,
Sure I scarcely could believe my eyes.

There was guns, big bounders, and Eighteen Pounders,
All banging away at the Four Courts there,
And along the roofs there were snipers sniping,
And bullets all whizzing through the air.

At some point shortly after noon, the long-awaited high explosive shells arrived from Carrickfergus, and were delivered to the 18-pounder positions in wooden crates packed with straw. Now that a decision had been made that there would be an infantry assault, the gunners at Bridge Street began to concentrate on punching a breach in the wall of the west wing overlooking Morgan Place, where it had been decided to make one of the two infantry strikes. The artillery men had already shown that the walls of the Four Courts could be breached by concentrated fire: the Winetavern Street gun had made a small breach in the south façade of the main courts building on the first day, and the Bridge Street gun had blown one in the western façade of the main block, under the dome, penetrating a wall that was almost a metre thick.

The breach that had to be made in the façade of the west wing facing onto Morgan Place required very accurate fire. Only about 98 feet (30 m) of this wall, between the south-west corner of the wing and the corner of the block of buildings that included the Four Courts Hotel, was visible to the gunners. The Four Courts Hotel block was occupied by the National Army, so the men operating the 18-pounder had to create a wide breach, in exactly the right place, without touching it. Since their tentative beginnings early the previous morning, they had learned how to operate their gun accurately, and they succeeded in getting all their shells onto the target. The pulverized masonry of the west wall began to cascade down the façade, bringing with it floor and roof timbers, until a scree of debris formed on the ground.

At about 1 p.m. a correspondent of *The Times* made his way along the side streets on the south of the river: 'to the street from which the Free State artillery is being served... the steady firing of the guns is gradually producing its effect. Fire has been principally concentrated upon the western wing of the Four Courts, and when I left towards 2 o'clock the top floor of this wing had been largely shot away for about 50 feet [15.2 m], and considerable damage had been done to the

This view from behind the Bridge Street gun shows clearly the accuracy required to create a breach in the west wing without hitting the Four Courts Hotel block, on the left in the distance.

floor next below. One could see bits of furniture lying strewn about in the wreckage through the gaping walls, and in the room there seemed to be shattered masses of deed-boxes scattered pell-mell about the ruins. One shot particularly which was fired about 1.30 had a devastating effect. A dense cloud of dust followed the shot and drifted like a heavy curtain of smoke across the building. While it was still hanging thick in the air we heard the heavy crash of falling masonry and when the dust had at last cleared away one saw that a large gap had been torn.'

The breach in the west wing of the Four Courts in Morgan Place, as it was about 2.30 p.m. on the Thursday: the dust from the collapse of the wall is just settling. This image shows the narrowness of the target that the crew of the Bridge Street gun had to hit: the Four Courts Hotel block, occupied by National Army troops, is the dark building seen on the left. This view also makes clear that the 18-pounders, when used with serious intent, were clearly effective against the walls of the Four Courts.

Irish Life reported that 'the great guns bellowed at longer intervals and the breaches in the walls gaped wider'. The reporter went on to say that Commandant-Gen. Lawlor, who was in charge of the Bridge Street gun, had had no sleep for four nights, and that the crews were weary, their eyes red from fatigue, their ears deafened from the repeated explosions. In spite of their exhaustion and lack of proper training, their success in manning the 18-pounder is clear to see from contemporary photographs.

The *Irish Independent* of the following day praised the men operating the guns, stating

it is a marvel, perhaps without precedent, that an artillery action went on, beginning on Wednesday morning about 4 o'clock, and continuing all through Wednesday, Thursday, and up to noon on Friday in the heart of the city, and from five distinctive positions, without doing any random damage to the persons or property of the citizens... when a large part of the Four Courts had been captured the artillery continued to work with precision and co-operation with the forces that had entered the positions – a feat, the difficulty of which can be realized by those who know the plan of the Four Courts.

West of the Public Record Office, in Lincoln Lane, off Hammond Lane, Padraig O'Connor's men were gathering in the afternoon sun, a scene that was photographed by a local man, Michael MacConneran. They stood in small groups chatting with one another, and in the photo below, the man in the foreground with his Lee Enfield slung on his shoulder, looking straight at MacConneran's camera, has a half-smile and looks relaxed, in spite of the battle before him.

The No. 4 gun, having been wheeled up to the western end of Hammond Lane, was dug in, and under the command of Peadar McMahon, his men commenced firing on the western façade of the Record House, which was framed between the buildings at the other end of the narrow lane. The tall wrought-iron boundary railings separating the building from the street, and

The junction of Lincoln Lane and Hammond Lane, facing north up Bow Street, before the assault began on the Public Record Office on Thursday afternoon. The tall building in the distance is Jameson's Distillery, which was used temporarily to hold prisoners after the surrender. In the June sunshine, what seems to be a very relaxed group of National Army troops waits for orders to begin the attack on the Public Record Office.

the inner railings around the basement area, were knocked over by targeting the granite plinths in which they were embedded. Then fire was concentrated on the west wall of the Record House, and a neat 10 square foot (3 sq m) breach was blasted in it in a very short time. In all, forty-eight shells were fired by the No. 4 gun.[10]

In anticipation of an assault on the west wing, the National Army troops in the Four Courts Hotel block began to concentrate their fire, peppering the Record House and the western end of the Headquarters Block (both of which overlooked Morgan Place) with raking volleys of machine-gun fire to dissuade snipers from showing themselves. The young men in the Record House, only a few yards away from the hotel, must have found it impossible to offer any defence, particularly after the No. 4 18-pounder located in Hammond Lane began laying down a barrage of HE shells against the western façade of the building. Soon the defenders, who had long since abandoned the Record Treasury owing to the exposure given by the large amount of glazing, were forced back from the west side of the Record House; they had to huddle in a first-floor room and in the basement on the east side of the building. One of them ran the gauntlet between the Record House and the main Four Courts building, bringing a message from his section leader, Tom Morrissey, to the garrison commander, Paddy O'Brien, saying that unless an offensive strike was made against the National Army men in the Four Courts Hotel block, he would be unable to hold out. It is likely, however, that O'Brien was not at the command post in the Central Hall. After the concentrated bombardment of the west wing, it was clear to the defenders that there would be an infantry attack into the breach that had been created at Morgan Place. O'Brien was most likely in the western end of the Headquarters Block, possibly in the third-floor toilet, from where there was a clear view of Morgan Place. There he set up a Lewis gun, and kept his head down, ready for when the assault began.

By this time a 40-foot (12.1-m) wide breach had been made in the wall of the western wing, and the spillage of masonry and timber had flowed out onto Morgan Place, crushing the 8-foot (2.4-m) high wrought-iron boundary railings and the defensive barbed wire that had been strung over them. It would have been impossible to remain safely anywhere in that part of the building during this concentrated shelling, and the defenders there had been driven back into the wing west of the dome.

At the appointed time of 4 p.m.,[11] bugles sounded 'cease fire' and the shelling, rifle and machine-gun fire from the National Army side stopped. On a signal, a first wave of about 100 National Army men, led by Commandant Joe Leonard, poured out of the Four Courts Hotel and adjacent buildings and raced along the quay and across Morgan Place, heading for the sloping scree of masonry that had spilled out of the building. Paddy O'Brien, high up in the Headquarters Block, now opened fire with his Lewis gun, 'with deadly effect', Commandant Simon Donnelly wrote later.[12] In fact, probably because of intense covering fire from the National Army troops in the back of the hotel, O'Brien managed only a few short bursts from the gun, and before the attack managed to get across the street,

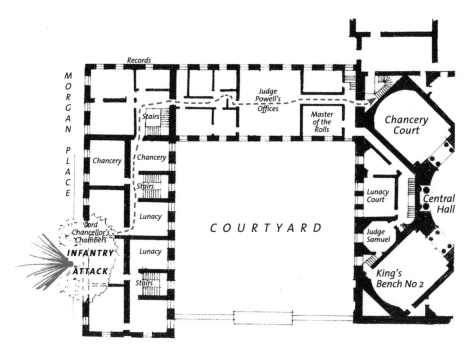

A plan of the second floor of the west pavilion of the Four Courts building as it was in 1922. Marked on the left is the breach made in the west wing by the 18-pounder at Bridge Street, where the National Army troops, after their rush across Morgan Place, had to scramble up the scree of debris into the first floor to gain access to the building. As can be clearly seen from the plan, at this level the men were limited to one route along which they could fight their way towards the Central Hall, through a series of doorways connecting small rooms.

Commandant Leonard and one of his men fell wounded, Leonard with a bullet in the knee. In an interview given to newspapers the following evening by Paddy O'Daly, he names himself as one of those in the vanguard of this assault, but there is no evidence that he was there. As the momentum of the charge continued, Lt. Downey took Leonard's place, leading

205

the men up the chaotic heap of loose rubble and lengths of timber into the first floor of the building and what remained of the Lord Chancellor's chambers.

Even if they had managed to obtain the plans of the building and examine them before the assault, which is doubtful, the chaos of destruction they found when they scrambled up into the ruined structure would not have been familiar. Rather than being a well-organized series of rooms connected by corridors, the building consisted of a rabbit-warren of stairwells and interconnecting rooms. Examination of the building plans, in conjunction with contemporary photographs, makes it clear that access to the rest of the building from where the soldiers had entered was confined to only a couple of possibilities. The plan of the three floors over basement of the west wing of the Four Courts was very convoluted, with poorly organized horizontal or vertical circulation routes. For instance, stairs that connected the first and second floors did not continue to descend to the ground floor and the basement.

Having entered the building into the ruins of the Lord Chancellor's office, different sections of the attacking force would have been detailed to secure and occupy the other three floors, somehow finding their way to the ground floor and basement, and up to the second floor, before any secure advance through the building towards the Central Hall could be carried out. The plan was to drive, by force of arms, the garrison ahead of them, pursuing them to the Central Hall and beyond.

At the time, there was no direct access from either the basement or the second floor to the Central Hall. Access was possible through the ground and first floors only, and even then, only indirectly. From the first floor where they had entered the building, the most direct route was to descend a stair in the north-west corner to the ground floor, and then follow one of the few straight corridors as far as the Chancery Court, off which was the Central Hall. Otherwise, they had to negotiate their way through a few offices and a small court-room to reach a sinuous corridor that led to a stairway which in turn led down to the Central Hall. This labyrinthine advance had to be made under constant fire from the defenders.

One can assume that the defenders, having stayed well away from the west wing during the bombardment, would, as soon as they heard the 'cease fire' bugle call, have returned to deal with the attackers. The fact that there were only two routes to the Central Hall should have made the building easier for them to defend.

It must have been a nightmare for the National Army men to attempt to make any progress in the dimly lit, dust-filled interior of the building, and in the fearful frenzy of close-up fighting three of them, George Walshe from Kilkenny, James Walshe from Monaghan and Patrick Lowe from Dublin, were shot dead. Fourteen National Army men were wounded, but with overwhelming numerical superiority, the attackers did make progress, climbing over rubble and furniture, making their way room by room, doorway by doorway, with much use of 'showers of hand grenades', flung ahead into open doorways to clear the rooms beyond. The defenders were forced into a chaotic withdrawal in the face of the superior firepower, and after the intense action of the first few minutes, some of them had already run out of ammunition. It seems that the rabbit-warren plan of the building which had hindered the progress of the attacking force, now served to hinder the defenders' retreat. It may have been that most of them were driven up to the third floor, from where there was no access into the main Four Courts, because, by the end of the first phase of the assault, thirty-three of them had been taken prisoner. Only three men now remained to defend the western wing.

Simultaneously with the assault on the western wing, a National Army force under Commandant O'Connor, assisted by Commandant McGuinness, assembled in Lincoln Lane, between Hammond Lane and the quays, to carry out their strike on the Record House. The breach had already been created in the western wall of the building, but O'Connor had arranged for Peadar McMahon, who commanded No. 4 gun, to fire two last rapid rounds as a signal for them to begin their dash down Hammond Lane. The soldiers must have been too near when this happened: Padraig O'Connor later wrote, 'the blast was dreadful ... it forced us back to the wall and then suddenly released us so that we staggered around'. Gathering themselves, however, they ran down the 100-yard (91.4-m) long, narrow lane, which would have been a true killing zone if the men in the Record House had been able to lay down fire. Yet although Paddy O'Daly, in an interview given to newspapers on the Friday evening, claimed that 'volley after volley spurted from the

The breach in the Record House, framed by the end of
Hammond Lane. The shellfire damage in the upper storey may
have been from the two shots arranged to signal Padraig O'Connor's
men to advance, and fired to deter the defenders from using
any of the windows overlooking Hammond Lane.

defender's guns', O'Connor said that not a single shot was fired
at them. Across Church Street they raced, and over the blown-
down perimeter railings. A 10-foot- (3-m)-wide and deep basement 'area', or light-well, now separated them from the breach
that had been blown in the wall. It had partly been filled with
the rubble from the breach above and, adrenaline-fuelled, the
attackers, led by O'Connor, scrambled down and across the
rubble before climbing up into the building. Seeing that there
was a door into the basement of the building from the light-
well, O'Connor posted two men to guard it.

Dust must have been hanging thick in the air as they surged over the rubble into the Record House. Facing them in the office they had entered was a door. They crossed the room and, probably after throwing hand grenades through the doorway to clear the room beyond, kept going and emerged into a large, roof-lit space, the Public Reading Room. They checked the doors leading off it, finding to the left an ante-room from which an iron door led into the Record Treasury, which was 'very large and had a glass roof'. There they found the 'munitions factory', with explosive materials and components, finished and half-finished, lying around. There were holes in the ceilings of the Record House, from which blankets hung down from the floor above. Padraig O'Connor assumed that these amounted to preparations for burning the building.

Through a door on the right from the Reading Room they found the elaborate Public Record Office stairwell. They had still not met with any resistance and were probably wondering if they had been enticed into a trap. It must have been a nervous time for O'Connor: it may well be that he was the only one of the attackers who was aware of the possibility of the building being mined for exactly this circumstance, and as soon as the maximum number of troops were in the building, he knew they might be set off. He did not know that most of the anti-Treaty garrison, probably shell-shocked by this time, were huddled in the room in the north-east corner of the first floor, farthest from the action, while the rest were in the caretaker's flat in the basement. Not taking any chances, however, the attackers probably used grenades again to clear the stairwell ahead of

How the Reading Room in the Record House looked during a normal day. Double height, it had an elaborately decorated cornice and a large roof light. The door under the clock led to the Record Treasury. Padraig O'Connor and his men would have entered the room through the door in the corner to its left. On the right of the photograph is Herbert Wood, deputy keeper of the Public Record Office.

them: the patched repairs made later to bullet and shrapnel damage in the Portland stone walls can still be seen. They found the defenders on the first floor. O'Connor described them as 'very shaken, a few in a state of complete nervous breakdown, a boys' unit I was given to understand… my men looked grim as they stood around with rifles and bayonets at the ready, a little uncertain what to do next.'[13] They had clearly expected a fight, and suddenly it was all over. The prisoners were bundled downstairs, out through the breach in the wall and taken, under guard, to the log yard of Maguire & Patterson's match factory.

The stairway in the Public Record Office (now the
Appeals Court) as it is today, showing old repairs to
bullet and shrapnel damage suffered in 1922.

McGuinness and his men now took up positions in the first-
and second-floor windows of the Record House, commanding
the yard between the Four Courts main block and the Headquarters Block. The yard was packed with cars and lorries that
had been commandeered over the preceding weeks. O'Connor's
men found an entrance to the basement of the Record Treasury
at the Bridewell end. They went down, and, in the darkness,
moved carefully through it and into the basement of the Record
House. Four or five members of the anti-Treaty garrison had
been sheltering there, and, realizing that their post was over-
run, they came out of a side door into the basement light-well
on the east side of the building and made a dash for the main
Four Courts building. Where they came out of the building was
almost directly under the window where McGuinness and his

men were stationed, and they shouted down at them to surrender. When the men kept running, they opened fire. Two young members of the Public Record Office garrison, Tom Wall and John Cusack, were hit, Cusack dying on the spot and Wall a day later. Wall was eighteen years old, but, in spite of his youth, he had seen action during the War of Independence, and had been jailed by the British before the truce. One of the Four Courts garrison, a man named Brogan, said later that he heard that the two youngsters had had their hands up when they were shot.[14]

Eighteen-year-old Tom Wall, mortally injured as he attempted to escape from the Public Record Office.

Paddy O'Brien had been aware, from early in the action, of the vulnerability of the Public Record Office post with its young, inexperienced garrison. In his book *The Singing Flame* Ernie O'Malley says that when O'Brien eventually received a desperate request for help sent over by Tom Morrissey, he decided that the building should be burnt; a conflagration of building and contents would create an effective barrier, at least for a while, against any attack on the complex from the Church Street side. Communications between the men in the garrison in the Public Record Office and those in the main Four Courts building were still very poor, and, unaware that there had been a successful infantry attack and the building had already been taken, O'Brien sent Lt. Ned Keller to withdraw the defenders and to set the building alight.[15] Keller had to keep his head down as he made a dash for the Public Record Office, and he probably did not notice that some of the fire he was dodging came from the building itself. When he arrived, however, he found the National Army already in occupation, and he was taken prisoner.

When the entire Public Record Office, House and Treasury had been searched and secured, O'Connor contacted brigade headquarters asking them to send engineers to come and deal with the munitions they had found. A party of soldiers worked briskly and removed fifty to sixty rifles and some small arms, a large cask of explosives and a cask of filament of mercury, fifteen shells, some finished land mines and fifteen unfinished landmines, thousands of detonators in cases and a 'huge' quantity of grenades. In a short time the fatigue party had 'cleared the building', and the materials were taken away and 'stored in pits at Smithfield Garage', about a quarter of a mile (400 m) away.[16]

Meanwhile, Commandant-Gen. MacManus, who had been stationed in the tenements in Church Street, came to O'Connor and told him that Commandant Joe Leonard had been wounded in the attack on the west wing, and progress had slowed down there. He got O'Connor's agreement to go around to Morgan Place to help out.

The anti-Treaty garrison in the Central Hall had lost contact with the section defending the west wing, so Paddy O'Brien went forward into the darkness looking for them, calling out the name of the section leader. He must have realized, before he went too far, that the National Army had taken the western end and, not wanting to become a prisoner himself, he soon returned to the Central Hall. The initial National Army attack had indeed secured much of the west wing, but the loss of their commandant, Joe Leonard, the death of their three comrades and the approach of evening must have slowed their impetus. After the initial attack, they paused a while to deal with their casualties and send back their prisoners.

When MacManus arrived from Church Street, he took over and quickly rekindled the troops' enthusiasm. He had them clear the rooms on the four floors that they had taken, checking for mines or hidden defenders, and securing their positions. While they were doing this, the men found a roomful of explosives and mines.[17] MacManus sent for the National Army's director of engineering, Patrick Kelly, to make the explosives safe, but as Kelly mounted the hill of rubble that had flowed into Morgan Place from the western wing he was hit by a sniper's bullet, which gave him a flesh wound in one arm but broke the other. He made it to the cover of the building, however, and MacManus put his broken arm in a splint made from the leaves of law books and timber ceiling laths, both of which were plentiful. Soon after, Kelly was taken away by ambulance. The explosives were left where they were. MacManus and his men, giving them a wide berth, settled into their posts and tried to get some sleep. In the morning, they would push forward again.

In the meantime, Ernie O'Malley and four men had gone into the west wing to engage the attackers, and, hearing men coming towards them, they crouched down and prepared to open fire. Luckily, they recognized the men's voices: it turned out to be their three comrades of the west wing section who had escaped capture by the National Army.

With the west wing lost, the garrison now worked to establish a new line of defence, probably at the doors into the Chancery Court that opened off the Central Hall. Everybody, including O'Connor and Mellows, joined in to build barricades using rolls of barbed wire, furniture and loose stones from the damage caused by the shelling. The place was dimly lit by candles on ledges and stuck into pieces of masonry, creating what O'Malley thought of as a Rembrandt etching. He went forward again into the west wing, in darkness, with Donnchadha 'Dinny' O'Brien, brother of Paddy O'Brien, and 'Chummy' Hogan. 'This is great gas', said Chummy as they felt their way along in the dark. They emptied their guns through doors to the left and right of them, and fired ahead, but there was no answering fire, so they returned to the Central Hall.[18]

A counter-attack, using mines to blow up the buildings they had vacated, was now discussed between Rory O'Connor, Joseph McKelvey and Paddy O'Brien. They still had plenty of mines, and O'Malley and O'Brien had previously talked about using mines and explosives to delay the advance of the National Army or against attacking parties. Seán Moylan, one of the defenders, said later that mines and incendiary grenades were laid at this time, but there is no report of the National Army men being hindered by booby-traps as they later advanced on the Central Hall.[19]

What remained of the defending garrison was tired and hungry, and food was very scarce. Paddy O'Brien felt that there was little point remaining any longer, and he suggested to O'Connor and the other members of the executive that they should make a surprise break-out from the complex: the garrison would fight its way, with 'The Mutineer' armoured car, along the streets towards St Mary's Abbey to the east of the Four Courts, where they understood Oscar Traynor's men held positions. He was overruled, however, by O'Connor, McKelvey and Mellows, who preferred to wait until the following morning, when they felt, if the water level was low enough, it might be possible to slip away through the old sewers.

★

At nightfall, as the sun set and darkness slowly fell, the shooting petered out. The pause in hostilities gave time for the commanders on both sides to review the situation. With the Public Record Office occupied by O'Connor's men, and MacManus's troops holding the west wing, the next target for the National Army was the Headquarters Block, the western end of which was less than 19 yards (17 m) from the eastern façade of the Record Treasury. What remained of the anti-Treaty Four Courts garrison, probably a little over a hundred men, settled down behind their barbed-wire barricades while some of them snatched a few minutes' sleep in the basement rooms in the east wing. Food had almost run out, and they had to make do with tea and biscuits seized during a Belfast Boycott operation. They fully expected that there would be another attack at dawn.

CHAPTER 6

FRIDAY, 30 JUNE:
THE LAST DAY OF THE SIEGE

Friday dawned dark and cloudy, with heavy showers of rain. At 5 a.m. the artillery started up again, firing five shells in quick succession. The Bridge Street gun had been moved to join the other at Winetavern Street, and now the troops of the National Army concentrated their fire on the eastern part of the Four Courts. Rory O'Connor had favoured the idea of the garrison slipping away unnoticed through the old sewers, but that morning it was found that they were flooded by the incoming tide in the River Liffey.

Commandant McGuinness and his men, with a Thompson sub-machine gun and a Lewis gun in the top-floor windows of the Record House, started the day by concentrating their fire on 'The Mutineer' armoured car in the courtyard below, as it drove up and down between the Four Courts building, the Headquarters Block and the large number of vehicles parked there. Earlier, its Vickers machine-gun had been damaged, but the crew had managed to jury-rig a Lewis gun in the turret and 'The Mutineer' had gone into action again, racing between the two courtyards and creating problems for the attackers. Commandant-Gen. Dermot MacManus was also pouring lead into 'The Mutineer' with a Lewis gun, from a back window in the west wing. Eventually, with its tyres almost ripped off, the car withdrew into cover between the Four Courts building and the Headquarters Block, and there the crew abandoned it and retreated inside. The courtyard was now completely commanded by National Army troops.

As always, Paddy O'Brien was in the thick of things, but when he received a head wound from shrapnel, it was serious enough to put him out of action. He did not wait to see what the leaders would do to replace him, but asked Ernie O'Malley to take over as the officer in charge. O'Malley agreed to do his best. He wrote later, in *The Singing Flame*, that they were beginning to suffer from the strain, and that he 'felt emotional surges' in himself and 'a desire to cry'. He said to O'Brien, 'An explosion may come at any minute. That will solve all our difficulties. We'll go up together.'[1]

O'Malley's first decision as commanding officer was to evacuate the wounded and the nurses and doctors from the hospital. Dr Jim Ryan did not want to leave, but O'Malley told him quietly that one of the reasons for evacuating was because the 'Munitions Block' was expected to blow up.

The west wing as it was on the Friday morning, before fires started. The National Army troops were in the west wing, and the garrison had been driven back beyond the Central Hall under the dome. To the left of the west wing, down Morgan Place, is the western end of the Headquarters Block, with its glazed penthouse. The munitions that caused the great explosion were stored on the ground floor of this building and it was from one of the upper-floor windows that Paddy O'Brien used his Lewis gun on the attacking troops, wounding Joe Leonard and another soldier. To the extreme left, past the Headquarters Block, the Land Registry Office can just be seen.

Another ceasefire was called, and the wounded, including Paddy O'Brien, were taken by ambulance to Jervis Street Hospital. The ambulance driver was Joe Connolly, who had been in the Citizen Army, the socialist force that had fought alongside the rebels in 1916. After the Treaty was passed, many of its members had aligned themselves with the anti-Treaty faction. As soon as O'Brien's head wound had been treated, Connolly arranged for him to be discharged and spirited away to his home by taxi.

At some stage that morning – Seán Moylan says 8 a.m., but other accounts suggest 11 a.m. – a fire began in the Head-quarters Block. O'Malley, in *The Singing Flame*, says that the 'Munitions Block had been on fire for some time.[2] However, because the 'Munitions Block' – in other words, the Record Treasury – had been in the hands of the National Army since the evening before, it is clear that O'Malley has mixed up the Treasury, which he previously called the 'Munitions Block', with the Headquarters Block, where the munitions were stored.

During the early hours that morning National Army troops had pressed forward from the west wing of the Four Courts. The details of this part of the battle are, perhaps, the least known, and it is not clear at what time the surviving members of the defending garrison were driven out of the Central Hall and into the east wing. Certainly, by about 11 a.m., most of the remaining garrison, hungry, exhausted and without ammu-nition, were holed up in the housekeeper's quarters in the cellars under the wing. Until it began to burn, a scattering of men still occupied the Headquarters Block and the Chancery Street gatehouse was defended. At this stage defensive fire was at best sporadic.

It would have been impossible for anyone watching the con-tinuing bombardment of the Four Courts not to believe that the garrison had suffered many casualties. Two members of

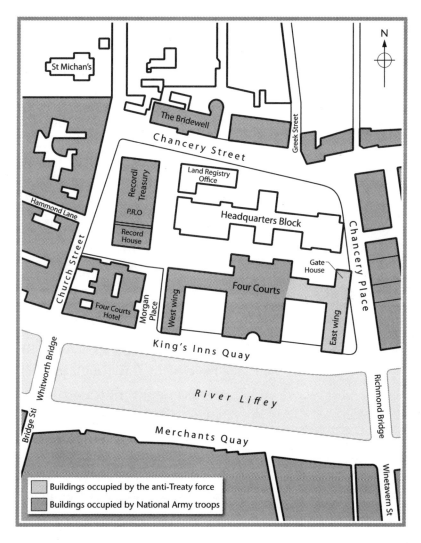

The situation after 11 a.m. on Friday, 30 June 1922.

Cumann na mBan, sisters Annie and Lily Cooney (later Mrs Annie O'Brien and Mrs Lily Curran), who were trying to get to the Four Courts to offer their help, somehow managed to find their way into Winetavern Street where they saw the 18-pounder gun manned by Free State soldiers:

we watched a soldier putting in a shell and we asked him what he was going to do with that. He expressed himself in very strong language about the people in the Four Courts, saying he would soon get them out of it with this. We argued with him about killing other Irishmen, but of course it was no use and we were ordered out of the danger zone.[3]

Commandant Simon Donnelly wrote that the fire in the Headquarters Block started at about 11 a.m. and was caused by 'incendiary bombs thrown into G.H.Q. Block in which was the chemical shop took fire owing to the inflammable substances in the building [and] the fire made great headway'.[4] Another member of the garrison claimed that 'heavy shelling from the Bridewell end began the blaze'.[5] This is most unlikely, however, because there is no record of any 18-pounder operating in the Bridewell area or Chancery Street at this time. The three-storey-over-basement Land Registry Office, which stood between the 'Bridewell end' and the Headquarters Block, would anyway have effectively blocked any 18-pounder fire from this side. The No. 4 gun, which may have still been located down Hammond Lane, could not have hit the Headquarters Block, because the trajectory of any shell fired over the roof of the Record House from Hammond Lane would have brought it to earth (or river) some place near the Custom House. At any rate, National Army troops had been in occupation of the western end of the Four Courts complex since the previous evening, and were in the process of advancing eastwards through the

Late Friday morning, the west wing is occupied by National Army troops, and the 18-pounder that had been stationed at Bridge Street under the command of Tony Lawlor has been moved to Winetavern Street. The two guns now concentrated on the east wing of the Four Courts into which the garrison had retreated before the attacking troops, led by Commandant-Gen. MacManus. Smoke can be seen rising behind the main Four Courts building, an indication that the Headquarters Block has started to burn.

complex, so it is most unlikely that the risk of using artillery on that general area would have been taken.

By 11.30 a.m. the fire in the Headquarters Block was visible from the south side of the river; 'a thin line of black smoke began to ascend from the rear of the building… By 12 o'clock the smoke had enveloped the greater portion of the huge place and had obscured it from view.'[6] However it started, the fire

225

spread fast, and those anti-Treaty men remaining in the building were ordered to evacuate.

According to the records, Dublin Fire Brigade received a telephone call from the police at 11.15 a.m. that Friday to say that firing had ceased at the Four Courts. The fire brigade chief, Capt. John Myers, ordered all available men and appliances to go there.[7] Fire was raging in the Headquarters Block when they arrived at the north side of the complex. Although they reeled out their hoses, they found it impossible to gain safe entry to the complex to tackle the fire, because it was setting off explosions, probably the 'barrels of petrol and paraffin' that O'Malley and O'Brien had stored in the building, or the 'chemical substances' mentioned earlier. Myers requested of Paddy O'Daly that a ceasefire be called, so that the spreading fire could be dealt with, but O'Daly refused, saying 'Ireland is more important than a fire in the Four Courts'.[8] Myers decided that his men would be best and more safely employed preventing any spread of fire to the buildings surrounding the Four Courts campus. Anticipating the end of the siege, a somewhat misleading statement was issued by Oscar Traynor's anti-Treaty forces, at noon: 'The Four Courts have been bombarded, smashed to pieces, burnt and gutted by Macready's 60-pounder guns and mines. There was nothing left for the gallant garrison to hold. All honour to them for having held it so long in a hail of fire. But the fight goes on!'

At a meeting at the National Army brigade headquarters in the Four Courts Hotel that morning, Commandant O'Connor was ordered to advance with his battalion from their position in the Public Record Office to capture the Headquarters Block. 'The Mutineer' armoured car was no longer controlling the courtyards between the buildings, so it was now safe to make a dash from the Public Record Office to a door at the south-west corner of the Headquarters Block. This was where O'Connor intended gaining entry to the building. He requested, and received, rifle grenades for use in the assault, although he subsequently did not get to use them. By the time he returned to his men in the Public Record Office, however, the Headquarters Block was burning; the fire had spread from the eastern to the western end of the building, and now it was 'blazing fiercely, the flames reeling across the 25- to 30-yard [23- to 27.4-m] gap that separated us'. The distance between the burning building and the Public Record Office was in fact nearer to 17 yards (15.5 m).

O'Connor had his attacking force of fifteen men lined up inside the Public Record Office with fixed bayonets. He commented that the heat that was radiating from the building opposite 'was unbearable', and he now saw little point in entering a burning building. He decided that, instead, he and his party would attempt to skirt around the left of the Headquarters Block and try to advance eastwards past it. He and his men missed death by moments. As they got ready to move out, 'an immense explosion rocked the building... everything seemed to come asunder... the men were lifted off their feet and sent spinning around'. He and the sergeant were thrown up in the air, and they landed together, the sergeant underneath saving him from the shock, and he saving the sergeant from the shards of glass that came raining onto his back and head, which fortunately, because they struck him flat, did not do great damage. The air was filled with black smoke and dust, and, fearing an immediate counter-attack, O'Connor scrambled to his feet and shouted out orders to evacuate the building.

Blinded with smoke and dust, and in many cases covered with blood from cuts, they all staggered out through the breach by which they had entered the building, some of them carrying their wounded comrades and collapsing on the Church Street pavement. Within minutes the wounded were attended by a section of Red Cross men.[9] One of O'Connor's men, who had been on the roof of the Record Treasury at the time of the explosion, was blown off and fell 30 feet (9.1 m), but was not badly injured because his fall was broken by stacks of papers.[10]

An *Irish Times* reporter was talking with Commandant-Gen. Tony Lawlor near one of the 18-pounders at Winetavern Street when the explosion occurred. From his description one suspects that he has had some military experience; written perhaps soon after the explosion occurred, his account rings with authenticity, and his identification of the 'locus' of the explosion is correct.

There was a thunderous roar, deeper in sound than any gun, which brought down in splinters any glass remaining in the neighbourhood, and part of the roof of the Four Courts seemed to lift itself into the air.

Black as ink, shot up, 400 feet [122 m] into the sky, a giant column of writhing smoke and dust; black as ink, and not more than 50 feet [15.2 m] in diameter at the base, it

A photograph taken moments after the 'great explosion'. The dome of
the Four Courts can be seen to the right of the tower of St Paul's church.

spread into a mushroom form some 200 feet [61 m] up, and
glared in the sun with lurid reds and browns, through which
could be seen thousands of great white snowflakes, dip-
ping, sidling, curtaying, circling, floating as snowflakes do.
But the shower was not falling. It was rising.

Higher it rose and higher again. All round us as we
stood 300 yards [274 m] away the bricks and mortar of
the great explosion were dropping like hail, but the great
white snowstorm eddied ever upwards till, at a height of
500 feet [152 m], the west wind ever bore the upward blast
of the explosion and the drift of snow swept, high up in
the air, down the quays in a slow slant towards Sackville
Street... What was the great explosion? Almost certainly it

229

was a mine or a magazine underneath the Probate Court and the Land Judges' Court which blew the whole of the upper storey and all the thousands of documents and forms contained therein into the air... Like most explosions its effect was freakish. Standing only 300 yards [274 m] away I hardly felt the impact in the air, while people fully 600 yards [549 m] distant from the focus on the other side were carried off their feet.

This reporter points out later in his article that the papers scattered around Dublin all dealt with probate, divorce or land judges' matters, material that would have been stored in the western end of the Headquarters Block.

Ernie O'Malley described in *The Singing Flame* standing near the Chancery Street gate with Donnchadha 'Dinny' O'Brien when the explosion occurred. The pillars of the gate shook, and he was thrown against the railings and fell to the ground with O'Brien, who he says told him that there would be another one shortly. He wrote that the 'Munitions Block' and a portion of the Headquarters Block went up in flames and smoke, although neither the Munitions Block (the Record Treasury), nor the western end of the Headquarters Block, where the explosion occurred, would have been visible to him if he had been at the Chancery Street gate.

Although a self-professed lover of art and architecture and thoroughly well-read in history and the classics, O'Malley had no regrets about the mayhem and destruction that had been caused by the explosion:[11] he only expressed concern about his own little library of books, maps, papers and notes and the clothes that he had left in the office he had requisitioned in the Headquarters Block.

Simon Donnelly wrote that he had been ordered to make sure that all their men were out of the Headquarters Block, and he and Father Dominic O'Connor were the last to leave the building.[12] Shortly afterwards, he said, there was a 'terrific explosion'. Calton Younger wrote that 'the shock of the explosion numbed all movement, all senses'.[13] The shock wave knocked to the ground some of the huge crowd of onlookers standing on the quays more than 1,300 feet (396 m) away, as an enormous plume of dark, bluish smoke rose into the air, as high, some said, as 2,000 feet (610 m), carrying with it myriads of fragments of paper that whirled around in the maelstrom like flocks of birds.

At the time of the explosion, about 12.30 p.m., National Army troops were in occupation of the western wing and the Central Hall of the Four Courts, having driven the garrison back into the east wing. The effects there were so violent that they thought that the explosion had been caused by a mine going off underneath the Central Hall: the stone floor was described as rising and falling like a wave, fragmenting and in some places collapsing into the vaults below. An official bulletin issued by National Army general headquarters talked of the Irregulars exploding 'a ground mine under the Central Hall'. It went on to say that all fifty of their troops there were injured, thirty of them being seriously wounded.[14] The Central Hall was about 87 yards (80 m) from the site of the explosion, with numerous protecting walls in between, so it is unlikely, as I will discuss later, that this scale of injuries occurred there.

The anti-Treaty garrison leaders knew that the detonation of the stored explosives was inevitable: the remaining members of the garrison, in the east wing of the courts, had been 'arranged' against a wall, as Máire Comerford put it, and 'orders, sterner than I had heard before, or since, held us in position... There was no announcement, that I recall, that the big explosion was coming; but nobody can have been in much doubt... The shock blew me back, the full length of my arms, then forward again, while dust and fragments scattered everywhere.'[15] Calton Younger wrote that the men in the basement 'had been expecting the explosion and had plugged their ears with cotton wool'.[16]

In Dobson's public house at the corner of Middle Abbey Street and Capel Street, 550 yards (457 m) away, a small force of Citizen Army men who had joined the anti-Treaty faction had gathered. They were preparing to cover the retreat that was expected from the Four Courts when they heard the explosion, followed by pounding on the street outside. This they thought was the sound of a large force of National Army troops running towards the pub to attack them, only to find, when they peered out, that it was the noise of many large books raining down onto the street from the sky.[17]

More than half a mile (0.8 km) away, in Grafton Street, the playwright Denis Johnston was with a gathering of friends in the popular Fuller's cafe when 'a most appalling crash shook the whole place and we could hear the sound of falling glass from the street outside. This was the huge explosion which blew up the central hall of the Four Courts just before it was captured.'[18]

Rosamund Jacob was in Tara Hall, a trade union building in Gloucester Street, nearly a mile (1.6 km) away, helping to make bandages, when 'a tremendous explosion... broke the glass in one window'. Some of the young women working with her were members of Cumann na mBan, and she was horrified that they seemed to revel 'in the whole thing in a horrible way'.[19]

A great shower of papers, legal documents and records of all kinds from the Headquarters Block was thrown hundreds of feet into the air in the explosion, and, lifted north-eastwards by the wind, began in time to fall to earth, like giant confetti, over a large area of the north inner city. Sackville Street was not yet the battleground it would become within days, and people there gathered the sheets of paper that snowed down from the sky. Half an hour after the explosion, charred pages from law digests and law reports were still falling in the Dollymount area, 4.5 miles (7.2 km) away from the Four Courts.

Some memories of that moment were eroded and corrupted by time. The two Cumann na mBan members we met earlier, the Cooney sisters Annie and Lily, wrote in their joint Witness Statement that they watched from the south side of the Half-penny Bridge:

> just then the shell was fired at the Four Courts and we saw the dome collapse and our hearts nearly collapsed too when we thought of all our friends there. We saw a shower of papers rising from the building. We thought none of the garrison

could have survived. The shop where we were standing shook from the terrific blast. We went back [to] one of the side streets to a height to see what damage had been done. We had a look and our thoughts were for the men inside.

The dome did not collapse until late that evening.

In the wake of the explosion, a shocked lull descended on the area, and for a while hostilities and activity ceased. The National Army might have expected a surrender to follow the explosion and the fires that were raging, but nothing happened, and after about half an hour, rifles and machine-guns opened up again, followed by the boom of an 18-pounder. What remained of the Four Courts garrison huddled in the basement under the Law Library in the east wing, covered with dust, their feet in water that seeped in from the river with high tide. There can have been little resistance left in them, with burning buildings to the north, the National Army troops pressing them from the west and the 18-pounders across the river. Although defensive firing was now impossible and had ceased, the garrison stayed put, the leaders still discussing among themselves what their next step might be, and arguing about whether to surrender or not. Rory O'Connor felt that they should, but Liam Mellows refused to take part in any discussions of surrender. His only comment was, 'The republic is being attacked here. We must stand or fall by it. If we surrender we have deserted it.'[20] Ernie O'Malley and 'Dinny' O'Brien were keen to break out of the Four Courts through the Chancery Street gate and occupy the houses and the Medical Mission across the road. They would have had the advantage of the dust and confusion following the explosion, and there were thirty men willing to take part, but the Medical Mission was occupied by the National Army, and with so much firepower lined up around the perimeter of the Four Courts, it would have been a suicide move.

During the calm that descended on the area following the blast, those tenement residents who had not been evicted by the National Army during the siege opened their doors and windows and peered cautiously out. Encouraged by the continuing silence, they ventured into the streets, gathering in little groups with their neighbours, gazing at the fires raging in the Four Courts, where clouds of billowing smoke were lit up by the lurid glow of the flames. An eyewitness commented about the group of locals that 'one could hardly describe their pitiable and terrible plight. Their pale and haggard countenances, strained and drawn and deeply lined, told the tale of sleepless nights of horror and anxiety, and silently spoke of the nameless terror for which they could not find words to express.'[21]

Padraig O'Connor was in a dazed condition after the explosion, and his memories of what happened in the aftermath are vague and a little surreal. This is not unusual; individuals exposed to blast can often display neurological symptoms, such as loss of memory, confusion, headaches or an impaired sense of reality. Today, Blast Induced Neurotrauma (BINT) is a well-studied condition with proven treatments, but it is likely that many of O'Connor's men, without the necessary treatment, would have suffered long-term neural damage. O'Connor remembered making his way back into the Public Record Office to make sure that all his men were out, and to retrieve his greatcoat, which he had left behind. He found his coat, but was 'hauled out' of the building for safety, one presumes, by a Capuchin friar. The next thing O'Connor remembered was sitting drinking tea, surrounded by 'a squad of women' in Benburb Street, nearly half a mile (0.8 km) away. He hurried back to his unit, and was told by Dermot MacManus that the garrison had surrendered. He entered the Four Courts complex again and wandered around the burning buildings. Finding 'The Mutineer' armoured car, he took from it a bag with 1,000 rounds of ammunition. O'Connor must have realized the importance of saving documents from the fire, for in one office he took a bundle of papers off a desk and stuffed them into the bag, but then had to make a retreat because the woodwork and the doors were beginning to burn.

In the courtyard, as the flames advanced, O'Connor came across a looter, 'working at frantic speed taking the engine off a motorcycle'. Over the previous two days looters had been shot at by the National Army, but this one called out, 'I may as well have it as the fire', and O'Connor left him to it, and 'legged it away from the fire as fast as I could'.[22]

The explosion had completely destroyed the western end of the Headquarters Block and the southern wing of the Land Registry Office. One of the panels of masonry between the tall windows of the Record Treasury collapsed, spewing bundles of ancient papers out into the courtyard. Most of the glazing

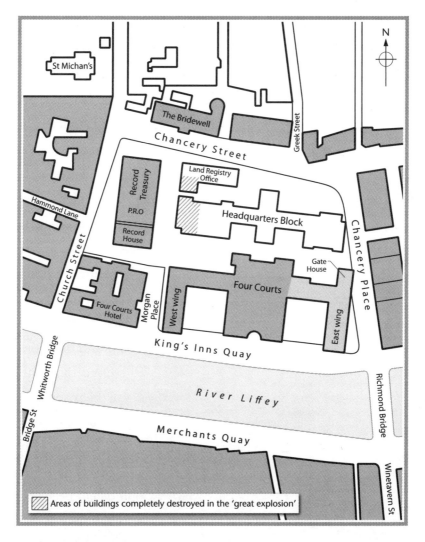

A plan of the Four Courts and the Headquarters Block, indicating the extent of the destruction caused by the 'great explosion'.

in the roof light and the windows shattered into smithereens, and the five storeys of shelves loaded with stored documents were exposed to the heat of the flaming Headquarters Block and the burning embers that flew out of it.

The original deputy keeper of records in Ireland, Samuel Ferguson, was proud of his achievement in cutting out every element in the construction that could be flammable, so that only the records themselves could burn, and he commented that 'these, I would observe, would be extremely difficult of combustion'.[23] It seems, however, that it was not long before the many stacks of desiccated old papers and parchments holding the history of Ireland began to smoulder. Although slow to start burning, the stored records provided an enormous amount of fuel: when Ferguson was gathering archival material in the 1860s to stock the Treasury, almost 169.6 tonnes (167 tons) of paper was delivered from the Custom House alone.[24] Eventually flickering flames appeared, producing a pall of thick white smoke that poured out of the building.

This photograph was taken after the siege, facing east towards
the surviving part of the Headquarters Block. On the left,
the eastern end of the Land Registry Office can be seen.

The explosion had blown the slates off some of the roofs at the rear of the Four Courts block itself, and before long the heat ignited exposed roof timbers.

About 2 p.m.,[25] medical teams that had been waiting nearby in a fleet of ambulances in preparation for the end of the siege, probably assuming that there would be no more fighting after the huge explosion, now converged on the Chancery Street gate. They were allowed in with stretchers to evacuate the wounded. Probably through one of the ambulance drivers, some of whom were members of the IRA, a message from Oscar Traynor was delivered to Rory O'Connor. Traynor said that his forces were unable to come to the aid of the Four Courts, and that the garrison must surrender to help him carry on the fight outside. He added, 'as senior officer outside, I take it I am entitled to order you to make a move that places me in a better military position... I take full responsibility.'[26]

The explosion had injured many of the National Army troops, and, with fires quickly spreading through the buildings, a general withdrawal was made from the complex at about 2 p.m.

The Capuchin priest Father Albert Bibby also arrived at the Chancery Street gate with the doctors and nurses. The courtyard inside the gate was scattered with rubble and lay under a pall of thick smoke, added to by billowing acrid plumes from a large motor car ablaze there. O'Malley described how Father Albert came into the guard-house at the gate to plead with Rory O'Connor and the rest of the headquarters staff to surrender, reminding them of Patrick Pearse's surrender at the end of Easter Week to save his men, and that what they had started in their rebellion continued after Pearse's death. Although O'Malley was wearing a green uniform, the priest also suggested that the populace at large might be turning against 'the soldiers in green', by which he meant the National Army. As Ernie O'Malley helped Father Albert out through the gates again, the priest still encouraging surrender, a correspondent of the *Freeman's Journal* edged as close as he could to listen to their exchange, and he reported:

> A tall young leader of the Irregulars, with his green uniform all thrown open at the throat, capless, covered with powder stains, and gripping his rifle, was refusing determinedly the prayers and appeals of the priest and the woman. 'No, no', said he: 'never', and shook his head. They would not surrender. The nurses bend forward, crowding around him – O'Malley was his name, as I heard, and the brown-robed friar made some particular appeal. I could not hear it amid the general din of falling beams and musketry reports from the flaming east wing. The young man scarcely moved. He said nothing, shook his head, and made motions that the interceders must go. 'Oh! Terrible, terrible!' said a voice, a nurse, I believe...

At about 2.15 p.m. there was another, and possibly two more explosions. Some reports suggest that these were caused by mines and occurred in the Record Treasury, but this seems unlikely. It is not good practice to store large amounts of explosives where the manufacture of explosive devices is taking place, and, anyway, the building had been cleared of munitions by Padraig O'Connor's men the evening before. If these explosions did occur in the Record Treasury, they may have been caused by the ignition of accumulations of gases in the densely packed archives.

In the east wing of the Four Courts, morale was low among the anti-Treaty men huddled in the damp, smoke-wreathed cellars, for so long listening to the crump of exploding shells. O'Malley wanted the headquarters staff to leave quietly and escape while he and 'Dinny' O'Brien stayed on to fight, but O'Connor and McKelvey refused. Typical of the fundamental confusions that had dogged the occupation from the first day, the question of who was in charge of the occupation, and who was prepared to take responsibility for what was to happen next, was discussed. Rory O'Connor, as chief of staff, seemed to be prepared to surrender, but was not prepared to order this. The men of the garrison were divided, some shouting 'Surrender!', others 'No surrender!' According to Ernie O'Malley, it was eventually he, as commanding officer, who finally made the decision to surrender, but he suggested they use up their ammunition first. While some of the men broke down and cried, others fired 'enraged volleys in the direction of the big guns along the quays'.[27] At about 3.30 p.m. a surrender flag was made from a white towel attached to a broom handle and poked out through the broken pane of a window.

Before long, some officers of the National Army, together with Father Albert Bibby, arrived at the Chancery Street gate where they met O'Malley. He told them the garrison wanted to discuss the feasibility of a truce, and he gave them a note to take to Brig.-Gen. O'Daly in the Four Courts Hotel, who, one of the officers said, was in charge. In the note it seems that O'Malley suggested to O' Daly that they should unite and attack the British before any more Irish blood was shed.[28]

All firing had now ceased and, according to O'Malley, the remaining members of the anti-Treaty garrison returned to the Central Hall under the dome. The National Army men had withdrawn an hour before, so this could be correct. His narrative of the events that ensued takes on a surreal tone when he writes that, while he awaited O'Daly's reply, he sat beside Rory O'Connor on the floor reading a pocket volume of Shakespeare's sonnets, one of two books he had in his pocket, the other being a work by Montaigne, the sixteenth-century French philosopher. He describes O'Connor as being 'like a Byzantine portrait, the dark blue-black shadows on his face recessing the lines', and tells how he quoted a version of part of Shakespeare's 'Sonnet XXV' for him:

> The painful warrior famoused for fight,
> After a thousand victories once foil'd,
> Is from the book of honour razed quite
> And all the rest forgot for which he toil'd.

O'Connor responded, 'Has he any more hopeful message than that?'

When Father Albert returned, he reported that Gen. O'Daly was not authorized to accept any conditions, that it had to be an unconditional surrender, and that the garrison should parade outside on the quay. A further conference was held by the leaders, and they decided there was no alternative remaining now but to surrender unconditionally. Father Albert was again driven to the hotel to bring this news to Gen. O'Daly, who ordered buglers to sound the 'cease fire'. The bugle order rang out several times, echoing around the streets and across the river through the silence, and a formation of National Army troops marched down the quays to Chancery Street to accept the surrender.

In an obvious reference to the way in which Paddy O'Brien, his predecessor as officer commanding the Four Courts garrison, had been continually undermined by the headquarters staff, O'Malley suggested that the army executive, having 'directed operations all along', should lead the surrender. This was only met by silence, and in the end O'Malley decided, as the officer in charge, to do it himself.[29]

After stacking up what arms and ammunition remained, the defenders doused them with paraffin and threw incendiary grenades onto them. Then the remaining garrison fell in two deep by sections, and at about 4.30 p.m., almost exactly sixty hours after the first shots had been fired, they marched out through the Chancery Street gate and down to the quays, where they came to a halt, surrounded by National Army troops. There are very few contemporary photographs of this moment: one photographer who was about to set up a tripod for his camera to record the event was warned by members of the garrison that if he did not move off, he would be thrown into the Liffey. One photographer did, however, get a picture of a group of young men walking

243

The Four Courts garrison being escorted down Chancery Place
by members of the National Army. The men in the front, close
to the wall, are remarkable for their youthful looks and
their neat dress: they look anything but exhausted.

past where Chancery Place meets the quays, loosely escorted by
a few National Army troops.

With the surrendering garrison was smoke-blackened and
dusty 'Ginger' O'Connell, much relieved to be free again. When
asked by reporters about his ordeal, he blithely replied, 'I didn't
like the noise... the food was running very short too.'[30]

The garrison was lined up along the river wall of Upper
Ormond Quay and Commandant-Gen. Tony Lawlor, who had
commenced the siege operating the Bridge Street 18-pounder,
inspected them. Liam Mellows wore a tough leather coat, and
Rory O'Connor was wrapped in a dark, heavy overcoat. The
other officers, nearly all of whom were dressed in trench coats
and leggings, had empty holsters on their leather belts. Younger
wrote that Ernie O'Malley, however, still had his pistol, and as
he made to offer it in surrender to Lawlor, he threw it over his

head into the Liffey.[31] While the *Freeman's Journal* describes the garrison as looking 'bedraggled, faces black with dust, fatigued but undaunted',[32] the photograph above seems to depict a youthful group, dressed in shirts and ties, wearing caps and overcoats. Lawlor sent for cigarettes to be distributed to the prisoners. O'Malley relates in *The Singing Flame* how he walked over to a Clare man among the National Army officers, Ignatius O'Neill, the man who had shelled the British headquarters by mistake, and chatted with him. Shaking his hand, O'Malley passed him some papers that O'Neill gave his word of honour to deliver for him. Another National Army officer who came and chatted with O'Malley was Dermot MacManus. 'His face was blackened. There were holes in his green uniform tunic, the edges were singed, it was open by the neck. "Damn good show," he said.'[33]

When Brig.-Gen. O'Daly arrived at the quayside, he was in an ugly humour and talked about shooting them all. It seems that he believed that the great explosion had been a deliberate attempt to kill as many of his men as possible. His attitude towards the Four Courts men, quite affable during the siege, when he personally had gone on a couple of occasions to plead with them face to face to surrender, had changed. In a telephone call to Gen. Mulcahy a couple of hours before, he had referred to the mine explosions as 'absolute murder by Rory O'Connor'.[34] Tony Lawlor tried to calm him down, and they had a 'stand-up row' on the quayside, which ended only when Lawlor told O'Daly that it should be him who should formally accept the garrison's surrender. O'Daly then approached Rory

O'Connor, but it was Ernie O'Malley who came forward and signed the surrender document.[35]

In the background, Máire Comerford, who had remained in the courts when the other women had been evacuated, retrieved her bike, wheeled it out, 'mounted it and rode away. Nobody stopped me. I cycled the short length of the street, through the North Lotts, crossed Sackville Street well down from the fighting that was still going on there, and entered by a rear door of the Hammam Hotel.' The Hammam was where Cathal Brugha had his headquarters: she had moved without difficulty from one battle zone to another. When shelling and fire brought fighting in Sackville Street to an end five days later, Comerford simply mounted her bicycle again and 'quietly leaked away'. She 'rode off through the smoke and the ruined buildings. I had stayed almost to the end, and I had cheated the enemy.'[36]

The fire in the Record Treasury had gained a complete hold by now, and melted lead from gutters and flashings poured into the flames like quicksilver. The roof timbers were the next to go, collapsing with the remaining slates they supported in showers of sparks, into the furnace below. As they did, they disturbed more of the tightly packed bundles of records in the steel shelving, bursting them open and exposing them to fire. The skeletal members of the iron structural frame remained, but not for long, for soon they too failed and, crumpling, bent down into the flames. As the many more tonnes of highly flammable paper and parchments ignited, the blaze became a veritable firestorm, producing a maelstrom of flames and white smoke that poured out of the top of the building and wafted

This photograph, taken by W. D. Hogan, is the clearest image I have
been able to find of the burning of the Record Treasury. On the left of
the photo, the eight-bay light-coloured façade of the Four Courts Hotel
can be seen: to its left, at the edge of the frame, the building with the
long row of windows exuding thick white smoke is the Record Treasury.
The west wing of the Four Courts, with its breach, can be seen halfway
between the Four Courts Hotel and the Dome, and it has not yet
begun to burn. Nelson's Pillar can be seen on the extreme right.

eastwards on the wind, a scene that was captured in a film of
the event.

After the ceasefire was blown and the garrison had paraded
out onto the quays, the *Irish Independent* reported, Capt.
Myers of the fire brigade led his men as far as he could into the
'central portion' of the Four Courts, but an explosion occurred
which injured three of his men. After ordering them out of the
building, he looked on as the prisoners lined up on the quays,
and Rory O'Connor, seeing who he was, warned him that there

were about 7 tons (7.1 tonnes) of explosives in the complex.[37] Myers had had to deal with the fires that consumed part of Sackville Street and Abbey Street in 1916, and was reported as saying that the Four Courts was 'a smaller job'. He added that at no time was he hindered in his work, but said that when he tried to persuade Gen. O'Daly to suspend firing so that something of the Four Courts could be saved, O'Daly replied, 'Ireland is more to me than the Four Courts.' In Chancery Place Myers' men did tackle, from the street, the fire that was spreading rapidly along the eastern wing, with flames bursting through the windows one by one until the whole façade was engulfed. Now and then there were explosions inside the complex, some of which were so violent as to throw onlookers to the ground. Capt. Myers told the correspondent from the *Irish Independent* that the Four Courts were 'doomed, and no efforts could possibly save it'.[38]

One wonders, however, why Myers made no effort at least to damp down the fire that developed in the Record Treasury, which could have been fought from the safety of Church Street. If this had been done, at least some of the documents stored there might have been saved. Some of the Dublin Fire Brigade personnel were members of the Citizen Army, and were clearly not only sympathetic to the anti-Treaty cause, but had actively assisted during the siege when they could. It seems certain that official communications between the IRA executive in the Four Courts and Oscar Traynor, Commandant of the anti-Treaty Dublin Guard, were facilitated by Citizen Army ambulance drivers coming and going from the courts, such as Joe Connolly, who, as we have seen, took the wounded garrison commander,

Paddy O'Brien, to Jervis Street Hospital for treatment, and then quietly arranged for him to be driven home before he could be arrested. One is also reminded of the burning of the Custom House in May 1921: there is evidence that when the fire brigade eventually reached the burning building the firemen's efforts at fighting the blaze had little enthusiasm. Not only did some of them assist the spread of the fire through the building, they recovered weapons left behind by the retreating Volunteers and passed them back to the Dublin Brigade.[39]

Capt. Myers decided that the danger of death or injury to his men from exploding mines or other munitions was great, so all the fires would have to be left to burn out, even that in the accessible Record Treasury. At this time, although its two wings were burning, the central building of the Four Courts itself was still roofed and structurally intact.

The surrendered garrison was divided into two groups and, after some discussion with Ernie O'Malley, the first group of about thirty, headed by O'Malley, Liam Mellows, Rory O'Connor and Seán MacBride, was called to attention. Then, led by an armoured car, it moved off between two lines of National Army troops with fixed bayonets, headed west along the quays and turned up Lincoln Lane, bound for Jameson's Distillery where they were to be held until more permanent arrangements could be made for their detention.

In the remaining group of about 100 men a tricolour was produced and waved over their heads, before they too, accompanied by armed troops, were marched off down the quays through the fumes and smoke from the burning buildings, surrounded and followed by an army of ragged, bare-footed boys and a considerable crowd. Along the way they were only loosely guarded, and they chatted with the onlookers. Members of Cumann na mBan mingled with the men, distributing refreshments and accepting messages and letters, which they promised to deliver. Two Volunteers, Tony Woods and Bobby Burns, had kept pistols concealed in their clothing during the surrender, and they were able to pass them to Cumann na mBan friends in the crowd without difficulty. Woods wrote afterwards, 'As I walked along the quays, leaving the burning building behind us, I could not think of it as the commencement of a civil war. To me, it was just part of a great adventure in which I was eager to play a part.'[40]

Jameson's Distillery had been Padraig O'Connor's base while he prepared for the assault on the Public Record Office, and its yard and out-offices were seen as suitably secure to hold the Four Courts prisoners until more permanent arrangements could be made. The most likely buildings and yard used to hold them were in a block on Bow Street, between Phoenix Street and New Church Street: today the north-east corner of the block has been converted into apartments, while the southern part has been replaced by a tram stop. The prisoners were ushered into a large yard, counted and their names taken, before they were dispersed into the buildings around the yard. There were some windows looking out on the street, which had rusted but robust iron bars.

A large crowd of people gathered around the windows on the street side and talked to the prisoners through the bars. Cumann na mBan member Annie Cooney was able to make contact with Mellows, McKelvey, Denis O'Brien and Seán Nolan, and she gave them the news that Paddy O'Brien was recovering and had avoided arrest. McKelvey wrote a despatch for Oscar Traynor which he passed to her for delivery. He warned her not to let it fall into enemy hands, so she stuck it into the top of her stocking and headed off to Sackville Street.

By now shooting was intense in other parts of the city, particularly in Sackville Street, heralding the next stage in the Civil War. Cooney, however, was able, like Máire Comerford a while before, to make her way through byways and alleyways to the back of the Hammam Hotel, and to deliver the despatch directly into Oscar Traynor's hands. She then returned to Jameson's Distillery and helped other women collect various items and goods the imprisoned men passed out of the window and wanted kept for them. Then off she went again, home this time, to prepare and bring back food for the men. They were very happy to get it; it had been a few days since any of them had eaten a proper meal.

Rosamund Jacob, having left Tara Hall, met Maud Gonne MacBride in the street. Maud Gonne (1866–1953) was the ex-wife of executed 1916 leader Maj. John MacBride, and mother of IRA director of operations Seán MacBride, who had been in the Four Courts. She had just arrived back from Paris where she had been publicizing the Provisional Government's efforts to establish a new state, on behalf of her friend Arthur Griffith.

Very concerned at the situation she found on her arrival in Dublin, MacBride was worried that it might be the beginning of a civil war. She decided to get a Women's Peace Committee formed to lobby both sides to seek a ceasefire before it was too late. Jacob joined her and a number of other women on a visit to the Lord Mayor of Dublin at the Mansion House, seeking his support, after which MacBride began to visit all the hospitals in an effort to find her son, Seán, whom she knew had been in the Four Courts and thought might have been wounded in the fighting. He was alive and well, but, as we know, was now one of the Four Courts prisoners in Jameson's Distillery.

Commandant Padraig O'Connor was ordered to go to Jameson's Distillery and take charge of the Four Courts prisoners, many of whom were old friends and comrades, such as Seán Lemass, Peadar O'Donnell and Paddy Rigney. He had been in Derry Jail with Lemass in 1920, and O'Donnell had hatched a plan to help them escape, by posing as a priest.

O'Connor and Paddy Rigney sat down together on sacks of grain and chatted as they had a smoke. It had been decided that the prisoners were to be moved to Mountjoy Prison, but after his chat with Rigney, it seems that O'Connor arranged that a particular door would be left unguarded, allowing Rigney to slip away. A little later, taking Joe Griffin, Seán Lemass and Ernie O'Malley with him, Rigney walked through the door and then through the distillery manager's house to reach the street and freedom.

Nearby an armoured car patrolled, but, unnoticed in the crowd that was gathered around the windows, the four men walked away. As soon as they were out of sight of the distillery they ran, putting as much space between them and Jameson's as possible. Joe Griffin and Paddy Rigney went their own ways, but Lemass and O'Malley decided to head together for Paddy O'Brien's house, a mile (1.6 km) away in the Coombe, and on their way they paused and mingled with the crowds along the quays watching the Four Courts burn. An old woman told them that the 'poor boys' inside had all been killed.

Later that day, the civilian prisoners in Mountjoy Prison were evacuated to other locations to make room for the Four Courts men, and that night the prisoners were all moved from the distillery and lodged in the jail. Since it was now to be a military prison, Commandant Diarmuid Ó hEigeartaigh, who had been acting as cabinet secretary, was appointed by the Provisional Government as military governor of the prison.

A *Freeman's Journal* reporter was allowed across the bridge to King's Inns Quay in front of the Four Courts at 4.45 p.m. by a tired National Army officer who commented, 'Glad it's over. They put up a great fight. You'll see that when you go over.' On the north side of the river the reporter met the Dublin Fire Brigade chief, Capt. Myers. Myers advised him to go back, and at that moment one of the mines in the complex went off 'with a noise only inferior to that of the great explosion which earlier had settled the fate of the defenders'. The newspaperman reported that the front buildings were not on fire, but 'every inch behind was a raging inferno.'[41] From contemporary cine film held by Getty Images Archival Images library, it is clear, however, that some cameramen and journalists took their lives in their hands and gained entry to the main Four Courts building before the fires had taken a complete hold.

Not long after the defeated garrison had been marched off, the air of the surrounding quays and streets no longer thick with bullets, thousands of Dublin citizens – men, women and children – rushed and pushed their way towards the Four Courts, down to the corner of Chancery Place, to Bridge Street, Church Street, Capel Street and every vantage-point from where they could view, close-up, the scene of the late battle and the continuing destruction of the buildings by fire.

One man marched from Lower Abbey Street playing the 'Soldier's Song' on a melodeon. A well-dressed young girl had

By late afternoon on Friday the west wing had been burnt out and fire was spreading to the main building.

a camera with her and told an *Irish Independent* reporter that she had taken a dozen excellent pictures, including views of flames bursting through the windows. In the abandoned shops and houses in the surrounding area some looting began, and at one stage soldiers had to fire a rifle volley over the heads of the looters to frighten them off.

The great massif of the Four Courts, looming smokily over the quays, was the centre of attention. Inexorably the flames spread and raced through the roofs and floors of the west wing, fed by the air pouring in through the gaping breach on the Morgan Place side. As the flames consumed the roof of the western wing, and it collapsed in clouds of sparks and smoke, the dome, on its Corinthian peristyle, stood aloof, rising above the smoke, as if unconnected with the horrific happenings all about it. From contemporary photographs, we can see that the only damage to the dome that was visible at this time was spalled stone where an 18-pounder shell had hit the drum, the many pockmarks left by bullets and some shattered windows. Although a number of reports mention shells from the 18-pounders striking the copper dome itself, there is no evidence of this, at least on the south side.

Shortly after 5 p.m. there was another large explosion, as the stored explosives discovered the previous day by Dermot MacManus and his men were deflagrated by the fire in the west wing. An *Irish Times* correspondent described how 'Debris enveloped in a great column of black smoke was blown a hundred feet [30.5 m] into the air. For many minutes there was a rain of blinding dust, and charred fragments of paper fluttered down into the streets for hundreds of yards around.' A survey of the Four Courts ruins early the following week showed that this explosion had taken place between the Crown and Hanaper's Office and the Lord Chancellor's office in the west wing.

By 6 p.m. the fire had enveloped the central part of the main building. Before long flames had begun bursting out of the high windows surrounding the drum of the dome, as the fire finally reached the coffered ceiling under the dome itself. High up over the Corinthian portico, black, oily smoke swirled around Edward Smyth's five massive limestone statues. They had survived the battle, although they suffered some minor damage during nearly three days of fusillades and shells. On the west side of the pediment, Justice still stood proud, although part of her face was missing. Moses, standing on the top of the pediment holding the Ten Commandments, was without a scratch, while an abandoned, torn and forlorn republican flag flapped above the head of Mercy to his left. Seated Authority at the south corner of the parapet, the severest-looking of the quintet, seemed to glower on the scene of destruction, while at the northern corner Wisdom reclined, ignoring all. The row of trees that had been recently planted along the quayside was in full summer leaf and seemed to be untouched by the violence.

That evening Clare Sheridan left Ireland from Kingston on the steamer to Holyhead, which was crowded with refugees. From the deck she could see the smoke from the burning Four Courts fill the sky over the city, and she remembered the young boys she had seen showing off their rifles there, and knew

Friday, after 6 p.m.: the interior of the dome is ablaze;
within an hour, the timber framing of the great copper
dome would burn and collapse into the interior.

that by now the Playboys of the Western World had played
their part.

Around 7 p.m., the watching crowd grew silent as there was
a sudden movement in the tall structure and, with a thunderous roar, the great green dome collapsed into the building, and
an immense mushroom of sparks, smoke and dust arose. The
flames then raced along the roof of the east wing, until then the
only intact roof remaining in the complex. It was not long before
it too collapsed, falling into what remained of the great Law
Library below and throwing up a shower of burning embers.

257

The fires in the Four Courts were still burning at 3 a.m. the following morning and, viewed from the *Irish Independent* offices, the scene was described as 'an awe-inspiring spectacle'.

CHAPTER 7

AFTERMATH

The newspapers of Saturday, 1 July, the day after the surrender of the garrison of the Four Courts, provide evidence of how, in spite of the momentous and destructive event that had happened and was still happening in the streets of the capital, normal life continued throughout the country, and indeed in much of Dublin itself. On the front page of Saturday's *Freeman's Journal*, under a spread of dramatic photographs of the burning courts and prisoners being escorted away by soldiers, a column entitled 'Social Programme' announced:

> Princess Mary Viscountess Lascalles and Viscount Lascalles gave a small dinner party at Chesterfield House, London, last night. Princess Mary has just recovered from an attack of Hay fever.

The Duchess of Rutland, who has now quite recovered from her operation for appendicitis which confined her to her house for seven weeks, was present at the opening of the Exhibition of Pictures of Jerusalem at Grosvenor Square, London.

An advertisement for Colleen Soap assured the public that 'there is no harsh mineral alkali in Colleen to shrink your skin – make it dry and rough', while another urged readers to 'come to Arklow for the ideal healthy, happy holiday', extolling the 'pretty countryside... excellent fishing, boating and tennis'. Readers are also warned to: 'Watch your feet! And use Tinori (corn cure and Foot Powder) to ensure you keep smiling during the holidays!'

From early that Saturday morning crowds of sightseers began to gather outside the cordon around the Four Courts. Most of the buildings had by now burnt out, but were still smouldering and smoking and, in spite of a brisk breeze, the air was acrid. With plenty of fuel still remaining, the archives in the Record Treasury continued to burn fiercely, fanned by the breeze into white-hot flames. From time to time, in different parts of the ruined complex, there was a rumble, a thunderous crash and a cloud of dust, as great sections of masonry wall collapsed. Now and then the crackle of exploding ammunition and the thud of mines detonating could be heard, discouraging those photographers who were looking for a chance to enter the complex.

How the Four Courts looked after the fires had gone out.
Note that the flag of the Irish Republic still blows in the wind,
over the statue of Mercy on the near side of the pediment.

The Provisional Government's publicity department issued a statement on the Saturday morning deploring the fact that nineteen of the prisoners captured in the Four Courts were only fourteen to sixteen years old: 'to put weapons in the hands of boys who have not yet passed the age when they must be called children, to send them out to loot and commandeer, to bid them spill blood and take human life is surely villainous work.' The fact that the War of Independence had been fought by IRA units that certainly included sixteen-year-olds had already been forgotten.

An *Irish Times* reporter chatted with the members of the National Army who were still at their posts around the Four Courts: 'Tired, very tired, they sat in the houses overlooking the place they had captured, full of stories, mostly inaccurate, for they had not the gift of scientific observation. Mostly young themselves, they were all insistent on the youth of their antagonists.' The reporter called them 'wonderful, lovable fellows, simple and kindly in every way. One of them gave me a little cartel of the *Virgin of Seven Dolours of Campocavallo*. "I don't know your religion, sir," he said, "but take this. A priest gave me two, and it might help you."'

Comment in *The Sunday Times* indicated the continuing sceptical attitude of the British establishment towards the Irish and their ability to govern themselves:

Can the Irish be induced to accept and obey any Government? They never accepted or obeyed British rule, and they may be so out of hand and demoralized as to be incapable yet a while of settling down under any system of authority, even a system of their own choosing. That doubt has to be resolved, and it can only be resolved if the Free State leaders nerve themselves to act throughout Ireland as they have acted tardily in Dublin. Strength and determination always win in the long run, and nowhere is their victory apt to be so complete as among a people with the leader-following instincts of the Irish.

The dust had hardly settled, literally, when on Monday, 3 July, Constantine Curran, in his capacity as registrar of the Supreme Court, arrived at the Four Courts to carry out a preliminary survey of the extent of the destruction, at the request of Hugh

Kennedy, the law officer for the Provisional Government. Curran was a courageous man: only three days after the fighting and conflagration, his inspection was not without risks from unexploded ordnance and collapsing structures.

In the main Four Courts building, he found the west wing gutted by fire and that considerable destruction had been caused by an explosion that had occurred in the middle of the block, between or under the Crown and Hanaper's office and the Lord Chancellor's office (see page 263). The east wing, with its fine two-storey Law Library, was completely burnt out.

The Central Hall was open to the sky, and the remains of the outer and inner domes, brought down by the fire, covered the floor. The court-rooms off the Central Hall were in ruins, but Curran found that the Lord Justice's chamber, at the north-east

The Central Hall of the Four Courts, open to the sky.

corner of the Central Hall, had survived 'practically intact'. The cellars under the main block were flooded in 'five or six inches' (12.7 or 15.2 cm) of water, though a large number of affidavits, judgments and court or chamber orders of the previous twenty years which had been stored in the cellars under the King's Bench offices, had only been partially damaged.

Of the Record Treasury, above ground, nothing remained but the walls, which enclosed a tangled mass of the cast-iron beams and columns that had once formed the galleries, distorted by the fire and fused together by the great heat. The fireproof doors between the Treasury and the Record House had been left closed, so the fire in the Treasury did not spread to the Record

The tangled remains of the Record Treasury. Through the opening in the masonry caused by the explosion in the adjacent Headquarters Block, the roof parapet of the Land Registry Office can be seen, with sandbag fortifications.

House. The latter, but for the breach in the Church Street façade, the holes that had been made in the floors and general bullet damage, had survived well, and most of the documents that had been there at the time of the occupation remained intact. Curran could see that the Search Room in the Record House had also been used as a munitions factory, but the files stored there were unharmed. Subsequently, it was found that some material stored in the vaults or basement under the Treasury was also relatively undamaged, in spite of the fire that raged above. Boxes of documents stored at the southern end were intact, though those in other parts had been damaged by the intense heat, with some 'reduced to the finest powder'.[1]

In the Record House, National Army men showed him an unexploded 'booby-trap' mine with wires attached to a door, which suggests that some of Padraig O'Connor's men had had a narrow escape, and the 'clear out' of munitions to pits at Smithfield Garage had not been completely thorough. It was Curran who had written to the leaders in the Four Courts, and even visited Rory O'Connor, voicing his concern about the vulnerability of the archive of documents stored in the Four Courts complex, and particularly in the Record Treasury. One can only imagine his disgust when confronted, on that July day, with the smoking ruins.

In later years, recalling his inspection of the Four Courts ruins, Curran commented, with regard to the array of statues that had stood in the Central Hall, that only one of them, that of Judge Whiteside, was repairable. 'I saw [them] under the open sky. Smyth's work fallen into indistinction, Lord Chancellor,

Statue of Henry Joy in the Central Hall.

Judges and advocates, broken and calcined. I stuck my thumb into Joy – he had the consistency of cream cheese.'*2

The wing of the Land Registry Office that extended south towards the Headquarters Block and which had accommo-dated the main stairs, had been completely demolished by the explosion, but the fire in this building was limited to a few rooms in its western end. Most of the records therefore sur-vived intact. The land commissioners calculated that there were about 10,000 land purchase agreements, 3,000 estate maps and 1,000 land certificates lodged there at the time.[3]

---

* Edward Smyth (1749–1812), sculptor, born in Co. Meath, was employed by Gandon on all his Dublin buildings; Henry Joy, Chief Baron of the Irish Exchequer 1831–8.

On 13 July an Office of Public Works engineer, John Chaloner Smith, was sent to inspect the ruins of the courts, to supervise demolition of dangerous sections of the buildings and to carry out any salvage works that seemed necessary. Work of clearing up the site began on 17 July, with dangerous walls and vaulting being taken down and cleared. It seems to have been assumed that some element of rebuilding would eventually occur, as reusable stone and other materials were neatly stacked in the courtyards. Chaloner Smith's main concern with regard to the effects of the explosions was what he referred to as 'the practical impossibility of saying how far the damage had penetrated... through the foundations and superstructure'.[4] In his opinion the only sensible thing to do was to demolish the greater part of the complex. When this work was completed, the ruins would be left in stasis until decisions could be made about the future of the site.

Leaving aside the loss of the contents of the Record Treasury, the enormity of the loss also of all the 'live' legal documentation, papers dealing with many thousands of legal cases, wills, securities and company and estate records, created a nightmare for the legal profession. The business carried on in the Four Courts complex had been disrupted since 13 April, and so, initially for what was believed would be a temporary period, but that had already gone on for over three months until the last days of June, the large staffs of the courts, the Land Registry Office, the Law Society and the Public Record Office had been accommodated in a maze of offices around the city. The courts sat in the King's Inns, with temporary offices rented in

Westmoreland Street, while the Law Society moved to premises in Molesworth Street.[5] Now, suddenly, with the destruction of the Four Courts complex, the disruption that was thought to be temporary became semi-permanent. Sir Thomas F. Moloney, who had been appointed Lord Chief Justice of Ireland by the British government in 1918, was at the forefront of efforts by the judiciary to get matters back to normal as quickly as possible. He made rooms in his home in Fitzwilliam Square available for the Lunacy and Minors' courts. Suitable accommodation was the first necessity, and from early in July efforts were made to find more permanent homes for the various courts and offices.

By October 1922, however, matters had still not been resolved. Moloney, writing to the chairman of the Office of Public Works, Sir Philip Hanson, complained that the Accountant General's office was still confined to one table in the King's Inns and the use of one room in the Bank of Ireland. He commented that these temporary arrangements were very unsuitable, and, since it would take some years to erect new courts of law, a satisfactory interim solution would have to be sought. Eventually space was found and made available in Dublin Castle, and from the Easter Term on 11 April 1923, all legal business was carried out from that address. With the urgency reduced, it was some time before any serious thought was given to the long-term problem of constructing new courts.

At the Four Courts site, repairs were carried out to the Record House, the building that had been the least damaged in the battle, and the housekeeper's apartment in the basement was converted into strong rooms for the storage of retrieved records and documents. John J. Tucker, the erstwhile foreman and housekeeper of the Public Record Office, now thrice evicted from his apartment, submitted a claim for damage and loss to his property, for the second time in six years, but this time under Section 15 of the Damage to Property (Compensation) Act 1923. He claimed the loss of a long list of items, including silver cigar and cigarette cases, Malacca canes, 2 dinner suits, 2 velour hats, 4 suits of clothes, a large doll's house, a perambulator, 2 pairs of ladies' knickers, 1 galvanized foot-bath, 1 rocking zinc bath, a Summer House, and furniture including a brass bed. The amount claimed by Tucker amounted to £260: he received £180.

The basement of the Record Treasury, which, as we have seen, had not been greatly affected by the fire above, was roofed over, heated and lit, and made available again for the storage of records at the end of 1923.

There was much debate and argument, at many levels, about what the future of the Four Courts site was to be. The Four Courts had been seen by some as a symbol of British imperialism and, in addition to those who were not unhappy to see the courts in ruins, there were many who would have liked to see the buildings levelled. After the widespread destruction of essential public buildings during the War of Independence and the Civil War, the new Free State government had to embark on a programme of replacements for many of them, including 98 coastguard stations, 147 police barracks and 10 post offices.

In addition, office accommodation had to be built or found for the new Houses of the Oireachtas (Irish Parliament) and the new departments of state.[6] Of the three important Dublin buildings that had suffered destruction – the GPO in 1916, the Custom House in 1921 and the Four Courts in 1922 – there was never any question that the GPO, the locus of the opening of the Irish Rebellion of 1916 and a national symbol, would not be restored. The Custom House had housed the Local Government Board, and it probably owed its restoration largely to the Free State government's need for office space. The Four Courts, however, almost as synonymous with British imperial power in Ireland as Dublin Castle, was larger than either the GPO or the Custom House, and the expense of its refurbishment would be considerable.

On 13 November 1922, the council of the Royal Institute of the Architects of Ireland wrote to the government informing it that it had passed a resolution 'recognizing the great historic, civic, and aesthetic value of the partially destroyed public buildings of Dublin such as the Custom House, the Four Courts etc., [and] desire to place on record their conviction that these buildings should be most carefully preserved, and, as far as possible, restored to their former condition'. The Office of Public Works took the time to prepare a well-considered report, in which it agreed that these buildings and others were considered to be stately and noble in appearance, and that it hoped the government would be prepared, 'in due time', to 'face the very heavy expense involved in preserving what can be preserved'. With regard to the Four Courts, the Office of Public Works was firmly of the opinion that, after demolition of most of the structures remaining, Gandon's building should be rebuilt.[7]

Since June 1922 there had been no shortage of ideas put forward about the future use of the Four Courts site, including the Greater Dublin Reconstruction Movement's proposal that the buildings should be restored and turned into an art gallery, and surrounded by a park. The idea that the site would be suitable for the home of the new Free State Oireachtas, the parliament of Ireland, got considerable traction, even to the extent that sketch plans for the new buildings were prepared by the Office of Public Works.

T. J. Byrne.

T. J. Byrne (1876–1939) was appointed principal architect of the Office of Public Works in 1923. He had built up a significant reputation as a housing architect in the early years of the twentieth century, and in 1919 had been appointed housing inspector in the Local Government Board, the British government's supervising body that oversaw local administration in Ireland and controlled the distribution of funding to local authorities. Byrne had never dealt with large building projects, and for that reason he might not have seemed an ideal candidate, at such a time, for the post of chief government architect. However, after the local elections of 1920 during the War of Independence, Sinn Féin had controlled most of the Irish local authorities, and its councils had bypassed the British-operated Local Government Board, dealing instead with the underground Local Government Department of the Irish Republic's Dáil. The Dáil Minister for Local Government was W. T. Cosgrave, and he had got to know T. J. Byrne, and become aware of his ability, during his time on the housing committee of Dublin Corporation. It is possible that Byrne took the job with the Local Government Board, based in the Custom House, to act as a mole on Cosgrave's behalf; he would have been in a position to pass to Cosgrave crucial information about the board's policies on such matters as funding plans, taxation and local government generally. He continued to advise Cosgrave on housing matters, particularly on the subject of rehousing Dublin's slum-dwellers, and the two men became friends. When the Provisional Government took over in 1922 and Cosgrave again took on the position of Minister for Local Government, Byrne was appointed acting chief of the new Local Government Housing Department. After Andrew Robinson retired from his post as principal architect of the

An inspection being carried out of the façade
of the west wing of the Four Courts.

Office of Public Works in February 1923, Byrne was appointed
to take his place.

In his new post, Byrne was responsible for many building
projects, but he took a particular interest in the Four Courts.
As an active member of the Royal Institute of the Architects of
Ireland, he had probably had a hand in the recommendation to
the government regarding the future of the GPO, the Custom
House and the Four Courts, and now, less than a year later,
he was in a position directly to influence their futures. The

new state had scarce resources, and the considerable expense of rebuilding works might prevent the commencement of the restoration of these buildings for a decade or more, so Byrne had to find imaginative ways to keep down costs.

The most complicated aspect of the restoration of the Four Courts was the reconstruction of the great dome and its drum, and the peristyle of twenty-four slender Corinthian columns on which the dome stood.

Byrne had inherited the recommendation that the whole lot should be demolished, but when he had scaffolding erected to allow a close examination he found that, although there were some structural problems and surface damage was severe, it would be possible to restore the drum and erect a new dome without great expense. His friend W. T. Cosgrave was by now chairman of the Free State government, and it is not unreasonable to suggest that Byrne persuaded him that Gandon's masterpiece could and should be restored, no matter what its future use might be, and with imagination and care the project could be carried out economically. The Office of Public Works report for the year 1924/25 states: 'we have proceeded with reconstructing the shell and central part of the old Four Courts building, the architectural amenities of the structure being carefully preserved', and by 1926 it had been decided, after much discussion, not only fully to restore the Four Courts, but to establish the Free State courts of law there.

The project proceeded slowly, in parallel with the reconstruction of the Custom House and the GPO. As the work progressed, many hidden problems were uncovered, some of them

This photograph indicates the severity of the damage to the area around the drum of the dome and, indeed, the drum itself, with its twenty-four slender Corinthian columns. Note the rather precarious scaffolding that T. J. Byrne erected to allow a close inspection of the structure.

dating back over 100 years to the original construction. Byrne himself referred to it as a task 'bristling with difficulties' which required a good mixture of imagination and technical expertise. The cost of replacing the twenty-four peristyle columns and capitals around the drum would have been prohibitively expensive, but Byrne discovered that while the outward faces of the capitals were badly damaged, those facing inwards were perfect. Until the funds became available to replace the capitals, he therefore decided simply to rotate them, bringing the undamaged faces to the outside, and turning the damaged parts to the wall where they could not be seen.

The original structure of the copper-covered dome had been an elaborate timber frame. T. J. Byrne was not only an architect, but also an engineer of considerable talent, and he kept abreast of the considerable advances that were occurring in structural engineering. He made the radical decision to use a relatively new material and an innovative structural system for the dome, designing a 6-inch- (15-cm)-thick reinforced concrete shell, something that had not been done before at this scale in Ireland. For the dome to work as a single homogeneous unit, it was necessary for all the concrete to be poured in place in one operation, and at more than 100 feet (30 m) above street level, the construction had to be carefully planned. For the first time in Ireland, an electric construction elevator was used to deliver wheelbarrows of mixed concrete to the dome level, where an ingenious one-way timber bridge system allowed a continuous supply of concrete to be barrowed to the placement site. Though not without its hazards, building the dome structure was successfully and safely completed by twenty men in thirty hours. As before, it was covered with copper.

Although few changes were made to Gandon's original design externally, Byrne replanned the interiors to modern office requirements and, in spite of a shortage of funds, the great Central Hall and the four courts were restored to something near their original splendour, using Irish materials where possible. The work was completed in October 1931, but, for security reasons, the reopening of the Four Courts took place without any formal ceremony.

T. J. Byrne's new reinforced concrete dome under construction, seen from the north-west. This photograph also shows the destruction to the north wall caused by the deflagration of the explosives that had been moved from the Headquarters Block to the west wing.

The north Solicitors' Block, used as the Headquarters Block during the occupation, was only partially rebuilt. The western end of the original building, where the great explosion took place, was left and later cleared, and is today a car park. The south wing of the Land Registry Office was rebuilt as before.

While the Record House was completely restored, and

today houses the Appeals Court, the tall and graceful Record Treasury with its fine fenestration was not rebuilt: in the 1970s a three-storey modern office block was erected on its ground-floor walls.

While it was possible to replace the buildings that made up the Four Courts complex, the most serious loss suffered in the fires in June 1922 was that of Ireland's records.

The Public Record Office had, before the occupation and siege, a staff of thirty-five, including the housekeeper, cleaners and the deputy keeper, Herbert Wood. When the occupation of the Four Courts began, temporary accommodation was provided for the PRO in government buildings and in Dublin Castle, so that its work, in so far as it was possible, could be carried on. The disruption created by having inadequate space in unsuitable offices in two locations in the city, and a reduced staff, made the smooth running of the office very difficult.

As soon as the site had been made safe, and material gathered up deposited in the records tower of Dublin Castle, cataloguing of the surviving documents got under way. At the time of the fire in June 1922, the Public Record Office holdings amounted to an estimated 12 million individual records. Fortunately, in 1919, Herbert Wood published a 300-page *Guide to the Records Deposited in the Public Record Office of Ireland*,[8] which at least tells us what the Record Treasury contained before it was destroyed. This list casts a sad light on what has been lost, on the 'black holes' that have, since then, frustrated the development of our understanding of many aspects of Ireland's history.

In his guide Wood reported that for some of what was lost – for instance the pipe rolls from the reigns of Henry II to Edward III – the only clues to the riches they contained lie in a catalogue laboriously made by the Public Record Office assistant keeper, M. J. McEnery, in which he wrote brief notes about their contents. These include comments such as 'These accounts are extremely interesting; they show what were the principal articles of food at the time; their prices, the places whence obtained and the steps taken to provide commissariat for armies and garrisons', and 'This account is very interesting as showing how men were recruited at the time, and where the government obtained its soldiers'. As Herbert Wood noted about the pipe rolls, 'what a flood of light their preservation would have thrown on the economic life in Ireland in the middle ages'.[9]

Aspects of more recent Irish history, such as the Great Famine from 1845 to 1849, also have critical gaps as a result of the fire. The national censuses of 1821, 1831, 1841 and 1851, which held an almost complete demographic record of Ireland in the period before, during and after the famine, down to the details of each family in the country and how the famine affected them, are among the records that were destroyed.

Great amounts of papers and documents, some relatively undamaged, fell from Dublin's skies for hours after the explosion and fire, and appeals were printed in the press requesting anyone who had found documents to restore them to official custody by handing them in to the Royal Society of Antiquaries in Merrion Square. The society provided a room on its premises for the receipt of such material, which it was thought would in the main consist of legal documentation blown into the sky when the munitions exploded in the Headquarters Block. The results of the appeal were disappointing, for although a number of people brought in documents or fragments, very little of any importance was recovered.

James F. Morrissey, assistant deputy keeper of the Public Record Office, reported in December 1928 that, 'To a great extent the loss is irreparable, but in certain respects much can be done to mitigate it.'[10] Work began almost immediately to recreate the Public Record Office: Herbert Wood wrote, 'The Irish Record Office is starting again like a new country almost without a history.'[11] Apart from dealing with surviving documents, the reduced PRO staff began to assemble, from every source possible, duplicate documents of all kinds to those missing. Between the opening of the office in 1867 and its destruction fifty-five years later, numerous historical and literary researchers had copied documents, preserving them in their notes or in published material. Work began to identify and source all these so that the originals could be replaced. A concerted effort was made to request a wide range of bodies and individuals to provide the PRO with copies of original documents that they might have made before the fire, such as parish records, wills, affidavits and grants of probate. In many cases the PRO received documents that it had not had before, such as a large collection of miscellaneous letters and papers for the period 1726–1868 which had been found in the chief secretary's office in

Dublin Castle, and 'bundles' of papers received from the chief Crown solicitor's department and the probate office of the high court. The Ordnance Survey office discovered duplicates of some 1851 census returns, and duplicates of some of the 1821 census returns were found in the sheriff's office. Many solicitors' offices, and private individuals such as Professor R. A. Macalister and Charles McNeill, deposited records, manuscripts, maps, deeds, wills and grants of lands for the making of copies for preservation.

Herbert Wood and his successor, James F. Morrissey, must have believed that one day the technical resources and finance might be available to restore the considerable number of pathetic bundles of sheepskin parchments, dating from the sixteenth and seventeenth centuries, which had been rescued from the cellars of the Treasury and other places in the Four Courts complex. During the years after 1922 these were painstakingly annotated, packaged up and stored away. Reductions in staff and lack of government funding meant, however, that progress was extremely slow, and it was not until the 1970s, when it became policy to cache all government records in the PRO, that matters began to improve. The Public Record Office became the National Archives in 1988, and the collection, storage and conservation of national records was put on a modern footing.

In recent years some 5,000 of the documents known as chancery pleadings contained in those bundles rescued from the Record Treasury cellars have been processed and conserved as part of a twelve-year conservation project being carried out by the National Archives of Ireland. Trinity College Dublin has been among the outside agencies that have been assisting in the restoration of records; over the past forty years, scholars there have succeeded in assembling copies of many of the destroyed documents, including as many as 20,000 items produced by the medieval chancery of Ireland, the secretariat of the Irish government, which issued letters and writs in the name of the king.

All the gaps in the records created by the destruction wreaked by the Record Treasury fire can never be filled, but many important documents were not lost because, for various reasons, they had never been deposited in the Public Record Office. Civil registration records, Catholic, Presbyterian and Methodist baptism, marriage and burial records and nearly half of the Church of Ireland parish registers, and the Griffith's Valuation (a comprehensive land valuation survey of Ireland carried out between 1848 and 1864) are still major primary sources on people, land and property in the middle of the nineteenth century, and, together with surviving fragments of those nineteenth-century censuses, provide alternative sources for historians. The London Public Record Office also holds many thousands of medieval documents that are replicas of those destroyed in 1922, including the correspondence and documents sent to London by Irish officials and copies or drafts of letters sent by the British government to Ireland.

The National Archives of Ireland, the National Archives of the UK, the Public Record Office of Northern Ireland, the Irish Manuscripts Commission and Trinity College Dublin are, at the time of writing, collaborating on a virtual reality reconstruction of the destroyed Record Treasury which they hope will be completed for the centenary of the destruction, and which will include a complete inventory of what was lost and what has been recovered from other sources.

CHAPTER 8

EPILOGUE

The destruction caused by artillery during the Battle of the Four Courts was limited and focused, and subsequently was comparatively easily repaired. The most severe and widespread structural damage was caused by the detonation of mines and munitions stored in the complex by the IRA executive, and the fires that spread through it. How these explosions and fires occurred has been argued about since 1922.

Photographic evidence, contemporary newspaper reports and the findings of T. J. Byrne, the principal architect of the Office of Public Works in charge of rebuilding the Four Courts, point to the location of the 'great explosion' being in one of the rooms in the Land Judges' Court at the western end of the Head-quarters Block, less than 65 feet (20 m) from the east façade of the Public Record Office. The explosion did not occur in the basement of the Public Record Office, as many historians have reported, and I can find no evidence that an explosion occurred in the basement under the Central Hall of the Four Courts, as Provisional Government propaganda insisted for some days after the event.

The explosion reduced the western end of the Headquarters Block and the south wing of the Land Registry Office to rubble. Much of the glass in the roof lights and the windows of the Record Treasury was shattered, and the blast destroyed one of the tall, slender panels of masonry on the east façade, exposing the building's interior.

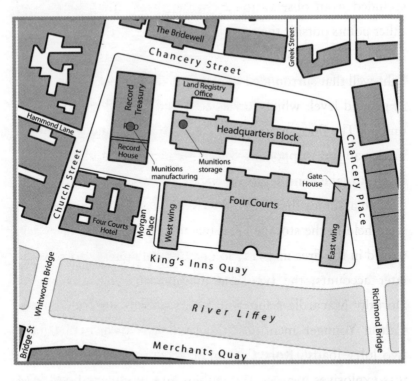

Location of munitions storage and manufacturing areas established at the beginning of the occupation of the Four Courts in April 1922.

While the anti-Treaty IRA bomb-makers may not perhaps have adhered to the comprehensive safety regulations of the Explosives Act 1875 when the decision was made to use the Public Record Office for the manufacture of hand grenades and mines, it seems they did opt to store the raw materials needed in the nearby Headquarters Block. This location was close enough to where the work was being carried out without being dangerously so. If there were an accident in the 'munitions factory', as there was when Seamus O'Donovan had his hand blown off, the main store of explosives should be remote enough for safety. The Headquarters Block was also reasonably secluded from observation from the surrounding streets and other points outside the complex, and access to the building was straightforward: there were two bridges crossing the basement light-well that surrounded the Headquarters Block to doorways at ground level, which lorries could be driven right up to, to unload. The floor construction of the building at the time was brick vaulting supporting a stone slab floor, structurally sufficient to take considerable weight.

One assumes that records were kept of the munitions that were held in the storage area, but these would have been destroyed in the fires in 1922, so one can only guess, from sparse later accounts, the type and amount of explosives stored. Dorothy Macardle refers to a 'great store of explosives', and Calton Younger mentions 'thousands of sticks of gelignite, two lorry loads'. Rory O'Connor, whose particular expertise was explosives, warned the Dublin Fire Brigade chief, during the surrender, as we know, that there were about '7 tons [7.1

tonnes] of TNT' in the building. Although his accounts of this last phase of the Four Courts battle are confused in places, Ernie O'Malley mentions that 'the tons of explosives in munitions might detonate, or the TNT, a half-ton of it, in the cellars'.[1]

When Thomas Johnson, leader of the Labour Party, interviewed Rory O'Connor, Joe McKelvey and Liam Mellows in Mountjoy Prison on 3 July, 2 tons (2.03 tonnes) of explosive material were mentioned.

When Padraig Gill, an experienced explosives engineer, examined on my behalf photographs and contemporary accounts describing the explosion, he ruled out the possibility that there were 7 tons of munitions involved. The detonation of 7 tons of explosives such as TNT or gelignite, Gill believes, would have caused complete destruction within an 88-yard (80-m) radius of 'ground zero'. This would have included the Public Record Office, the Land Registry Office, the Four Courts Hotel, the west side of Church Street, the Bridewell police station, the entire western wing and much of the central Four Courts. Most of the soldiers stationed within this perimeter, including members of the garrison, would have been killed, and this would have amounted to scores of combatants. He is of the opinion that the damage depicted in contemporary photographs was caused by considerably less than half a ton of TNT. The possibility that some of the munitions that had originally been stored in the Headquarters Block were, at some point during the siege, moved across to the west wing, may explain this. The movement of explosives, possibly on the Thursday, is mentioned by garrison member Andy Cooney, although his account of the location is somewhat vague. He does describe, however, packing the explosives in biscuit tins, which were stacked tightly in a room, 'right up to the roof'. Dorothy Macardle also mentions the movement of munitions 'to the south side', although she says this was done on the Friday morning, which cannot be correct, because the National Army was already in occupation of the west wing by then.[2] These moved munitions are almost certainly the 'store of explosives' that Calton Younger reports being discovered in the west wing by Commandant-Gen. Dermot MacManus and his men on the Thursday evening: they remained there until they exploded shortly after 5 p.m. on the Friday afternoon.[3]

Padraig Gill also addressed the question of how the explosion

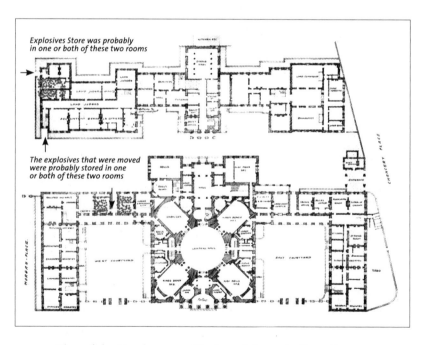

Plan of the Headquarters Block and the main Four Courts building, indicating the probable locations of stored explosives on the morning of Friday, 28 June 1922.

was caused, whether by remote electrical switch or by the fire that was raging in the building at the time. A leaflet issued by the general headquarters of the National Army on 4 July stated that the explosion was caused by a mine, 'and that it was Connected', meaning that the mine was deliberately electrically detonated. The statement went on to say that Ernie O'Malley had 'assured Brigadier-Gen. O'Daly "That the Mine was Exploded by the Irregulars", and he went on to express 'regret that the casualties among the National Army troops were not greater'. This may simply have been (National Army) propaganda: O'Malley, in his book *The Singing Flame,* admittedly written years after the event, claims that he told Commandant-Gen. Dermot MacManus, during the surrender, that the anti-Treaty forces did not 'fire a mine'.

There is no record of any member of the anti-Treaty garrison admitting to detonating the explosives or even knowing who carried it out. While, in a number of sources, there are mentions of an explosion being expected, one can reasonably assume that this is because, given the fierceness of the fire in the Headquarters Block, everyone who knew about the store of explosives would have been aware of what might happen when the fire reached the munitions. There is no mention of an explosion being expected at a specific time, as there might be if the detonation had been planned.

The deliberate detonation of the explosives would have required a manufactured 'mine', connected by wires to a remote electrical switching device. Typical at the time would have been a steel box with a tee-shaped plunger, which, when depressed, operated a high-voltage magneto, which in turn generated an electrical current down wiring to the detonator in the mine, setting off the main explosive. There were certainly a number of engineers in the Four Courts, including Rory O'Connor, with experience in setting up such a device, and there was no shortage of explosives or detonators. Ideally, what would also be required would be a location from where to operate the switching device that had the locus of the explosion in view, but was sufficiently remote from it to be safe. At the time of the explosion, there seems to have been no such location that was not in the control of the National Army, other than, possibly, inside the Headquarters Block itself, but this building had already been cleared of personnel by Simon Donnelly some time before, and was now on fire.

Padraig Gill asserts that it should have been possible to ascertain, through a careful forensic examination of the site of the explosion after the event, whether or not it was caused by a 'connected mine': in such explosions it is usual for the wiring to survive. With the fighting intensifying in other parts of the city on 30 June, however, the army and the authorities had other matters to think about, and we can assume that no such examination ever took place.

Based on the photographic evidence depicting 'ground zero', and the fact that no one was killed when the explosives detonated, Gill leans towards the conclusion that they were not electrically detonated, but were deflagrated by the heat of the fire. Under normal circumstances TNT will melt at a temperature of 80°C (176°F). If the temperature is then raised to over

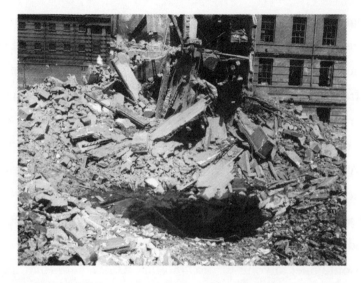

Ground zero of the 'great explosion'. This photograph was taken looking north towards the Land Registry Office. In the centre ground at the far side of the crater are the destroyed walls, concrete floors and roof slabs of the south wing of the Land Registry Office. To the left, the Bridewell can be seen across Chancery Street.

220°C (428°F), the melted TNT will explode, or, as it is more properly termed, deflagrate. According to Commandant Padraig O'Connor's account, just before the explosion, the western end of the Headquarters Block was 'blazing fiercely, the flames reeling across the 25 to 30-yard [23 to 27.5-m] gap that separated us', and 'the heat inside the Record Office was unbearable.'[4] Barrels of petrol and paraffin had been stored in the Headquarters Block, and with accelerants of this sort, there is little doubt that the fire could have achieved the necessary temperature to deflagrate the stored TNT. This would have created a powerful shock wave that blew outwards and upwards, lifting up the western part of the building to a quite considerable extent, before gravity reasserted itself, and the entire three-storey structure above the cellars collapsed in a heap of rubble. The south wing of the Land Registry Office close by was similarly destroyed. Later surveys indicated the foundations of the Land Registry Office were shifted 'bodily, in some places so as to be completely outside their old position',[5] which would mean a horizontal shift of just over 3 feet (1 m).

A deflagration is similar in many ways to an electrical detonation, but the pressure wave resulting from deflagration is subsonic, as opposed to the supersonic wave that an explosion produces. A supersonic pressure wave is far more lethal than a subsonic one: anyone within its range would suffer considerable internal injuries, including ruptured alveoli in their lungs, and they would quickly die from suffocation. Gill, nevertheless, would expect that a deflagration of the scale of that at the Four Courts would have left many of the men in the Public Record Office badly injured owing to their proximity to the site of the detonation. The only mention of troops being 'seriously injured' in the explosion is in a communique issued by National Army headquarters, and this refers only to those who were in the Central Hall at the time. While these men would have physically felt the force of the explosion, there were numerous walls and rooms between them and the blast and they were three times farther away from the source than the men in the Public Record Office. There is good reason to believe, therefore, that the soldiers who were seriously injured were some of Padraig O'Connor's men in the Public Record Office rather than those in the Central Hall; indeed, given their closeness to 'ground zero', it is remarkable that none of them

This photograph was taken south of the blast location, looking north: the crater in the floor is just beyond the heap of rubble behind the destroyed motor car. In the background is the Bridewell, on the extreme right the truncated south wall of the Headquarters Block, and filling the left to centre is the eastern wall of the burnt-out Record Treasury.

were killed. O'Connor himself and the men with whom he was going to launch an attack on the Headquarters Block were probably saved serious injury because they were lined up in the entrance area of the PRO, or in the basement below it, as remote as one could be in the building from the blast.

When Thomas Johnson interviewed the leaders of the IRA executive in Mountjoy Prison on 3 July, he was 'positively assured' that no mine was fired by the garrison, and was told that 'The explosion arose from the ignition of 2 tons of explosive material either by shells or by flames from petrol stores which had become alight.'[6]

With regard to the possibility of shells fired by the National

Army setting off the explosives, there was only one location from which a direct hit by an 18-pounder on the west end of the Headquarters Block might have been possible, and that was in Chancery Street in front of the Bridewell, a very exposed position for a piece of artillery. Although an 18-pounder had been stationed in the Chancery Street area earlier in the siege, and had fired a number of shells at the Headquarters Block, it had been withdrawn, and there is no evidence that it returned, so it would not have been there at the time of the explosion. Considerable efforts were also made throughout the siege to ensure that National Army artillery would not target areas close to where their own troops might be located. Even if there had been a gun in the Chancery Street area on the Friday morning, then, with the impending advance by Padraig O'Connor's men from the east side of the complex, it is most unlikely that it would have been aimed at a building already occupied or about to be occupied by National Army troops from the close-by Public Record Office.

What caused the fire to start in the Headquarters Block, the fire that probably caused the 'great explosion', is another question that has been asked over the years. Calton Younger wrote that one of the Four Courts garrison snipers said that it was 'heavy shelling from the Bridewell end' that 'began the blaze'.[7] As mentioned above, I have found no references to an 18-pounder operating at the 'Bridewell end'. An examination of the plans of the complex also shows that there is no clear view of the Headquarters Block from there because the Land Registry Office lies between it and the Bridewell.

There were some suggestions that the fire was caused by incendiary shells fired into the building. High explosives, shrapnel, smoke and armour-piercing 18-pounder shells were available in 1922, but I can find no evidence of an incendiary type being so.

There is no doubt, however, that Ernie O'Malley and Paddy O'Brien had 'barrels of petrol and paraffin... stored in the cellars and in dark corners, unknown to the rest of the Headquarters Staff',[8] and there seems to be no question, from O'Malley's account, that both he and Paddy O'Brien had every intention of burning the Four Courts and the Public Record Office rather than surrender the complex. Seán Moylan also confirmed that 'barrels of paraffin were brought into the courts on the Sunday before the attack, and men were sent to distribute them among the buildings'.[9] If one wished deliberately to burn the Headquarters Block, an efficient way to do it would have been to set fires in each of the stairwells. This would provide efficient vertical routes for the fire to spread to roof level, and horizontal routes for the fire to spread along corridors. There was a clear corridor from one such location leading to the room or rooms in which the munitions were stored.

Right are two photographs of what remained of the western end of the Headquarters Block, taken after the siege, which may hold clues about the behaviour of the fire in that part of the building. In photograph A it can be seen that, although the central corridors and the roof were destroyed, the first and second floors survived the fire. In photograph B flame and smoke staining can be seen over the ground-floor windows,

A. The remains of the Headquarters Block, taken looking east.
The rubble in the foreground is all that remained of the western end
of the building. While the remaining first- and second-floor structures
survived intact, the floors of the central corridor that provided a
horizontal conduit for the spread of fire have been destroyed.

B. This photograph of the surviving southern façade of the
Headquarters Block, taken from the main Four Courts building,
shows flame and smoke damage over the ground-floor windows;
there are no similar markings over the upper-floor windows.

but not over the first- or second-floor windows. These images might suggest that the fire at that end of the building was at its most fierce on the ground floor, where it probably began, but before it destroyed the floors over, it spread along the ground-floor corridor to reach the munitions store, and vertically up the stairwells to reach and destroy the roof and the upper-floor corridors. The blast may well have quenched the fire at the western end, before the upper floors were burnt.

It seems reasonable to suggest, therefore, that the most likely cause of the fire in the Headquarters Block was the deliberate ignition of the contents of some of the barrels of petrol and paraffin mentioned above, in key locations such as stairwells, which would have ensured the rapid spread of the fire.

In spite of the ferocity of the Battle of the Four Courts in June 1922, involving the widespread destruction of buildings and the discharge of an enormous number of bullets and shells, there was a remarkably low casualty rate. The early figures for the National Army counted three dead, and five officers and fifty troops injured, although later it was reported that as many as seven were killed. It seems that three of the occupying garrison were killed and about twenty were injured.

The Irish Civil War, a conflict that was to continue for more than ten months, began with those first shots fired in the early morning of 28 June 1922. The conflict started hesitantly, with little rancour, and indeed with much sympathy between combatants. A deep sense of betrayal, felt on both sides, however, combined with what I believe was post-traumatic stress disorder among those young men who had spent the previous four years fighting and killing for a cause, led, within months, to a savagery on both sides that we can find hard to understand. Maybe their condition can be summed up by the lines W. B. Yeats wrote about the men of 1916:

Too long a sacrifice
Can make a stone of the heart.[10]

During the conflict some 540 National Army men were killed, and although historians disagree on the number of anti-Treaty men and, indeed, civilians who died, it is generally thought the figure might be between 3,000 and 4,000. Many of the leaders were dead by the time the fighting petered out in May 1923. While Michael Collins and Liam Lynch died in action, others, such as the leaders of the Four Courts occupation, Rory O'Connor, Joe McKelvey, Dick Barrett and Liam Mellows, were executed.

Arthur Griffith was a man who had been used to a healthy lifestyle, swimming at Sandymount and walking in the Dublin mountains. Since the period spent negotiating the Treaty in London, he had enjoyed little exercise and had been under considerable and continuing stress. He suffered from insomnia and was physically run down, which revealed itself in an attack of tonsillitis during the first week of August 1922. His friend and doctor Oliver St John Gogarty persuaded him to rest for a few days in St Vincent's nursing home on St Stephen's Green, and while there, on 12 August, he had a brain haemorrhage and died. He was fifty-one.

On 12 July 1922, thirty-two-year-old Michael Collins, regarded as the best man to deal with the deteriorating situation, became commander-in-chief of the National Army. He told the cabinet that he would not be able to continue in his ministerial roles until further notice, so W. T. Cosgrave took over as Acting Chairman and Acting Minister of Finance. Many of the best-known photos of Collins show him in uniform, but it was a uniform that he was to wear for less than forty days more before he was fatally injured during an ambush in Co. Cork on 22 August 1922. He was a man of exceptional organizational ability who ran a highly effective intelligence network that helped to destabilize British rule in Ireland. When consulting his papers while carrying out research for this book, I was impressed by Collins' documentary output, his voluminous correspondence, articles, speeches and plans for Ireland's future, and wondered when the man found time to sleep. He seems to have had that rare mind that can deal with the big picture while simultaneously taking care of all the details; he prosecuted the war with prodigious energy, but when he saw the possibility of peace, he worked tirelessly for it. Brilliant, charismatic, secretive, forward-thinking, Michael Collins has become an almost legendary figure, and speculation about what path Ireland would have taken through the twentieth century, if he had lived, continues to this day. The gun-carriage used for his funeral to Glasnevin Cemetery was one of the 18-pounders that had been used in the siege of the Four Courts.

Although a general election had taken place in June, it was not thought safe to have the first sitting of the Third Dáil until 5 September 1922, and three weeks later the Public Safety Bill was passed, giving military courts far-reaching powers that included execution for giving assistance to the 'Irregulars', as the anti-Treaty men were increasingly being called, and for the possession of arms. The British government was doubtful that the new law would be strictly enforced, and was surprised when the first executions were carried out on 17 November. These were, however, the first of many, and they brought a strong threat of reprisals against elected members of the Dáil from Liam Lynch, chief of staff of the IRA. The first such reprisal was carried out on 7 December, when the Dáil deputy Seán Hales was shot down in the street on his way to a meeting of the Dáil at Leinster House. Immediately, the cabinet took the decision to be ruthless in its reaction to the murder of an elected representative, and, after much agonized discussion, imprisoned anti-Treaty leaders Rory O'Connor, Liam Mellows, Joe McKelvey and Dick Barrett were selected for execution, in retaliation. O'Connor and Mellows, in particular, had continued their campaign from prison, tireless in their letters and messages of encouragement to the anti-Treaty IRA in its efforts to undermine the Provisional Government. This, together with their leadership roles and their direct involvement in the outbreak of the Civil War might have marked them out, but it is difficult to understand why McKelvey and Barrett were also chosen, other than the idea that the four men represented all four provinces of Ireland.

Minister for Justice Kevin O'Higgins signed the execution

order: Rory O'Connor had been best man at his wedding only fourteen months before. The four were given little warning, only sufficient time to write last letters, before being taken out of their cells and shot the following morning. The members of the firing squad were in shock at what they had to do, and it appears that some of them deliberately missed. The officer in charge had to give the *coup de grâce* to Mellows, and to ensure that they were all dead, he had to fire nine shots from his revolver. The *Nation* newspaper in New York described the deaths as 'murder, foul and despicable, and nothing else'.

Emmet Dalton was with Michael Collins when he was fatally injured in the ambush at Béal na Bláth. He had seen much death and destruction in his short military career, but the shock of seeing his great hero die in such a way must have affected Dalton badly; in November 1922 he resigned from the army for reasons he never revealed. He worked as clerk of the Irish Senate until 1925, after which he went through a tumultuous period in his life, drinking heavily, and working as a salesman of encyclopaedias, Scotch whisky and weighing scales. He eventually became involved in the film industry, and enjoyed a successful career in the business, becoming a founder member of Ireland's first film studio, Ardmore Studios, outside Dublin. He died on his eightieth birthday in 1978.

In spite of his ordeal, J. J. 'Ginger' O'Connell was back at work in National Army headquarters on the same day he was released from incarceration in the Four Courts. He stayed in the army after the Civil War, and held a number of important posts until he died of a heart attack in February 1944.

Brig.-Gen. Paddy O'Daly served throughout the Civil War, but the Dublin Guards under his command were implicated in a number of atrocities during the conflict, particularly in Co. Kerry. After one particularly horrifying incident in which O'Daly's men tied eight anti-Treaty prisoners to a mine and then detonated it, he himself was appointed to oversee the army enquiry into the matter. The enquiry found that no one was to blame. He was one of three Dublin Guards officers involved in a 'reprisal' against two young Kerry women, which involved beating them with belts and rubbing motor oil into their hair. No witnesses were found to give evidence to an enquiry, and there were no charges. O'Daly left the army, however, in 1924, and was given full military honours at his funeral, after his death in January 1957.

Ernie O'Malley continued his fight for the Republic until he was captured in a dramatic shoot-out in Dublin in November 1922. He was severely wounded in the gun battle, and it is likely that he would have been one of the many anti-Treaty men who were executed during this period but for the fact that he was gravely ill. He suffered a long recovery and imprisonment, during which he went on hunger strike for forty-one days. He was one of the last anti-Treaty prisoners to be released following the end of the Civil War. After attending University College, Dublin, he went abroad, living for periods in New Mexico and New York. He returned to Ireland in the mid-1930s and wrote a number of books dealing with his experiences during the War of Independence and the Civil War. Later, he travelled around Ireland interviewing hundreds of old comrades, pro- and anti-Treaty alike, and filled numerous notebooks describing their experiences. His war injuries affected his health all his life, and he died at the age of fifty-nine in March 1957. He was given a state funeral.

Padraig O'Connor, after giving courageous service and leadership in the assault on the Four Courts, was, only days later, in the thick of the fighting again, to oust anti-Treaty forces from their last Dublin stronghold east of O'Connell Street. Before the end of July 1922, he had been involved in a number of actions in Co. Tipperary, including the taking of Tipperary town from the anti-Treaty IRA. During a military operation in August 1922 he was again in the midst of things, in Co. Cork, where he was wounded by a hand-grenade explosion. After recuperation, he resumed his duties at Beggars Bush barracks in Dublin, and perhaps it is an indication of how highly his loyalty and commitment to the Provisional Government was regarded by headquarters that he was selected to be the officer commanding the firing squad that executed Erskine Childers, the director of propaganda for the anti-Treaty IRA. O'Connor was appointed to the general staff in March 1923 and became director of training in 1925, before resigning his commission in 1927. On the outbreak of war in Europe in 1939, he was called up and served in the army, much of the time as commanding officer of 46th Battalion based in Waterford, where he was much loved. He died in May 1953 and is buried beside his wife, Nellie, in Bluebell cemetery, Co. Dublin.

Liam Lynch rallied the southern brigades of the IRA and prepared to hold and defend a 'Munster Republic', south of a line between Limerick and Waterford. The National Army moved at speed and strength, however, to take Lynch's headquarters at Limerick on 20 July 1922. The following day Waterford fell, followed by the towns of Carrick on Suir and Clonmel. In a sea-borne attack, the National Army landed men in Co. Cork on 8 August and they went on to take Cork city. Lynch was now forced to disperse his forces into the countryside and carry on a guerrilla war. Executions and reprisals led to a series of increasingly vicious atrocities on both sides. In April 1923, Lynch and a number of comrades were surrounded by troops of the National Army in the Knockmealdown mountains in Co. Tipperary, and he was mortally wounded in a firefight. He died in St Joseph's Hospital, Clonmel, aged twenty-nine, on 10 April 1923.

After the death of Liam Lynch, Frank Aiken became IRA chief of staff. A ceasefire was declared, followed by an order from Aiken on 24 May 1923 to all anti-Treaty forces to dump their arms. Éamon de Valera issued a proclamation telling them that further sacrifices would be in vain, and that 'military victory must be allowed to rest for the moment with those who have destroyed the Republic.'[11]

As time passed, and the country settled somewhat uneasily into getting on with making its way in the world, the unsavoury facts of what had happened during those terrible months of the Civil War were buried away deep in the national psyche. There was no appetite to confront the unpleasant truths, which may have been a factor in the continuance of a civil war mentality that must have stunted for years the development of politics in Ireland.

As early as 1924, P. S. O'Hegarty, in his book *The Victory of Sinn Féin*, suggested that 'our deep-rooted belief that there was something in us finer than, more spiritual than, anything in other people, was sheer illusion, and that we were really an uncivilized people with savage instincts. And the shock of that plunge from the heights to the depths staggered the nation.'[12]

For comfortable citizens of a free and prosperous twenty-first-century Ireland, it is almost impossible to appreciate what dominated the thinking of the average Irish man or woman in 1922, let alone to understand the powerful dream of a republic that a small cadre of idealists nurtured through the sometimes vicious fighting and killings, activities that many of them felt deep guilt about for the rest of their lives. They particularly resented that the terrible things they had had to do to gain a republic seemed to be for nothing, when some of their erstwhile comrades were prepared to shake hands with the British oppressors and swear an oath of allegiance to the British king. These comrades, however, believed that democracy was at stake, and hardened their hearts to what had to be done to save it.

Democracy did survive in Ireland. Four years after the end of the Civil War the staunchly anti-Treaty politician Éamon de Valera formed a new political party called Fianna Fáil, meaning 'Soldiers of Destiny', and in the general election of June 1927, it won forty-four seats. De Valera and his colleagues presented themselves at the Dáil and took the oath of allegiance that had been a major cause of a civil war, dismissing it as an 'empty formula'. In the general election of 1932, during a decade that witnessed the demise of democracy in Italy, Portugal, Spain, Greece and Germany, Fianna Fáil became the largest party in the Dáil, and, with the support of the Labour Party, formed the government of the Irish Free State.

The author inspecting recent damage to one of the original Corinthian capitals just below the dome of the Four Courts.

ACKNOWLEDGEMENTS

This book could not have been written without the assistance of many, whose help I greatly appreciate. My agent, Jonathan Williams, suggested that a paper I had written about the 'great explosion' should become a book, so I am grateful to him for lighting the fuse. Diarmuid O'Connor generously shared the archive of his fascinating uncle Padraig O'Connor, and Cormac Lalor patiently took me through a short course on the use of the 18-pounder gun. Padraig Gill introduced me to the fascinating world of explosives. Dr Ciaran Wallace guided me in my understanding of the period, and Dr Peter Crooks assisted me in the complex matters of pleadings, pipe rolls and parchments. Susan Murphy, Eugene Lynch and Helen Priestley of the Courts Service assisted in getting me access to the Four Courts complex, and Fergus McCormick of the OPW Architects Department arranged access to the works currently being carried out to the Four Courts dome. My thanks to Patricia Parfrey, Parish

Administrator of St Michan's Church, Colum O'Riordan and the staff of the Irish Architectural Archive, Dr Brian Kirby of the Irish Capuchin Archive, Cillian MacDonnell of the Law Society, Aideen Ireland, Gregory O'Connor, Tom Quinlan and Zoë Reid of the National Archives, John Timmons of the RTÉ Archives, Mary Broderick of the National Library, Aoife Torpey of the Kilmainham Gaol Museum, Orna Somerville, Sarah Poutch and Leanne Harrington of the UCD Archives, Maurice Kealey and the late John Byrne.

NOTES

Chapter 1

1 Peter Ellis, *Eyewitness to Irish History*, Wiley, Hoboken, NJ, 2004, p. 82.

2 Terence de Vere White, *Kevin O'Higgins*, Anvil, Dublin, 1966, p. 48.

3 G. B. Kenna, *Facts and Figures of the Belfast Pogrom*, The O'Connell Publishing Company, Dublin, 1922.

4 Tom Garvin, *1922: The Birth of Irish Democracy*, Gill & Macmillan, Dublin, 1996, pp. 58 and 59.

5 Todd Andrews, *Dublin Made Me*, Mercier Press, Dublin & Cork, 1979, p. 207.

6 Donal P. Corcoran, *Freedom to Achieve Freedom: The Irish Free State, 1922–1932*, Gill & Macmillan, Dublin, 2014, p. 88.

7 John P. Duggan, *A History of the Irish Army*, Gill & Macmillan, Dublin, 1991, p. 71.

8 Tom Barry, *Guerilla Days in Ireland*, Irish Press, Dublin, 1949, p. 227.

9 Sir Henry A. Robinson, *Further Memories of Irish Life*, Herbert Jenkins, London, 1924, p. 325.

10 J. A. Pinkman, *In the Legion of the Vanguard*, Mercier Press, Cork, 1998, p. 87.

11 Address to the Irish Society at Oxford University, 31 October 1924.

12 Bureau of Military History, Dublin, Truce Liaison and Evacuation papers, LE/B/4.

13 Mulcahy Papers, University College of Dublin Archives (hereafter UCDA), P7/A 25 and P/7/A/483.

14   Ibid., P7B/39.
15   Dorothy Macardle, *The Irish Republic*, Corgi, London, 1968, p. 616.
16   Joseph McGarrity Papers, National Library of Ireland (hereafter NLI).
17   Macardle, *The Irish Republic*, p. 6.
18   Ernie O'Malley, *The Singing Flame*, Mercier Press, Cork, 2012, p. 89.
19   *Irish Times*, 25 May 1922.

Chapter 2

1   Caroline Costello (ed.), *The Four Courts: 200 Years*, Incorporated Council of Law Reporting for Ireland, Dublin, 1996, p. 160.
2   Letter from Liam Lynch to his brother Tom (NLI MS 36,251).
3   Mulcahy Papers, UCDA, 7/A/556.
4   Peter Crooks, 'Reconstructing the past: the case of the medieval Irish chancery rolls', in Felix M. Larkin & N. M. Dawson (eds), *Lawyers, the Law and History*, Four Courts Press, Dublin, 2013, p. 296.
5   A memorandum to the law officer from Mr Glover of the Land Registry Office dated 20 July 1922.
6   Simon Donnelly's unpublished handwritten account of the siege, written one year afterwards, at the request of Oscar Traynor, while interned in Gormanstown Camp: National Archives of Ireland (hereafter NAI) MS 33063 acc 4715.
7   Uinseann MacEoin (ed.), *Survivors*, Argenta Publications, Dublin, 1980, p. 45.
8   Una Daly, Witness Statement 610, Bureau of Military History, Dublin.
9   Andrews, *Dublin Made Me*, p. 225.
10   Letter from Liam Lynch to his brother Tom (NLI MS 36,251/27).
11   O'Malley, *The Singing Flame*, p. 71.
12   Una Daly, Witness Statement 610, Bureau of Military History, Dublin.
13   O'Malley, *The Singing Flame*, p. 132.
14   *Hansard*, 31 May 1922.
15   R. B. McDowell, *Land and Learning: Two Irish Clubs*, Lilliput, Dublin, 1993, p. 95.
16   MacEoin (ed.), *Survivors*, p. 127.
17   NLI, MS 15,369.
18   O'Malley, *The Singing Flame*, p. 103.
19   UCDA, O'Malley Notebook, P17/87.
20   Calton Younger, *Ireland's Civil War*, Fontana, London, 1982, p. 319.
21   Pinkman, *In the Legion of the Vanguard*, p. 86.
22   Macardle, *The Irish Republic*, p. 664.

23   Seán MacBride, *That Day's Struggle*, Curragh Press, Dublin, 2005, p. 57.

24   Macardle, *The Irish Republic*, p. 666.

25   Duggan, *A History of the Irish Army*, p. 86.

26   Kevin O'Higgins, *The Civil War and the Events Leading up to It*, Talbot Press, Dublin, 1922.

27   Mulcahy Papers, UCDA, P/7/B/96.

28   Tim Pat Coogan, *De Valera*, Random House, London, 1993, p. 310.

29   Duggan, *A History of the Irish Army*, p. 79.

30   Desmond FitzGerald Papers, UCDA, P80/851.

31   Tim Pat Coogan, *Michael Collins*, Arrow, London, 1991, pp. 123–4.

32   Maurice Craig, *Irish Bookbindings 1600–1800*, Cassell & Co. Ltd, London, 1954, p. 4.

33   NLI MS 22,433.

34   Florence O'Donoghue Papers, NLI, MS 31,249.

35   O'Malley, *The Singing Flame*, p. 147.

36   Seán Brunswick, Witness Statement 898, Bureau of Military History, Dublin.

37   Younger, *Ireland's Civil War*, p. 327.

38   O'Malley, *The Singing Flame*, p. 135.

39   MacEoin (ed.), *Survivors*, p. 127.

40   O'Malley, *The Singing Flame*, p. 112.

41   General Macready's Report to the British cabinet, 3 June 1922.

Chapter 3

1   Mulcahy Papers, UCDA, P7/B192/72.

2   Macardle, *The Irish Republic*, p. 668.

3   Keith Jeffrey, *Field Marshal Sir Henry Wilson, A Political Soldier*, Oxford University Press, Oxford, 2006, pp. 264–7.

4   Ibid., pp. 256–60.

5   Liam O'Briain, Witness Statement 784, Bureau of Military History, Dublin.

6   Letter from Lloyd George to Michael Collins, 23 June 1922, NAI, TSCH/3/S1570.

7   Padraic Colum, *Arthur Griffith*, Browne & Nolan, Dublin, 1959, p. 339.

8   Clare Sheridan, *In Many Places*, Jonathan Cape, London, 1923, p. 43.

9   Florence O'Donoghue, *No Other Law*, Irish Press, Dublin, 1954, p. 256.

10   T. Ryle Dwyer, *Big Fellow, Long Fellow*, Palgrave Macmillan, London, p. 307.

11   Charles Desmond Greaves, *Liam Mellows and the Irish Revolution*, Lawrence & Wishart, London, 1971.

12   Colum, *Arthur Griffith*, p. 367.

13   Ibid. and Ernest Blythe, Witness Statement 939, Bureau of Military History, Dublin.

14   Ernest Blythe, Witness Statement 939.

15   Greaves, *Liam Mellows and the Irish Revolution*, p. 46.

16   Patrick J. Little, Witness Statement 1769, Bureau of Military History, Dublin.

17   Sheridan, *In Many Places*, pp. 44–8.

18   O'Donoghue, *No Other Law*, p. 256.

19   *Irish Times*, 28 June 1922.

20   Younger, *Ireland's Civil War*, p. 321.

21   L. O'Carroll, Witness Statement 314, Bureau of Military History, Dublin.

22   General Sir Nevil Macready, *Annals of an Active Life*, Hutchinson, London, 1924, p. 527.

23   Undated radio talk by Lt.-Col. Niall Harrington, NLI MS 40,662/2.

24   Seán Boyne, *Emmet Dalton, Somme Soldier, Irish General, Film Pioneer*, Merrion Press, Dublin, 2016, p. 101.

25   Younger, *Ireland's Civil War*, p. 319.

26   O'Malley, *The Singing Flame*, 2012, p. 103.

27   Greaves, *Liam Mellows and the Irish Revolution*, p. 342.

28   O'Malley, *The Singing Flame*, 2012, p. 122.

29   James Cunningham, Witness Statement 922, Bureau of Military History, Dublin.

30   Andrews, *Dublin Made Me*, p. 207.

Chapter 4

1   Macardle, *The Irish Republic*, p. 678.

2   Seán Prendergast, Witness Statement 755, Bureau of Military History, Dublin.

3   *Freeman's Journal*, 28 June 1922.

4   Diarmuid O'Connor and Frank Connolly, *Sleep Soldier Sleep: The Life and Times of Padraig O'Connor*, Miseab Publications, Dublin, 2011, p. 92.

5   O'Malley, *The Singing Flame*, p. 102.

6   *The Times* [London], 29 June 1922.

7   Donnelly's unpublished account, NAI MS 33063 acc 4715.

8   Boyne, *Emmet Dalton*, p. 143.

9   Undated radio talk by Lt.-Col. Niall Harrington, NLI MS 40,662/2.
10   Michael Hopkinson, *Green against Green*, Gill & Macmillan, Dublin, 1988, p. 116, and Mulcahy Papers, UCDA, P7/B/106–110.
11   Mulcahy Papers, UCDA, P7/B/106–110.
12   Macready, *Annals of an Active Life*, p. 656.
13   Younger, *Ireland's Civil War*, p. 324.
14   Ibid.
15   Macready, *Annals of an Active Life*, p. 658.
16   *Freeman's Journal*, 28 June 1922.
17   Donnelly, unpublished account, NAI MS 33063 acc 4715.
18   O'Malley, *The Singing Flame*, p. 102.
19   Ibid., p. 129.
20   O'Malley, *The Singing Flame*, p. 122.
21   Geraldine O'Donel, Witness Statement 861, Bureau of Military History, Dublin.
22   Máire Comerford, unpublished manuscript 'The Dangerous Ground', UCDA, LA18/43.
23   Donnelly, unpublished account, NAI MS 33063 acc 4715.
24   UCDA, P88/72.
25   Greaves, *Liam Mellows and the Irish Revolution*, p. 346.
26   Annie Farrington, Witness Statement 749, Bureau of Military History, Dublin.
27   Maurice Walsh, *Bitter Freedom*, Faber & Faber, London, 2015, p. 354.
28   Ibid.
29   Sheridan, *In Many Places*, p. 51.
30   Ibid., p. 52.
31   Mulcahy Papers, UCDA, P7/B/107.
32   *The Times*, 29 June 1922.
33   Comerford, 'The Dangerous Ground'.
34   Bernard Share, *In Time of Civil War*, The Collins Press, Cork, 2006, p. 33.
35   Younger, *Ireland's Civil War*, p. 324.
36   Macready, *Annals of an Active Life*, p. 656.
37   Comerford, 'The Dangerous Ground'.

Chapter 5

1   Cable from Churchill to Collins, 28/06/1922 quoted in Tim Pat Coogan's *Michael Collins*, p. 332.
2   *Irish Independent*, 30 June 1922.

3   *Irish Times*, 8 July 1922.

4   O'Connor and Connolly, *Sleep Soldier Sleep*, p. 95.

5   Conclusions of a cabinet meeting, held at 10 Downing Street, London, on Tuesday, 4 July 1922 at 11.30 a.m.

6   Younger, *Ireland's Civil War*, p. 326.

7   Macready, *Annals of an Active Life*, p. 656.

8   *Irish Independent*, 1 July 1922.

9   Undated radio talk by Lt.-Col. Niall Harrington, NLI MS 40,662/2, and *Freeman's Journal*, 1 July 1922.

10   Michael MacConneran, a photographer who observed the bombardment.

11   Brig.-Gen. O'Daly, in the *Galway Observer*, Saturday, 1 July 1922; some accounts give 3 p.m. as the attack time.

12   Donnelly, unpublished account, NAI MS 33063 acc 4715.

13   O'Connor and Connolly, *Sleep Soldier Sleep*, p. 97.

14   O'Malley notebook, P17b/98.

15   O'Malley, *The Singing Flame*, p. 139.

16   O'Connor and Connolly, *Sleep Soldier Sleep*, p. 98.

17   Younger, *Ireland's Civil War*, p. 329.

18   O'Malley, *The Singing Flame*, p. 143.

19   O'Malley notebook, 17b/87.

Chapter 6

1   O'Malley, *The Singing Flame*, p. 146.

2   Ibid., p. 147.

3   Mrs Annie O'Brien and Mrs Lily Curran, joint Witness Statement 805.

4   Donnelly, unpublished account, NAI MS 33063 acc 4715.

5   Younger, *Ireland's Civil War*, p. 329.

6   *Irish Independent*, 1 July 1922.

7   Las Fallon, *Dublin Fire Brigade and the Irish Revolution*, South Dublin Libraries, Dublin, 2012, p. 87.

8   Eoin Neeson, *The Civil War in Ireland*, Mercier Press, Dublin, 1966, p. 73.

9   O'Connor and Connolly, *Sleep Soldier Sleep*, pp. 99 and 100.

10   *Irish Life*, 14 July 1922.

11   O'Malley archive, Trinity College Dublin, No. 384, MS7850 907.

12   Donnelly, unpublished account, MS 33063 acc 4715.

13   Younger, *Ireland's Civil War*, p. 330.

14   Commandment O'Daly's account of the fighting two days later suggests 'at least 20', while Younger suggests about 40.

15 Comerford, 'The Dangerous Ground'.

16 Younger, *Ireland's Civil War*, p. 331.

17 R. M. Fox, *The History of the Irish Citizen Army*, James Duffy & Co., Dublin, 1943, p. 220.

18 Bernard Adams, *Denis Johnston: A Life*, Lilliput Press, Dublin, 2002, p. 57.

19 Diaries of Rosamund Jacob, 1897–1960, NLI, MS 32,582/1-170.

20 O'Malley, *The Singing Flame*, p. 151.

21 *Irish Times*, 8 July 1922.

22 O'Connor and Connolly, *Sleep Soldier Sleep*, p. 101.

23 *The Eleventh Report of the Deputy Keeper of the Public Records of Ireland*, 1879, p. 10.

24 R. B. McDowell, *The Irish Administration 1801–1914*, Routledge & Kegan Paul, London, 1964, p. 279.

25 *Freeman's Journal*, 1 July 1922.

26 O'Malley, *The Singing Flame*, p. 151.

27 Ibid., p. 155.

28 Ibid.

29 Ibid., p. 157.

30 Younger, *Ireland's Civil War*, p. 331.

31 Ibid.

32 *Freeman's Journal*, 1 July, 1922.

33 O'Malley, *The Singing Flame*, p. 160.

34 Mulcahy Papers, UCDA, P7/B/60.

35 Younger, *Ireland's Civil War*, p. 331.

36 Comerford, 'The Dangerous Ground'.

37 Fallon, *Dublin Fire Brigade*, p. 88.

38 *Irish Independent*, 1 July 1922.

39 Ibid., p. 78.

40 MacEoin (ed.), *Survivors*, p. 323.

41 *Freeman's Journal*, 1 July 1922.

Chapter 7

1 C. P. Curran's Report to the government law officer, Hugh Kennedy, dated 3 July 1922, NAI, AGE/2002/16/475.

2 Costello (ed.), *The Four Courts*, p. 167.

3 Land Commissioners' Report to Hugh Kennedy, government law officer, 20 July 1922, NAI, FIN/1/11/2.

4 T. J. Byrne, 'Some Reconstruction Work at the Four Courts, Dublin', talk given by Byrne, Chief Architect of the Office of Public Works to the Institution of Civil Engineers of Ireland, in January 1928.

5   Costello (ed.), *The Four Courts*, p. 161.
6   *Irish Times*, 3 April 1924.
7   Letter from the Commissioners of Public Works in Ireland to the Secretary, Ministry of Finance, NAI, FIN 1/674.
8   His Majesty's Stationery Office, Dublin, 1919.
9   Herbert Wood, 'The Public Records of Ireland before and after 1922', *Transactions of the Royal Historical Society*, Fourth Series, Vol. 13, 1930, p. 43.
10   *The Fifty-fifth Report of the Deputy Keeper of the Public Records and Keeper of the State Papers of Ireland*, Government Publications Office, Dublin, 1929.
11   Wood, 'The Public Records of Ireland before and after 1922', p. 48.

Chapter 8

1   O'Malley, *The Singing Flame*, p. 148.
2   Macardle, *The Irish Republic*, p. 684.
3   Younger, *Ireland's Civil War*, p. 329.
4   O'Connor and Connolly, *Sleep Soldier Sleep*, p. 99.
5   Byrne, 'Some Reconstruction Work at the Four Courts, Dublin'.
6   Letter from Thomas Johnson to the Secretary of Dáil Éireann, 4 July 1922, NAI, FIN/1/11/2.
7   Younger, *Ireland's Civil War*, p. 329.
8   O'Malley, *The Singing Flame*, Mercier Press, Cork, 2012, p. 103.
9   O'Malley notebook, P17b/87.
10   From 'Easter, 1916'.
11   Macardle, *The Irish Republic*, p. 781.
12   P. S. Hegarty, *The Victory of Sinn Féin*, University College of Dublin, Dublin, 1998, p. 88.

IMAGE CREDITS

INDEX

Illustrations are in *italics*. All places are in Dublin unless otherwise stated.
FC refers to Four Courts. NA refers to National Army.